C000010660

Tears Before Bedtime

By the same author:

A YOUNG GIRL'S TOUCH

BORN LOSERS

A LOVE MATCH

Tears Before Bedtime

By

Barbara Skelton

Hamish Hamilton London

HAMISH HAMILTON LTD

Penguin Books Ltd, 27 Wrights Lane, London W8 5TZ (Publishing & Editorial)
and Harmondsworth, Middlesex, England (Distribution & Warehouse)
Viking Penguin Inc., 40 West 23rd Street, New York, New York 10010, U.S.A.
Penguin Books Australia Ltd, Ringwood, Victoria, Australia
Penguin Books Canada Limited, 2801 John Street, Markham, Ontario, Canada L3R 1B4
Penguin Books (N.Z.) Ltd, 182–190 Wairau Road, Auckland 10, New Zealand

First published in Great Britain 1987 by
Hamish Hamilton Ltd

Copyright © 1987 by Barbara Skelton

All rights reserved. Without limiting the rights under copyright reserved
above, no part of this publication may be reproduced, stored
in or introduced into a retrieval system, or transmitted, in any form
or by any means (electronic, mechanical, photocopying,
recording or otherwise), without the prior written permission of both
the copyright owner and the above publisher of this book.

British Library Cataloguing in Publication Data

Skelton, Barbara
  Tears before bedtime.
  1. Skelton, Barbara——Biography
  2. Authors, English——20th century——
  Biography
  I. Title
  941.082'092'4   PR6069.K36Z/

ISBN 0-241-12326-7

Typeset at The Spartan Press Ltd, Lymington, Hants
Printed in Great Britain by
Butler and Tanner Ltd, London and Frome

To Jocelyn and Clive Donner

Contents

List of Illustrations

Unless otherwise indicated, the pictures are by
courtesy of Barbara Skelton.

◇◇◇ Chapter I ◇◇◇

Family

Mummy was a beauty. She had very blue eyes that she liked to compare to the violet hue of hydrangeas. Not that she was particularly vain, but she craved admiration. When she met Daddy, she belonged to a repertory company, the members of which were known as the Gaiety Girls, renowned for looks rather than for talent. Following the trend of other young men of good family in those days, my father courted actresses. When my mother was playing in *The Merry Widow*, he called on her backstage, carrying a bouquet. Years later, she complained that was how he had frittered his money away.

My father Eric and his elder brother, Dudley, were child orphans. Their mother had been a direct descendant of the playwright, Sheridan, and at the age of twenty-one each boy came into an inheritance. Eric was a delicate, gentle man with sad brown eyes, slim and well built with beautiful hands – *'les attaches fines'*, I think, is the French expression. An honourable man and witty, he had a very weak character, and no outstanding ability except as a sportsman. A keen cricketer, he had played in the second eleven for Sandhurst.

My mother's instant summing up of any man depended on whether or not she considered him to be a 'gentleman'. Those who did not qualify were either 'blackguards', 'cads', or 'dagos', but mostly they ended up like 'Daddy' being just a 'poor devil'. It is doubtful if Mummy would have been able to define the term gentleman as well as the Regency courtesan, Harriette Wilson,[*]

---

[*]Harriette Wilson, born Dubochet, was the daughter of a Swiss clockmaker. Her *Mémoires*, published in 1825, opens with: 'I shall not say how or why I became, at

who claimed, 'A man is a gentleman who has no visible means of gaining a livelihood or because he's a Lord, and the system at White's Club, the members of which are all choice gentlemen, of course, is and ever has been, never to blackball any man, or one who ties a good knot in his handkerchief, keeps his hands out of his breecher pockets, and says nothin'!'

I was born on the night of Mummy's twenty-sixth birthday and handed over to Nanny, in whose care I remained throughout the formative years. Mummy claimed that she had been 'such a tiny little thing', it had been a difficult birth, forceps being employed. It is doubtful if she felt much love for her child. My feelings became more extreme. But, towards the end of her life she inspired pity and, according to George Sand, love and pity can't be separated.

In their early married years, my parents lived near Henley in a white clapboard house with a garden sloping down to the river. Then, punting was all the rage. Snaps of Mummy show her tightly belted into long white dresses with velvet laced-up booties, her long hair plaited round her head, as she reclined sensuously under a parasol in a punt, while Daddy, wearing a boater, stands manipulating the pole. While stationed in Barbados he contracted malaria. Then, after a severe heart attack, he was invalided out of the army altogether. For as long as I can remember, my father was considered an invalid, unable to take a very active part in life.

We moved about a good deal, living in rented houses, holidays being spent with my maternal grandparents in one of those four-storied semi-detached houses lining Hythe seafront. Each house had a strip of garden that joined the promenade, and when the sea was rough the waves would sweep over the garden gate and lash against the French windows, depositing giant pebbles in their wake. The kitchen was in the basement, meals being carried up to a sitting cum dining room furnished in heavy Victorian oak. We ate seated round an oak gateleg table, above which hung a frilly red chiffon lampshade, so that, when seen from the promenade, the room resembled the interior of some red light district.

The Marine Parade house was invariably full. My mother had four sisters, Hilda, Elca, Vera and Greta, all married bar Aunty

---

the age of fifteen, the mistress of the Earl of Craven. Whether it was love or the severity of my father, the depravity of my own heart, or the winning arts of the noble Lord, which induced me to leave my paternal roof and place myself under his protection, does not signify: or if it does, I am not in a humour to gratify curiosity in this matter.'

Greta whose flirt had been killed in the First World War. Aunty Greta never left Hythe. She remained with my grandparents all her life, cooking superbly, Mrs Beeton style: a Sunday roast with batter pudding, steak and kidney pies, boiled beef and dumplings, cheese straws with drinks, and sponge cakes for tea being the ritual. All the aunts chainsmoked and spent the mornings studying the racing form. They then made bets with a local tobacconist. Should there be a large gathering, as at Christmas, after dinner, a green baize cloth was spread over the gateleg table; everyone played roulette, poker or *vingt-et-un*, and money changed hands. Before going to bed, Aunty Greta came up the stairs carrying a loaded tray of hot drinks.

When anyone spoke of the house, it was always referred to by its number. 'We're going to forty-two,' my mother would say and, because of the sea, staying with my grandparents was always a treat.

Grandma could barely read or write, but like many grandmothers she seemed to me to be an angel of goodness. What happy memories! – picnics together in the woods, coming back laden with primroses and bluebells and her delicious teas of home-made strawberry jam, and freshly baked warm scones spread with melting butter and thick Devonshire cream. Alas, as I grew older her ignorance and friendly questioning irritated me. Whenever I think of Grandpa, he is already over eighty, wiry and sprightly, with a certain rickety energy. The only remark of his that I remember is that he couldn't eat bananas; they upset his digestion. When too old to play bowls, he took up gardening and walked to an allotment on the outskirts of the town, coming home at dusk laden with various produce of his own planting: some tomatoes, a cabbage, an abundance of artichokes or a prize marrow of colossal dimensions. He lived on a pension from the postal service and on retirement had been awarded a floridly designed certificate, claiming him to have been an impeccable civil servant, which remained on display between two Town Crier prints on the mantelpiece. But, with his bright blue eyes and slightly flushed complexion, Grandpa looked more like a retired seaman.

He was of Danish descent. His sister, Great Aunt Greta, could barely speak English. A tall formidable lady with a deep guttural voice, when visiting forty-two she remained seated by the fire doing very fine crochet work. Otherwise, she sang in operas. She was on her way to tour the United States, travelling in the *Titanic*, when the ship struck an iceberg. One of the few survivors, as her lifeboat rowed to safety, Great Aunt Greta sang hymns and was later given an award for bravery. My grandparents lived to celebrate their diamond wedding anniversary.

I used to love the crunch of the smooth brown pebbles as in summertime we stepped onto the beach to lie in the shade of a slimy green wooden breakwater just in front of the house. We'd take a picnic basket and lunch there, sheltered from the wind. I collected milk stones and at low tide paddled about the sand gathering mussels. Shoals of porpoises flipped past on the horizon. Dymchurch lighthouse flickered in the distance. At night, lying in a four-poster, one could hear the lap of the sea as the waves rolled over the shingle. Then, a horse-drawn tram ran along the seafront as far as Sandgate, and the narrow High Street of Hythe was full of old pubs and antique shops. Nowadays, red buses thunder through and a stream of traffic runs parallel to the canal bank. Ugly beach huts line the promenade, where at high tide men squat with fishing lines. Even the Ladies' Walk, once a haven for lovers, is now a treeless barren waste.

Bun-faced, with slanting sludge-coloured eyes, I was probably a great disappointment to my parents. My hair looked as though it had been trimmed round a pudding basin and I wore a fringe. But I kept on·smiling until my mother sat down at the piano, when I flew at her screaming with jealous rage. Aged four, during luncheon, after being refused a second helping of roast beef, I ran at her with a carving knife.

I was banned from the table and locked into the attic, and Aunty Hilda's husband, Uncle Dicky, came up to console me. A schoolmaster, he was very fond of children, though he never had any of his own. Whenever trouble brewed, I sought his company, and spared him my usual term of abuse to grown-ups, 'You silly old elk!'

Soon after the attack on my mother, wearing a boy's sailor suit and a red tam-o'-shanter, I walked out of the house. It made a lasting impression on my mother. For years she went on recounting how, from her bedroom window, she had seen me bobbing along the cricket pitch as I strode purposefully into town.

One Easter, we were staying with an aunt in Cheltenham and Daddy took me into the town, where we saw three ducks wagging their heads up and down, seated on three large Easter eggs. When told the ducks were not for sale, that I couldn't have them, I created such a scene that a crowd gathered and a policeman had to help Daddy drag me away.

When left in the care of this dreaded aunt, an underling took me

4

to play on some public swings, whereupon a rash appeared on my hands. It was never clear whether the rash had been caught on the swing or from touching a hairy caterpillar, but I was considered to be unclean and, to prevent the door handles becoming contaminated, I was again locked into a room. It seemed to be a universal form of punishment in those days, locking children up to brood on their wickedness. Perhaps I had answered back, determined to have the last word, a habit that caused my father to suffer a great deal of anxiety.

Such a difficult child clearly needed more discipline. At the age of four, I was sent as a border to a nearby convent. Besides being less costly, a Catholic school was thought to be more strict. Having inherited Daddy's aptitude for games, I was soon handling a hockey stick. Whenever I fell and grazed a knee, the nuns plied me with sweets. Brighton rock and sherbert sucked through a liquorice stick were then a childhood treat, though it is doubtful if that is what the nuns produced. After breakfast, when the other pupils trooped up to class, I lingered behind to eat the remains of the nuns' buttered toast. Then, exacerbated by fear, lest someone should come in and catch me at it, I'd rub on the edge of the refectory table while conjuring up a fantasy of falling into a bed of stinging nettles. I developed a crush on a very plain girl, called Marjorie. I would creep into her bed or lie curled on her lap in a foetal ball, which was interpreted as precocious sexuality meriting instant spanking.

Then, when my sister Brenda was born, we settled into a large basement flat in a dingy London block not far from Hyde Park. The sitting room curtains had a design of red and yellow tulips, and in one of the window panes was a circular black patch where someone had kicked in a football. As pedestrians hurried past, one could hear the clank of a manhole. Above the mantelpiece hung a Victorian painting of Sir Walter Raleigh sitting on a deserted beach gazing longingly out to sea. A dining room at the back of the flat had Chippendale chairs and looked on to a yard of dustbins.

Our mongrel terrier Peter excited great admiration by accompanying my father to the War Office and finding his way home alone. My sister's Irish nurse had coarse red hands with long brittle fingernails that were always getting chipped during our fisticuff fights in the kitchen. For, at this stage, it was Brenda who incited my jealous rages. Wearing a *cloche* hat, the nurse would wheel Brenda's pram into the park, while Peter trotted alongside. I carried the picnic basket containing a thermos of tea, tomato and cucumber or jam sandwiches. Once at the Round Pond, with nurse settled on the grass, I'd take the pram, saying I was going to watch the little sailing boats and, once out of sight, pinched Brenda's bare calves, so that screams prevailed all the way back to Hyde Park Mansions.

The nearest convent, Sion, was in Chepstow Villas. The entrance hall was dark and cavernous with candlelit Virgins in niches. The school uniform was a white silk blouse and black gym tunic with a coloured sash. Out of doors one wore a wide-brimmed cream Panama hat. The English and maths mistress was a brisk little nun who always came bustling into the classroom nervously adjusting her wimple. She must have been a good teacher, for I began to excel at maths. She would read out any essay that appealed to her. One subject I chose was the fantasy life of the cabby parked on the corner of Chepstow Villas. Whenever one passed, he was invariably asleep perched high up behind his horse, a whip in his hand and his mouth ajar.

Daddy paid extra for me to take piano lessons. At the end of school concerts, I and another girl would play duets. I collected rosaries. In chapel, I loved kneeling before the altar, waiting to have a wafer placed on my tongue and sipping Christ's blood from the goblet of Madeira. Surprisingly enough, no one ever tried a conversion. And, although I often played truant, having saved up bus fares by walking to school in order to spend an afternoon in the local 'fleapit' watching Garbo and John Gilbert, I was very happy at Sion.

Mummy had retained an old bachelor admirer from her theatrical days, the *Times* theatre critic, who gave us free tickets; whenever we went to the Palladium to see *Peter Pan*, he got us a box to ourselves. But what Brenda and I enjoyed most was being taken to Barnum's circus every year. When Brenda reached an age to attend Sion Convent, she was made to walk with me; in that way I saved up two bus fares. Everything went well until the age of puberty, when I rouged my cheeks and used Mummy's tweezers to pluck out all my eyebrows. One day, a pale saintly-looking nun was rifling through our desks when she came across a bundle of love letters I had written to myself, but signed 'Fred'. I was expelled in disgrace.

When Brenda developed asthma, Daddy moved us all to a healthier atmosphere, high up in a new modern block off Baker Street. Their concern over Brenda's health, and the comings and goings of medical men induced a bout of anorexia. I would eat nothing but Ryvita and lettuce leaves. A doctor recommended exercise. Every morning, before anyone was awake, I walked briskly round the outer circle of Regent's Park, and went on starving myself. So Daddy packed me off as a boarder to Ashford High School. On autumn mornings, all the girls aimed to be the first one down to gather up the walnuts that had fallen in the school grounds overnight. At hockey, I started off the match . . . one two three and clack clack clack. I was then so tall that at netball all I had to do was stand on tiptoe to drop the ball into the net.

At this stage, Uncle Dudley came to the fore. He was then a major in the RAMC. During holidays, I and my bicycle were despatched to some army base. My uncle was a great womaniser, much to Aunt Nancie's grief. They had a son, Richard Brinsley. That side of the family always considered my father had married beneath him, whereas we would ridicule Uncle Dudley's medical ineptitude. Once, he prescribed a remedy for colds and the instant the bottle touched the table, the cork flew up to the ceiling. He was not a weak man like Daddy, but rather formidable. Aunt Nancie was kind and puritanical. She considered *Jane Eyre* an immoral book for children. She was rich and, staying with them, life became quite luxurious. A maid brought up an early morning cup of tea with two thin slices of bread and butter. I would remain in bed reading Jeffrey Farnol, Mazo de la Roche[*] and Thomas Hardy until a gong announced that breakfast was on the table, where scrambled, poached or fried eggs with sausage and bacon were being kept warm on a hot-plate. Everyone dressed for dinner; a butler served at table and the meal terminated with a ritual glass of port. But my appetite was never appeased and, being too shy to say so, I would bicycle off to the nearest chemist, and spend any pocket money on malt and cod-liver oil that I mixed with Bemax in the secrecy of my room.

Horrified by my ignorance, Uncle Dudley tutored me in French. The sentence '*Pierre est allé au bord de la mer*' still rings in my head. I also learnt to play bridge. I developed a crush on Cousin Dick who was timid, with twerpy good looks. We would be put together in the open dicky of Uncle Dudley's two-seater. Uncle D was fanatical about cars. At the beginning of the century, he had driven a Citroën as far as Iran and back. He loved to travel and at the end of his life, a widower and retired from the army, he travelled round the world as a ship's doctor.

The first sexual attack came from Uncle Ivan, the handsome

---

[*]Author of the family saga, *Whiteoaks*. Farnol was another immensely popular novelist.

Armenian husband of Mummy's pretty sister, Vera. One summer at Grandma's Uncle Ivan came into my room and plunged a hand under my nightdress. Not taking this as a warning, the following day I accompanied him into the town. While driving along the High Street, he said I'd find some sweets in his trouser pocket, but all I found was a hole and something warm and slithery.

That summer, there must have been a large gathering at my grandparents'. One evening, with everyone seated in an upstairs sitting room dominated by a piano, I was asked to play the *Moonlight Sonata* for Daddy, poor Daddy who had been paying for piano lessons all these years; but, although used to performing at school concerts, I was unable to strike a note. All piano lessons were stopped and I remained Little Misunderstood.

After the break-up of Aunty Vera's marriage to Uncle Ivan, forever after referred to as 'that dreadful dago', Vera became the mistress of a Catholic solicitor who had a wife and children. On weekends, he and Aunty Vera drove down from London to stay at the Imperial Hotel. But Sundays were spent with Ma, as my grandmother was called. I used to brood on Aunty Vera's scandalous situation. She appeared so glamorous with her sports car, pretty clothes and wide-belted high-collared pure camelhair coat. Grandma used to criticise her for using too much make-up and annoy her by saying, 'You looked so much prettier, Viv, when you had a natural look.'

Finally, Aunty Vera remarried a querulous alcoholic, then the Governor of Lagos. When he retired, she bought a cottage on the outskirts of Hythe But she still spent most of her time on the Marine Parade. She would arrive, bounding up the stairs and bursting into the sitting room with the joyful welcome of 'Hallo, girls'. And that is how the aunts always thought of themselves, 'the girls', until well into their eighties, when each one died.

Plagued by ill health, Daddy also retired and settled in the neighbourhood. We lived next door to Saltwood Vicarage; and close by stood a Gothic church. We became a family of hermits, with Daddy's health the ruling topic. And, whenever the church bells tolled, he would recite some ditty from an Irving play that ended, 'Oh, those goddamned bells.' His days were spent tapping the weather gauge, reading *The Times* and taking afternoon strolls with the current dog. After Peter, it was a sheep-killing cocker spaniel. And, every evening at six o'clock, he turned on the radio to listen to the news. A great worrier, he was always fretting about bills. Most of his inheritance went in the Wall Street crash. He was a great disappointment; I even fostered the idea he was not my real father – a common misconception among father-fixated children, according to some clever Freudian. My mother went on reliving her glamorous past, repeating anecdotes about Gertie Millar,[*] the actor Reginald Denny and Michael Arlen.[†] 'I remember him taking me to a ball . . .' she'd say, 'and on the way home we stopped at a cab stall for a cup of coffee. He was carrying a rolled-up umbrella, and pointing to a doughnut he spiked it with the tip of his umbrella saying, "I'll have that one" . . . He was a very dapper little man.'

She had long given up the piano. A large aviary was built into the garden and she bred budgerigars. There was nothing my mother could do well. Not even cook. We seemed to live on sausage and mash, being easy to prepare and cheap.

I would go by bus to a convent school in Folkestone until one day my father flew into a rage because I had blocked the washbasin with camomile flowers, a hair-bleaching device. So I was packed off to school as a border until fifteen, when I left school altogether and took to wandering about the nearby woods with a book, followed by the postman's son, a Heathcliffian character with a mongrel dog. We never spoke except to say good evening and, while I sat reading about Becky Sharp, he squatted close by, explaining to Daddy afterwards that he was doing it for my own good. I had another admirer, whom we named The Egg Man, rather as one might say, The Elephant Man, who came round every week with a poultry van.

Then, Daddy agreed to pay for my keep in a YWCA hostel in London and I left home for good.

---

[*]The actress who became Countess of Dudley.
[†]Author of *The Green Hat*.

◇◇◇ Chapter II ◇◇◇

YWCA

In the early days of their marriage, my parents had made friends with a neighbouring millionaire whose wife had also been a Gaiety Girl much admired by Daddy. Sidney had inherited a fortune from margarine. Being a director of Gooch's, a large general store in Knightsbridge, he arranged for me to be taken on in the model dress department, where my job was to fold up the clothes in tissue paper and put price tags on the models in the window. As I was determined to buy a pure camelhair coat with a high collar like the one Aunty Vera wore, I'd save up my wages and at lunchtime, standing among the coat racks in the basement, drank milk through a straw. Knowing me to be a director's protégée, the head saleslady sometimes took me to a teashop in Sloane Street. When she discovered that the customers preferred seeing the clothes draped on me rather than on a hanger, she recommended me to take a modelling course; and that was how, on evenings in Oxford Street, I learnt how to twirl round corners with outstretched pleading arms like someone balancing an invisible tray.

At weekends, seated on the windowsill of my cell in the YWCA, I'd gaze down at the traffic and long to go home. On fine days, at lunchtime, I went into Hyde Park with a book. One day, while sitting reading on a park bench, no doubt attracted to the bleached hair and over-made-up face, a handsome Guards officer from the nearby barracks approached. The following day he suggested an evening rendezvous. The meeting place turned out to be a *louche* hotel off Leicester Square, where he had hired a private room and ordered champagne. Even so, I resisted all attempts on my virginity, merely laddering a pair of silk stockings in the fray on the four-poster bed. Mummy would have rated the officer a 'Perfect Gentleman'. The following day, three pairs of silk stockings were deposited at Gooch's information desk. The Guards officer, alas, never turned up in the park again.

The next chance meeting took place on a bus top. Peter was Austrian and so good-looking he could have been a film star, though he claimed to be secretary to Lady Asquith, and lived in a furnished room off Notting Hill Gate. Evidently his wages were small; all we ever ate were cakes. On Sundays, in a borrowed car, we drove to Guildford and went riding. Peter, on the other hand, never laid a finger on me. One day, maybe out of wishful thinking, I told him I had been raped and then aborted, and that was why Daddy had banished me from home, which so scared Peter that I never saw him again.

Tina engaged me in conversation one evening while we were both lining up with our trays in the hostel canteen. Petite, bossy, with an obscene red mouth and ginger hair, Tina taught ballroom dancing on stiletto heels at Costelanni's Famous Dancing School in Regent Street. On weekends, we would take the train to Basingstoke where I was kept busy cleaning her mother's cottage windows. According to Tina who was a good deal older than me, one should never sit idly brooding. These were formative years still; and her endless activity made a deep impression on me; she was always on the go, sewing dusting, knitting and reading aloud Somerset Maugham's short stories; he remained her favourite author. Tina's childhood had been spent in Tientsin, where her father had been Governor, and she clearly identified with Maugham's heroines.

Thinking she rendered me a service, she introduced me to her boss Mr Costelanni himself; but all he did was to take me to a greyhound track, and introduce me to a nauseous concoction of champagne and Guinness known as Black Velvet. All tracks, whether horses, cars, or dogs, bore me to distraction. All I enjoyed was the appearance of the little men in white aprons, carrying buckets, who circled the track, shovelling.

At this stage, Aunty Vera would lend me her cyclamen satin evening dress, Sidney's chauffeur would collect me from the YWCA, and Sidney, the family friend, and I would dine at either Scott's in Piccadilly, Odennino's or the Savoy Grill where, after dinner, we moved to the edge of the dance floor to watch the cabaret or danced sedately to a foxtrot or a tango.

11

In high heels, I was a good deal taller than Sidney. Dapper, white-haired, impeccably dressed, when not wearing a dinner jacket, with a red carnation in his buttonhole, he would appear in green tweed or oatmeal, a silk handkerchief in his breast pocket and brown and white co-respondent shoes. On Sundays, his chauffeur drove us out to a golf club. Exceedingly clean, smelling of Hermès eau-de-Cologne and cigar smoke, reserved and devoid of conversation, Sidney's main interests were golf and business. As well as having a wife, a house in Grosvenor Square and a villa in Cannes, though not a promiscuous man, he had always maintained a mistress.

One weekend, his chauffeur drove us to Brighton. On Saturday afternoon I wandered into a fortune teller on the seafront. Noting a smudge on my middle finger, she counselled me to go on writing, but failed to foretell the loss of virginity that night in a suite of the Royal Albion. Although I felt no loss or regret, I never boasted of my alliance with this father-substitute – my father's best friend, what's more – done to spite daddy, the same clever Freudian later said.

I moved into a large flat in Crawford Street. Sidney furnished it in pale green with an Axminster carpet and green velvet curtains. A Bechstein followed. Piano lessons resumed. I was given an allowance, half the amount he had settled on his wife, according to Sidney, who thought he was being fair to both of us. Furs followed . . . a white ermine cape, two silver fox stoles, one slung over each shoulder with their jaws snapped together. On my birthday, the chauffeur deposited a sports car at the kerb. I had outdone Aunty Vera. Then the chauffeur drove us round Europe. A suite at the George V. Champagne luncheons at Fouquet's. Afternoon drives in the Bois. Shopping in the rue de Rivoli. Josephine Baker at the Folies Bergère. Holland. Belgium. Italy. Gelati. Ghiberti. The Ethiopian crisis. In Bologna, tomatoes were thrown at the chauffeur seated at the wheel of the Alvis. In Rimini, the hotel was full of Italian beauties dining with German officers *à la* Stroheim. In Basle, we lodged in the Hôtel Trois Rois. In the evening, from my hotel window, I could see the workers leaping into the river, their arms held high, hands clutching some garment as the swirling current swept them homeward. In Monte Carlo, I developed a passion for water-skiing. Then, on our way back, in the Villa d'Este, alone in my hotel room, gazing out at the moon, I stood draped in white ermine and, without understanding why, burst into tears.

Back in London, an abortion was dealt with cleanly in a nursing home. Accompanied by Sidney's ex-mistress, a recuperation took place in Madeira. It was very agreeable swimming from the rocks of Reid's Hotel in February. While the duenna gave bridge parties in the hotel lounge, I carried on with the band leader in the surrounding countryside. Cynicism had set in. The duenna advised me to get a life settlement out of Sidney. Feckless like my parents, I was not cut out for that sort of thing. The future would take care of itself!

It was I who terminated the affair, for no rhyme or reason other than boredom. An unemotional man, Sidney never questioned the decision. Being an original shareholder of Wimbledon, every year he went on giving me two Centre Court tickets. And we went on meeting for lunch or dinner until, many years later, he married again, for a third time, the last lucky bride being his Irish housekeeper. They moved to Ireland to breed race horses.

It was never known what Daddy had thought of the affair. But Mummy, forever after, whenever Sidney was mentioned, referred to him not only as a swine, but 'that dirty old man'.

✧✧✧ Chapter III ✧✧✧

First Love

In those days, like Jane Austen's heroines, what most girls dreaded was eternal spinsterhood. Uncle Dudley had become the general in charge of medical services throughout India. He wrote inviting me to stay. I bought a lot of pretty clothes from a small boutique in Bond Street. One of the evening dresses was deep red in the style of a sari with a short red bolero trimmed with sequins. Then, with a first-class ticket, I boarded the *Viceroy of India*. When the ship docked in Marseilles, the future King of Egypt and his mother came aboard. One night, there was quite a scandal when the band appeared and a tipsy passenger tried to drag the Queen Mother onto the dance floor. It was dark when we docked in Alexandria and the ship was surrounded by hundreds of lit feluccas. The fellaheen were celebrating Farouk's return. A red carpet was lain along the gangplank, and shouts and laughter continued throughout the night.

When the *Viceroy of India* docked in Bombay, there was Uncle Dudley leaning on a shooting-stick on the quay dressed in khaki shorts and a topi, a row of medals on his chest, among them the DSO. As the passengers disembarked, he adjusted his eyeglass, anticipating my appearance. After dining in the air-conditioned restaurant of the Taj Mahal Hotel, we visited a nightclub full of sailors dancing together. The following morning we left for Poona, four hours drive away. Then Poona was almost a dirty word, being a synonym of Anglo-Indian bigotry. You only had to mention Poona for people to jeer and it was included in many music hall jokes. In fact, it was a very pretty hill station filled with barracks.

14

We entered the drive of a white bungalow covered in bougainvillaea, where Aunt Nancie awaited us holding a Welsh terrier. I was looked after by an ayah, who washed my hair, took charge of my clothes and for breakfast she brought me a paw-paw with fresh limes. Otherwise, the meals remained scrupulously British. We always dressed for dinner. The first course was a clear soup with croutons. While we were eating, brightly coloured lizards ran along the walls or peeped out from behind the picture frames. The first evening, when I appeared wearing the red sari dress, my aunt was shocked. To her Indians were an inferior race and it struck her as odd that anyone should wish to imitate their way of dressing. I slept under a mosquito net and was usually awakened in the morning by a series of bugle calls coming from the nearby barracks. Very soon Uncle Dudley had found me a retired race horse. On late afternoons, I'd set out for a leisurely canter round the compound. After trotting docilely out of the drive, the stallion (if he did not throw me a short way up the road) broke into a canter and headed for the racecourse. Once there, he galloped round, with me clinging to the mane until, thoroughly exhausted, he trotted back to his bag of oats. This caused my relatives such anxiety, particularly as I refused to go out wearing a topi, that they found me a riding companion. Colonel Rice and his steed clopped into the drive. The Colonel had a reputation for being a fine horseman. He taught me how to handle the reins, grip well and keep my heels well down. Then, off we would set for a leisurely canter out of the compound into the surrounding countryside, through stretches of sugar cane and villages full of yapping pye-dogs. We would return at dusk, the sky a blaze of red, while on either side of the track Indians squatted over camp fires preparing their evening meals. But I was still bucked off, for the stallion would be bitten by horseflies between the buttocks and break into a gallop. Before long I was anxious to give him up; and, as a consolation, someone presented me with a tame leopard.

The great event of the week was the Poona race meeting, when Uncle Dudley went round to groups of moustached officers, introducing his 'beautiful niece from England'! Should I be driven down to Bombay, I stayed with a naval commander whose sister I had met on the ship. Bombay has an intolerably humid climate. At night, one lay pouring with sweat, listening to the screech of peacocks in some nearby garden. But it was very pleasant at lunchtime, when one drank chotah pegs in the Bombay yacht club, where the atmosphere was far less stuffy than the 'Whites Only' Poona gatherings.

One evening, my uncle took me to a circus and after the performance we visited the animals' stalls, where we came across a young man stroking an elephant's trunk. We liked him so much that my uncle invited him back to lunch. But my aunt found him callow and ill-mannered, for he had a habit of reclining on the arm of a chair and talking with a cigarette dangling out of his mouth. He was clean-shaven, moreover, and consorted with Indians.

Charles was a captain in the Royal Engineers and had enlisted on a scholarship to please his parents. He was not at all happy in the Indian Army, wrote poetry and had a passion for T S Eliot. On my birthday, Aunt Nancie gave a big party. As a birthday present, Charles parted with his copy of Eliot's early poems, from which he liked to read aloud. In the evenings, we sometimes dined together at a dismal Poona hotel.

Charles had two horses, a pye-dog and a broken-down old car. We would drive into the country taking a picnic, a gramophone and his pye-dog; his syce brought up the rear with the horses and we would ride back, until one day Charles fell ill with dysentery and had to go into hospital.

Meanwhile, Uncle Dudley, who had now and then to travel through India checking on medical supplies, was due to appear at a conference in Lucknow and decided to take me with him as co-driver. He also thought it would be a good opportunity to show me something of the Indian scene. We set off in an open Citroën, a turbaned bearded Sikh servant on the back seat with the luggage, and drove for days without seeing a living creature, except cows, or an occasional red-bearded holy man. As we drove fast through the villages, we left any washing that had been spread out on the ground coated with dust; and one had the impression that old people were being literally pushed beneath our wheels. At lunch-time, we'd picnic under a banyan tree by the side of the road and, when we had a puncture, it was Uncle Dudley who changed the tyre. After lunch, my uncle moved to the back seat to snooze. Once, when I took over and the car stalled in the middle of a river, out of nowhere a band of Indians suddenly appeared and pushed the car to the farther bank. Every evening, we would arrive dust-coated at one of the Dak houses that are posted all over India. The rooms were clean and bare, with a washbasin and a jug of lukewarm water. Outside, pecking about a dusty yard, were a few scrawny hens, one of which we ate for dinner.

The sunsets were so beautiful, with the sky a blaze of red, that I suffered the same despair and sense of loss that had reduced me to tears in the Villa d'Este; and, wherever we arrived for the night, a letter from Charles awaited me. One night, in a rainstorm driving through a jungle, a tiger, blinded by the headlights, leapt onto the bonnet.

Back in Poona, Charles had just come out of hospital, where he had lost a lot of weight. Monsoon time was approaching; and, as my aunt insisted I should return to England, we all drove down to Bombay and a farewell dinner took place at the Taj Mahal Hotel. The next morning, my aunt and uncle and Charles escorted me to the docks; and there I said goodbye to my relations. But Charles accompanied me onto the ship and we talked of soon meeting again, as he was determined to leave the army. Then he kissed me goodbye and the *Viceroy of India* sailed. When we were already far out at sea, Charles suddenly walked into my cabin; and from that moment he became a stowaway. The cabin steward befriended us and brought Charles meals from the ship's kitchen. Sometimes we sat on deck sheltered from the wind, planning our future, and how, as soon as the ship docked in Aden, we would disembark and wend our way to Suez, and thence get back to England. The third day at sea, however, the captain received a message from Poona HQ informing him that he had a deserter on board. Some pukka sahib going home on leave had seen Charles on deck and reported it. The ship's captain was a kind man; Charles was allowed to remain in the cabin; but, when the ship docked in Aden, he was to be put under arrest.

It was night time and raining when the ship reached Aden, but we remained anchored well out. A patrol boat then chugged from the shore; three men boarded the ship, entered the cabin and took Charles away. I stood on deck in the drizzle and, leaning against the handrail, watched the patrol heading back until the rear light had completely vanished. I returned to the empty cabin; and henceforth was ostracised by all the Anglo-Indian passengers. But there was always the cabin steward and the captain invited me to join the other guests at his table.

Back in India, a court martial was held, at which Uncle Dudley was obliged to appear as main witness. Charles's long hospitalisation might have been used in his defence and a plea that he was not entirely responsible for his behaviour. He himself no doubt hoped he would merely be dismissed. In fact, he was banished to the North West Frontier, where the British were at war with a religious fanatic, the Fakir of Ipi, whose followers were called The Rebels.

When I got back to England, my father had already received a letter from Uncle Dudley. I was a disgrace to the whole family, I learned, selfish and ungrateful AFTER ALL THEY HAD DONE FOR ME. Poor Nan was so upset; it had affected her health; for details of the scandal had spread throughout India, while Uncle Dudley never wished to see or hear from me again.

A month later, when I was staying with my parents in the country, my father as usual tuned in to the six o'clock news and we heard a voice say he had a special announcement to make – on the North West Frontier of India, a relief force of British troops, carrying supplies, had been ambushed while passing through a narrow gorge. The convoy of officers and men had been taken by surprise and, as they climbed out of their open trucks to take cover, all shot down and killed. There were no survivors. The names of the dead officers were read out, including that of Charles Langford Hinde.

Back in London, I found a letter, the last Charles had written. Enclosed were several snapshots of us taken on the ship. There was one of him on deck, leaning against the handrail, smiling and seemingly careless, wearing an open-neck shirt, his hair blown about by the breeze; and one of me sitting in a deckchair, vainly engrossed in varnishing my fingernails, in preparation for our flight to Suez. His letter, written on Taj Mahal notepaper in the form of a poem, was headed *On The Way To The War*.

> I have been moved
> moved to the core
> of my fantastic soul
> the visit to the Viceroy proved
> most heart searching
>
> there was Shilston wondering
> how I knew he had a son
> offering advice as he had done
> before
>
> the bandsmen barmen and hordes of pursers
> and above all your cabin steward
> we talked in your cabin for a while
> of this and that but mostly you
>
> I think I even raised a smile
> but it was utterly dejecting

thank god I am rejecting
all good advice and trying to get home
and we will meet again

both there and in this Indian hotel I have
been feeling things; between which and remembering them
there is a whole world's difference

as the ship came in, slowly toward the pier, I might have been
in Aden again
the rain falling and a tug taking me away from you forlorn
well loved standing and . . .

tonight I go north
we were supremely happy in that dreadful ship, in other
circumstances perhaps joy
would be too near perfection. There is always hope.

Charles on the way north to the war.

◇◇◇ Chapter IV ◇◇◇

The Lost Girls

'They valued their independence; for they belonged to
a section of war-time society whom I called "The Lost Girls",
adventurous young women who flitted around London,
alighting briefly here and there, and making the best
of any random perch on which they happened to descend.'

Peter Quennell, *The Wanton Chase*

I resumed modelling, at Fortnum and Mason, Stiebel and Hartnell, where I made friends with Louise who had been a model for Epstein and Augustus John. She was beautiful, wore her long hair pulled sharply back off a heart-shaped face and was very prudish, sharing the opinion of a Frenchman who once claimed sex was an undignified function for his *organe noble*. Louise had other affections and a rather refined way of talking. As though to play down her physical attributes, she grimaced a great deal and when laughing covered her densely boot-blacked eyes with a rather governessy hand. She had been christened Mary, but adopted the name Louise at a time when anything French was considered to be terribly chic, and Maurice Chevalier was singing, 'Every little breeze seems to whisper Louise . . . just to be near you thrills me through and through . . . can it be true someone like you could love me . . . LOUIEEESE.'

Our favourite meeting place was the Guinea pub in the mews behind Hartnell's, much frequented by jockeys. Beasley was rather tall for a jockey and later became a trainer. The one time he rode an outsider at enormous odds, I was not tipped off. Aunty Vera, enamoured of anything to do with a racecourse, would drive us down to stay with him in Newmarket. Beasley was an extremely generous man; even after making an abortive attempt in spotlessly pressed pyjamas to creep into my bed, he went on giving splendid presents.

Louise was married to a painter turned art-critic for the *Evening Standard* and they lived in an attic studio in Charlotte Street where I was first introduced to *la vie bohème*. Her husband Michael Sevier, rarely spoke but constantly hummed. Rather than use an ashtray, he'd walk the entire length of a room in order to flick ash behind a piece of wall furniture. In the evenings, he haunted the Café Royal and stood over people humming until invited to join their table. Another habitué of the Café Royal then was Goronwy Rees. He once joined the writer Peter Quennell and me for dinner and, while Peter was engrossed in paying, managed to slip an invitation to lunch between the pages of my book.

On her way home from Hartnell's Louise invariably stopped off at the bar of the White Tower, and any pub-crawlers who amused her would be taken back to the studio and given a pot luck meal. The studio was invariably full of odd people. One regular, the Austrian Eugene Ledebur, had a beautiful check Tyrolean hunting jacket with knobbly leather buttons; and he gave it to me. Daddy always discouraged us from buying him a present, saying it was a waste of money; but he so much admired this garment that I gave it him; and it became known as Daddy's jacket, and remained on him in tatters until the end of his days.

Louise had a lover, Olgin, who had property in Berlin and used to drive her round in a flashy little sports car. At the outbreak of war he joined up in the Pioneer Corps and Louise always referred to him as poor bloody O or PBO for short. One evening, the three of us stood at the bar of the Eight Bells and Bowling Green, where we were joined by a young man Louise immediately labelled 'Miss' Becher, as he had a rather mincing manner. Miss Becher had a brother in the Indian Army, so he had already heard about the Poona scandal and its sad consequences. Neither handsome nor brilliant, but a thoroughly decent fellow, Miss Becher was so good natured and ready to conform we termed him Slave.

Becher became my first serious suitor. He liked to spend his money on going to the best restaurants and introduced me to nightclubs, the Nest in Soho and the 400 in Leicester Square. At the 400, which was unlicensed to sell alcohol after a certain hour, one joined what was termed a Bottle Party and on entering the club you bought a bottle which was labelled with your name, and when you left in the early hours the level of the alcohol was scrupulously marked on the bottle for you to claim the next time you went.

Another follower at this time was a Dutch theatrical producer who took me to Amsterdam to meet his family. His sister was an artist and a friend of Goering. Demeester wore a pince-nez and rather flamboyant clothes in the style of the late nineties. Once, in a fit of jealousy, he leapt onto the windowsill of my Cumberland Court flat and threatened to jump into the moving traffic. The third suitor was a travelling salesman. A hearty fellow who somehow lacked *esprit*, he would fly off to West Africa and send postcards saying 'travelling north tomorrow' or 'am now travelling south'.

Silver fox fur stoles had become a streetwalker's get-up; so I transformed mine into a collar and cuffs and a muff to go with a sleek black coat, the remainder becoming a fur hat to which I added a peacock's feather. One lunchtime, while walking along Berkeley Square, the Rahvis sisters engaged me by shouting down from their showroom window. But they made me model in a wig shaped like earphones and I didn't stay there long. A hopeless model, anyway, the one person who seemed to appreciate me was Schiaparelli as my dimensions conformed to the hourglass silhouette. Once, after sacking me for remaining in Monte Carlo waterskiing instead of returning to fit an autumn collection, she re-engaged me. Schiap was the most inventive designer of that period. Unlike Hartnell, whose showroom was a blaze of chandeliers, Schiap's surroundings were very simple – plain settees with shocking pink cushions. She lived with her daughter above the fitting rooms at 36, Upper Grosvenor Street. The boutique was on the ground floor. Then, the French reckoned to be smart you had to wear black. Schiap started the colour combination of black with *café au lait*. She created every detail, the belts, buttons, hats and costume jewellery. The staff were all French except for a Czech tailor. Whenever I was about to twirl, the head saleslady, Madame Madeleine, would invariably exclaim, 'Ouf! Elle est complètement VIDE, cette fille.'

We were allowed to borrow the clothes in the evening and buy the models cheaply, at the end of each season. One ankle-length coat I bought, already ordered and rejected by Marlene Dietrich, had an enormous beaver collar and hem, but proved so hampering whenever I ran to catch a bus that the fur was lopped off and made into a jacket which years later was still being worn in a hamseen in the Sinai desert.

Schiap's model girls were very mixed. There was one pig-faced American, Sally, very tall and chic; a Danish beauty, married to Adrian Conan Doyle,[*] who kept a cobra that they fed on live rabbits; and a Russian, Luba. But the most beautiful girl was a Norwegian called Gerda, who had been a Ziegfeld Follies showgirl. Blonde and blue-eyed like my mother, they had similar values in life. One was that you should marry for money, though neither of them was tough enough to attain her ambition.

It was about this time that I bought a cottage in Kent for £400. There was a garden back and front with damson and apple trees. In springtime it was filled with clumps of daffodils and scented narcissi. The cottage was oak-beamed and, on Daddy's advice, a porch was built on with seats and painted white. The upstairs rooms had dormer windows. A path led up to a white gate that opened into a lane bordered by meadowsweet. Opposite, on a slightly higher level, was a field; and, when approached from the field, Cot appeared to have a face, the dormer windows being hooded watchful eyes. From my bed, I could see the farmer tilling with a horse-drawn tractor and as the wheels turned the tractor made a clicking noise like the latch of the gate being opened, so that I would rush to the window to see whom it could be. The only visitor, in fact, might be PC Boot. His constabulary was about five miles away and he liked to drop in to keep an eye on things. Having propped his bicycle against the hedge, he would stamp up the garden path, pausing now and then with his hands on his hips to gaze quizzically down at the unruly flowerbeds. 'Been digging, mate, I see,' he'd say; 'I was just passing and I brought these,' and he'd produce a smelly bag, out of which he tilted some home-grown runner beans. He was a big man with enormous buttocks and sticking-out ears, and he walked with splayed feet like a duck. Should any friend arrive to stay Boot always addressed him as 'Gov'.

Weekends, Gerda and I and her chow dog, Bumpser, would drive down in Gerda's open blue Fiat. We would set off along the Old Kent Road; shop on the way in Wye, then drive on to Hastinglea, the closest village to Cot that consisted of nothing but a public house and a general store, Tappendens, where you could find anything from a corkscrew to a bag of dates. From Hastinglea, one descended into a wooded valley redolent of fox and stink-

---

[*]Son of Sir Arthur Conan Doyle.

fungus, rooks squawking overhead. At the bottom was a deserted cricket pitch and a stone ruin. Then one mounted a steep incline with meadows either side full of browsing cows. Round a sharp bend at the top stood a Gothic church, filled with stone effigies of the Honeywell family. The churchyard was dominated by a ninety-year-old yew tree, its branches supported by ropes. At Elmstead crossroad was a large farm and a three-forked sign-post indicating the way to Canterbury, Wye and Hythe; then, up the garden path. On either side of the open fireplace in the sitting room were built-in cupboards; there was a wall-to-wall carpet, a sofa covered in chocolate glazed chintz . . . bookshelves. A gramophone. A calypso group. The Inkspots . . . 'Do I worry when the ice-man calls . . . Do I worry when you stay home every night and read your magazines . . . Do I lose any sleep over you . . . You know GODDAMNED well I dooooooooooooooooo.'

One evening, I was sitting in a corner of the bar in the Berkeley Hotel, awaiting Becher, when a Rhett Butler figure swung past trailing a pair of dachshunds. With a flashing smile that later earned him the pseudonym 'the Grinning Ape', he came over to announce we had met at some party. As well as womanising, photography turned out to be his prime pursuit. He became a regular visitor to Cot, driving down in a girlfriend's roadster, bringing goodies from Fortnum and Mason, and records. In those days, one walked a lot. There was a charming pub with a log fire, run by Mr Fox, that we termed the Foxhole, an ideal distance across the fields for a pre-luncheon drink. With the threat of war, the Grinning Ape joined up in the Supply Corps. He looked even more dashing in uniform. While training in the north, he wrote suggesting I put our names down in the Caxton Hall Registry. Happily, I did not take this proposal seriously. Soon after Gerda and I, on opening a newspaper, saw him grinning beside the roadster, about to drive away on his honeymoon. As soon as he got back, he came tearing round anticipating an amorous renewal; and Gerda forever after referred to him as 'That Bastard'.

Mummy taught one nil. Tina had stressed you must keep your hands busy all day doing something *utile*. Louise's way of filling a void was to be continually on the go swigging and making rendezvous with no matter whom . . . My resort was laughter.

◇◇◇ Chapter V ◇◇◇

The War

That last winter before the war Gerda and I went skiing in Davos, where glamorous Gerda became the toast of all the sportive Teutons. The last summer was spent in St Tropez with Luba and her son, Jean-François Bergery, a very clever little boy of whom I was much in awe. Among our Schiaparelli clothes, I remember a satin swimsuit printed in cockles and seashells, and a large black Panama hat with velvet ribbons.

When war finally broke out, Schiaparelli had already closed her salon and gone back to Paris; Luba and I were sharing a tiny top floor flat above a grocery store on the corner of Kinnerton Street. My quarters were the attic, a triangular room with candy-striped wallpaper, white furniture and matting. As she was a perfectionist, Luba's room was never furnished and contained nothing but a bed. She had, and still has, superb taste and a charming Russian accent, her sentences invariably interjected with 'Darling'. My chosen companions were always a good deal older than myself; and Luba became such a maternal figure that, whenever we separated, I lapsed into a depression. She had two sisters, Lukey, and the brightest and maddest, Katyia, a costume designer, very extravagant and always in debt. All three girls had been beauties. Their father, Krassin, had been a friend of Lenin. When Stalin came to power Krassin despatched his family to Sweden, and they never returned to live in Russia. Krassin became the first Soviet Ambassador to London and later Ambassador to Paris where Luba married the radical socialist, Gaston Bergery. After Stalin's death, the Soviets recognised Krassin as having been an important economist and a statue of him now stands in his native town Kurgan in Siberia.

One of Luba's first visitors to Kinnerton Street was a Frenchman who came over with de Gaulle. A banker, Monsieur Boris had been the Chef de Cabinet du Ministre des Finances under Léon Blum. During the war he worked with the Resistance leader Emmanuel d'Astier de la Vigerie, who became Luba's second husband. A talented writer, and Minister of the Interior in the provisional French Government under de Gaulle in Algiers, Emmanuel d'Astier was a distinguished figure. In politics he veered towards the Left. Throughout the war he had a *nom de plume* and moved between England and occupied France, carrying messages from the French Resistance. Separated from his wife in Paris, his advances rejected by Luba, Monsieur Boris was desperate for a woman and I seemed to fit the bill. When Luba evacuated herself to Devon with her son, Jean-François Bergery, Kinnerton Street was disbanded and Georges Boris took me to live with him in Shepherd's Market. A balding stocky man with a pale reptilian face, Georges Boris was kind and intelligent and had boundless energy. Every morning, he prepared the coffee, then dressed in army uniform and a képi and, carrying a briefcase, walked briskly out heading for the French headquarters, where he relayed broadcasts to the French people.

Standing at the window, I would watch him stride away, then utterly exhausted return to bed and go on dozing. Monsieur Boris's knowledge of English was about equivalent to my French. But, like many Frenchman I have known, he was an extremely jealous man. Once, at a party, I was sitting beside another Free Frenchman, when Georges came across the room and slapped my face. But then, I was in love with him, so the gesture was pleasing.

We saw quite a lot of the beautiful Lee Miller of *L'Age d'Or*[*] fame and Roland Penrose. Though Roland was divorced from his French wife, Valentine, she lived with them in Hampstead. It was an agreeably relaxed household. There was no demur should two luncheon guests decide to take an afternoon nap in their double bed. Lee was working for *Vogue*. She tried to turn me into a

---

[*]A surrealist film made by Luis Buñuel in cooperation with the painter Salvador Dali.

photographic model, but in all her pictures, I looked like a deadend kid.

It was during the Blitz with its sticks of bombs; six in succession were dropped. We would listen for their approach and, just as the sixth was about to fall, Monsieur Boris had a habit of flinging himself flat on the carpet. We did, in fact, have a very narrow escape in the middle of the night when a bomb fell on the pub next door and everyone in it was killed. We merely suffered shock, as the walls of the flat caved in, and everything was embedded in dust and plaster. The rest of the night was spent with Luba's sister, Katyia. Then Georges took a flat above the Mirabelle, a very popular underground restaurant, on the corner of Curzon Street, and life went on. As though to seek oblivion, we led a hectic social life. Pre-luncheon drinks in the Curzon Street Sherry Bar, luncheons at the Ritz, the Coquille, the Ecu de France or the Coq d'Or in Mayfair. When we were not at the 400, we frequented a vast vulgar nightclub off Berkeley Square; the Conga had a revolving dance floor. Or one went to the Suivi or the Jamboree and, of course, there was always the Players' Theatre Club, where the walls were covered in Feliks Topolski's prancing horses and Peter Ustinov was the principal performer. Or we might have drinks with Augustus John in the French Club, run by a lady called Olwen, where Louise did her war work behind the bar.

Madame Boris had been informed of our affair. She had written to say that she only hoped Georges was living with someone *'digne de lui'*. His closest friend, another Free Frenchman, shared a flat with a streetwalker on Bond Street. Everything went well until Georges started negotiating for his wife to come over and I began dining out on my own. Then there were scenes; Georges was always in a rage or distant, while I became increasingly depressed, until one day I packed my belongings and left.

The family had returned to London and were living in Cranmer Court. In spite of his bad health, Daddy had rejoined the War Office, for he felt it to be his duty to participate in the war effort. Sister Brenda was packing parcels, war work she shared with Melinda Maclean. My furniture came out of storage and Mattli, the dress designer, offered me the top floor of his house in Hertford Street. Michael Sevier, then divorced from Louise, hummed about the floor below, until one night he came back drunk and died climbing the stairs.

The main cause of Georges's jealousy had been a mystic gentleman-farmer separated from his wife, the famous beauty

27

Euphemia.* Ned Grove had built his own house, a white bungalow surrounded by meadows. He wore an eyeglass, was tall and distinguished, and might have been quite handsome but for a clownish snout.

On a weekend, I would take the train to Salisbury, change for the village of Binley and, once, when I stepped out of the train, Euphemia attacked me with her handbag, until Ned appeared to intercede. Ned's mysticism took the form of sentimentalising over Joan of Arc who he claimed had been in direct contact with God. In spite of this, however, visits to the farm were always extremely agreeable. Ned made his own bread, churned butter and brewed elderberry wine which, when drunk before a log fire on winter evenings, seemed strangely potent. One time, his friend, Hugo Pitman, arrived with a freshly caught salmon. It was so delicious that, when he found me raiding the larder in the middle of the night, Ned labelled me 'Mouse'. He was a charming man, if rather intense. When the spring came, we were always out of doors gathering hay, feeding the animals, taking long walks to the post office for Ned to pick up his mail. The relationship remained chaste; and this aggravated Ned. The last visit, returning to London on a sunny May morning, carrying a basket of fresh eggs and vegetables, I mounted the stairs of Hertford Street and looking up saw a patch of blue sky. The roof had received a direct hit in one of the fiercest raids on London and the whole of the top floor was wiped out. Rummaging about amongst the ashes, where my desk had been, I found under the rubble all my jewellery intact and with it my diamond ring.

Deprived of all possessions, I became a night flitter, using Cranmer Court as a base for letters and telephone messages. Sometimes I stayed with Gerda in her charming Culross Street house, with Feliks Topolski in his studio off Warwick Avenue, overlooking the canal where barges drifted past the window, or with Louise in Ebury Street until we had a serious falling out over a French opium smoker who frequented the French Club. We named him Chopin, and he was so addicted to his pipe that, when taken to Cot, he never considered it odd to be put in the spare room, while someone else shared my bed. Far from it, not only did Cot become

---

*Euphemia Grove was first married to the painter Henry Lamb. She is described by Frances Partridge in *Everything to Lose* as being at the age of sixty 'really beautiful still; she has a splendid pair of blue eyes, a classical nose and a skin that keeps its bloom and softness'.

his *clos de bonheur* but, in an enamoured state, he took his darling *trésor* to Cartier and spent all his money on a diamond bracelet. As it was too ornate for wartime wear, I never knew what to do with this lavish gift; and it was carried around, gloated over from time to time, in a straw basket containing paraphernalia like spoons and knives and the rations, until one day Louise claimed the Frenchman was being exploited. She grabbed the basket and retrieved his valuable present, whereupon Chopin came to his senses, gave up smoking opium, and grew fat and pompous. Whether it was due to disillusionment or drink, Louise became increasingly bitter. If someone she didn't like was mentioned while she was polishing glasses, she literally spat across the bar. PBO had joined up in the Pioneer Corps and been transferred to Wargraves, so her permanent escort became Sir Simon Schuster, a rich elderly financier with a toothbrush moustache, whom she named 'Schoolboy'. Louise towered over this pinstriped figure and his rolled umbrella. They were an odd couple, seen all over London leaping in and out of taxis on a permanent pub-crawl.

It was not until 1941 that I was summoned to appear before a call-up board. In perpetual dread of being put into the WAAFs or the WRENs, I set about finding a serious job. Peter Quennell and Gerda worked at the Ministry of Information. Hoping that I also might qualify for a censorship job, I went to apply. I was carrying *The Spoils of Poynton*, so when asked by the interviewer who was my favourite author it seemed apt to reply 'Henry James'. 'That elephantine trunk continually chasing after a garden pea!' sneered the interviewer, and showed me the door. Eventually I got a job driving trucks for the MTC. Then, when my old seducer Sidney acquired a factory of nuts and bolts, he gave me the job of doling out the men's wages. It meant taking a train from Waterloo to Sudbury every day. The factory had once been a large garage. The office was situated above the machines, where the manager, his wife and a secretary sat drinking endless cups of tea. Luncheons consisted of powdered eggs and chips brought over from a canteen. The wages had to conform to the Union Rate System which meant working out two thirds or one fifth of one and sixpence.

Once a week, Sidney appeared smartly dressed in a dark blue suit and a blue woolly overcoat, with a trilby tilted over one eye. As soon as he entered the factory, all the workers stopped singing and the machines came to a halt After poking about and questioning them, he was eventually coaxed back into the office and handed a cup of tea and a cheque book. Then, the manager's wife helped him back into his blue woolly overcoat and, giving his trilby a final tilt, Sidney groped his way down the perpendicular stairway and sped off in the direction of the station.

◇◇◇ Chapter VI ◇◇◇

Yugoslavs

The first time I saw Peter Quennell was at Gerda's in Culross Street. He came round one evening bringing Cyril Connolly, who was then editor of *Horizon* magazine, and the two men of letters were sharing a flat in Drayton Gardens. With his Byronic attitudes, wit and blond quiff Peter struck me as being a romantic figure, an impression that was soon dispelled when I knew him intimately. Peter loved the country and soon became a steady visitor to the cottage.

It was about this time that a Yugoslav friend, Dimy, offered me the job of secretary to the Yugoslav government in exile. Their office was in Kingston House and by then I was sharing a second floor flat above an antique shop in the Brompton Road with an odd girl who, for some reason, never got called up. I then had a passion for brewing stews, the dominant ingredient being potatoes, which were sometimes eaten seated on the edge of the bed or the carpet, and shared with Peter Quennell, a journalist Anthony Cotterill, or a guerrilla Yugoslav doctor, whom we termed the 'Horse Thief'. Another member of the entourage was a practising lawyer until he got called up. I had met Captain Brien How in a curious way, as we both alighted from a bus outside the Café Royal. Brien had a caustic sense of humour, but he was rather stodgy and, because of his ashen complexion, Peter always referred to him as 'Cold Veal'.

Diary

I awoke early. Sour grunts from Miss Morris when I looked into her room. Brewed some tea, using the stale leaves, as the rations have run out. A dreary weekend. Saturday was spent gloomily eating huge platefuls of tagliatelli at the Speranza, with Peter dismally reciting Dryden's translation of Horace, 'Happy the man, happy he alone, he who can call today his own,' and where Peter was attacked by Nika Hulton who accused him of spreading nasty gossip. Sunday, Peter spends his morning in the telephone booth opposite fixing himself up with free meals. Washed my hair and then rushed off to meet Feliks Topolski at the cinema; he arrived late so we trailed about the streets in the rain without speaking and eventually saw a very bad film, the life of Schubert.

Lunchtime I met Cold Veal at the Bunch of Grapes. Found him seated at the bar gazing into space; as torpid as ever; so I left him and went back to the flat where Miss Morris made me a fish pie. Cold Veal again in the evening for a drink. He was still sitting in the Bunch of Grapes staring into space. He came out of a coma to attack me, saying I was unworthy and led a pointless existence. When he saw I was not interested he lapsed back into a coma. Peter appeared, very screechy and tiresome; baited Cold Veal. Very much the gloating victor with a vanquished foe. What a pair!

Last night Miss Morris threw a party. It had been threatening for some time. She greeted her guests wearing a plum-coloured brocade dinner dress made specially for the occasion out of curtain material. Later, I took the Yugoslav ministers off to the Café Royal for dinner. One of them had just arrived from Yugoslavia; he had been with the guerrillas and had escaped through Turkey and Bulgaria. We sat up on the balcony drinking wine and toasting the Chetniks. The conversation consisted of solitary chords. '*Encore du vin*,' gurgle gurgle, '*Aux Chetniks*,' '*A Mihailovic*'.

Went to bed early and slept until eleven o'clock. Woke to hear Miss Morris running up and down stairs singing. I lit the gas fire, turned on the bath, made toast and tea. We walked across the park to Feliks's studio. A friend of his arrived at six. They talked about the tank situation in Libya where the Germans have guns that can fire a greater distance than ours. They said the Russian successes were due to the slow retreat which meant they suffered gigantic losses in material and manpower. The young man was a great admirer of Feliks's work and we all picked out drawings for a Polish paper in the order we liked best. Feliks gave me a 'roasted pyramid' to eat when I got home, but I was too stuffed with caraway bread, meat balls and herring paste. He lent me *Scum of the Earth* which I took away with *English Wits*, a book I left at the studio months ago when I was in the process of installing myself there. Quite a nice day really although I intended reading Peter's *Byron*.[*]

Japan has declared war on America and Great Britain. I suppose now all the Japs will be moving out of Kingston House. Miss Morris was maddening this morning as I was dressing and insisted on prattling away from her bed that she had been listening to the radio stations until five in the morning. She was boasting in some way, trying to impress me that she was sufficiently bright to take in the news.

Kingston House was swarming with Japs rushing about in dapper black suits. When I came back at lunchtime several of them were standing looking grim and defiant beside their suitcases in the hall. Tarzo (our doorman) noticed I had changed my hair. 'Hair change. No like,' he said, 'Me, no change,' pointing to his own frizzy head. Wrote to Peter Q. Stayed in this evening and had a stew with Cotterill. He has been the only person concerned about the Jap news. His serial in the *Express* will not be included tomorrow. Miss Morris is worried about the parties for the New Year. Thinks that the news will affect them.

Cotterill came to see me at the office looking shamefaced and embarrassed. After standing in the hall for several minutes at a loss for anything to say, he then produced two packets of cigarettes as a peace offering. Evidently his behaviour of last night had been worrying him. He told me he was off to Brighton and would I have dinner on Thursday; as I had had a telegram from Peter saying he would be back that day I had to refuse, so Cotterill said he would return from Brighton Wednesday.

Went home, had a bath and put on a new face and black dress, as I was dining with Feliks. Miss Morris tried to persuade me to wear my tarty red fox cape; but I explained it made Feliks feel like a sugar-daddy out with a moll. I had to wait for him at the Café Royal and was late myself, anyway. I ordered a large double whisky and

---

[*]*Byron, the Years of Fame* (1941).

read *Scum*. When Feliks arrived, the usual food discussion. We had a filthy dinner, and diluted red wine. Clive Entwistle came in with his stooping walk looking like a hunted animal on the prowl. He seemed to have toughened up since being in the army. Feliks did a drawing making me look benevolent and homely. He made Clive look like someone supervising the coconut shies. I gave Feliks my compact to do a drawing of himself. He did a pair of black button eyes gazing out in pain and bewilderment. Then we all bundled into a bus as the taxi situation was hopeless.

The Horse Thief seemed embarrassed when he arrived in the office and shuffled into his little room after saying a hasty *'dobar dun'*. He explained later that he had come round to the flat just before midnight to find the door shut. I told him a policeman had shut it. An unsatisfactory day. Bought two very pretty scarves at luncheon. Did mending when I got home. Cotterill arrived at nine just when I was about to fry some fish and potatoes. He was two hours late but offered no explanation. After placing his hat on the kitchen table he stood by the sink and gazed at me. Miss Morris appeared. I told them both I was retiring to my room. They trooped up after me carrying trays. We sat in oppressive silence. Cotterill departed. Miss Morris then produced her poems and with a pretence of coyness asked me if I could bear her to read them as I lay in the bath. I thought of other things. Cotterill reappeared penitent and forlorn. So we parted friends.

Peter telephoned at eleven to say he was back. Why only one letter from me while he was away? We arranged to meet in the evening. Cotterill rang. The Horse Thief presented me with two packets of Players. Arrived home in the evening to find the flat in chaos. Cold Veal came to see me. He just sat staring into space. I left him and rushed off to have a fitting for my coat; and a re-varnish at Antoine's. There is a new Tony at the office. His name is Sveto and he is very willing, proud and pretty. Italy and Germany declared war on America. No one seems either surprised or indignant.

What a messy existence! What chaos! What indecision! I feel depressed and unsettled. What to do? Mixed feelings about Peter Q, though he gets a habit. I like to have him for a feeling of security and Feliks for his company. There will have to be a choice sooner or later. At lunchtime I went to Carlos Place and had a fitting for the check material. The dress designer Jo Mattli told me he had seen Feliks dining at the Café Royal with a very lovely girl. The description sounded like the left-wing Janetta.* It's glamorous to be left-wing these days. Lunchtime, I ate fish and chips at a snack bar and worried a great deal. Arranged to dine with Cotterill. Peter telephoned to say he would come to the flat at eleven. Feliks rang to suggest he did the same thing.

Today I woke up at eight o'clock feeling rested. It was still dark outside. There was nothing to eat in the kitchen so I searched Miss Morris's room for the biscuit tin where I knew she had a store of leftovers from her party. Judging by the disappearance of soap and toothpaste, she had gone away. Peter read Cotterill's little book *What No Butter?* while I ran the bath. He thought the descriptions of routine family life sounded too grim and was amused by the endless tea-drinking. I asked him to get my meat ration from Cooper's, but he said he didn't think he could appear at MEW with a parcel of meat. I said who would know it was meat?

Friday night I was taken by a girlfriend, Freeny, to have drinks with some of her old Putney friends who had risen in life and were now installed in Berkeley Square. They all seemed to have made their fortunes in the coal trade. Cases of bourbon whisky and gin were produced. A lot of them were called Charlie; one of them was referred to as Brassy Reynolds, another Ronnie Batter and another Lex Busby. I took Cotterill with me and we dined afterwards at the Berkeley on minced chicken and water ices. Then so as to avoid Feliks who was coming round at ten we went to the pub next door where I had a large brandy and a pork pie as I still felt hungry. Feliks had brought me a copy of *Scoop*. Peter arrived at the flat at eleven, tipsy as ever but very gay; Cotterill seemed rather put out but took it well. I hope I have not lost a new slave, he is so sweet and reminds me of a Disney faun with his funny sticking-out ears and enormous dimples.

---

*Janetta Slater, who later married Robert Kee.

Miss Morris has a slight cold and has decided to remain in bed. I went in to see her and found her heavily pinked and mascaraed, wearing a most elaborate peach nightdress, with bracelets jangling to the elbow. Peter Q's frequent visits last week produced such sulks that I thought I might have to leave. But to appease and impress her we presented her with a copy of his new book. Persistent charming on his part had no effect, so now whenever he sees her he breaks into forced hysterical giggles, 'You are rather sweet, aren't you? . . .' Feliks, on the other hand she likes; he ignores her affectedness and makes no attempt to play up to her. A terrible *cafard* today. Feliks has just phoned to say that bitch Louise is on her way to see him on the pretext of collecting a coat. This morning Peter was intolerably grumpy and complained he felt ill and sick; the kitchen smelt so appalling, he said if it was not cleaned out plague would set in. Cotterill and Cold Veal telephoned. All Sunday it poured with rain. Peter came round at twelve with the Sunday papers; he told me that, with the aid of a policeman, he had been ringing my bell at four in the morning, then being very tipsy had fallen over twice before finding his way home. We lunched at the Queen's with some friends of his called Rayner. Then we went back to the plague centre and I read *Scum*. Dined on hare and salad at the Café Royal on the balcony, and were quite surprised not to find Connolly on the same bus when we went home. Cold Veal told me that I am so preoccupied with pleasing my vanity that I have no thought for anything else and then I wonder why I am so dissatisfied and that, if I want to make anything of my life, I must change my values. Feliks phoned to tell me he is the best of friends with Louise and that they spent the afternoon comparing funny anecdotes about me. I really am sick to death of both of them.

A very messy day. Tidied up the plague spot. Peter came round at teatime and later took me to have drinks with Mrs Bainbridge. Her flat was furnished style *poule de luxe* with pieces of black net draped round the bed and sparkling tropical butterflies sewn onto the curtains. I left early and took a taxi to Kingston House to collect the Horse Thief. We saw a Russian film and dined at the Cigale. My fixation about him is wearing off.

It seems that every three months I go through a period of bad conscience and remorse when everything appears to go wrong and everyone is against me. Cotterill and Cold Veal telephoned. PQ grumpy still. Cotterill persevering still and Cold Veal still working on his recovery campaign; trying to make me feel unworthy. After adopting a solicitous attitude, condescendingly pointing out my faults, he then sits smugly back to see the reaction. Having made the mistake of loving someone as worthless as myself, I am not going to be allowed to get away with it scot free.

Feliks and I had a delicious dinner of boiled beef cut in thick slices with spinach and then some heavenly spiced cakes at the Esplanade Hotel run by a Russian Jew, full of rich German refugees. When we arrived back at the house there was Feliks's stooge Anthony. Feliks and Anthony together are a tiresome pair. I resented their attitude in trying to keep me quiet in a corner with a book. In spite of my arriving with a basket full of face creams I decided to go home, and anyway Peter Q was calling at eleven. I walked with Anthony through the blackout. It was a lovely night, very warm and foggy. We crossed over the bridge towards Paddington Station where we halted to peer over the top of the wall and saw the station below, hazy in the fog, looking as though lit by luminous balloons. We cried out for a taxi several times but there were none about, so we wandered on through the station yard; there were rows of carts covered by canvas tarpaulins lined up for the night, cobblestones underfoot and horsey smells about. When we reached the station it was nearly midnight, the platforms were infested with gnomey porters unloading and piling up trucks. Anthony came back to the flat and had some tea. When he had gone I sorted out some papers. Peter accused me of being a gerontophile. The flat gets more and more sordid. I arrived at work late and found no one there but the secretary, Mr Litvinne. A very Christmassy atmosphere, especially yesterday when Mr Fish rushed backwards and forwards carrying hampers, crates of whisky and tinned food. Mr Fish is a Jewish Czech black-marketeer. He can produce anything from a six pound ham to a case of sardines out of his briefcase at a moment's notice. The Food and Supply Ministry owes its existence to the inexhaustible energy of Mr Fish. It is the great festival day of the Greek Orthodox Church and after the ceremony a feast is being provided at the apartment of the Minister of Food and Supply. Lunchtime I went home and reheated the stew of the night before last. After reading *Scum* rushed off to Harrods. Swarms of people shopping. Queues in the tobacco department. Buying, buying, buying. I made for the tie counter. Orgies of ties. The assistant did her best to be helpful; she produced box after box; Peter has a taste for dowdy ties so I eventually decided on a hideously dim one with a diamond pattern in blue. All the way back to work I kept holding it up and decided to change it. One pair of stockings arrived from Sidney. What meanness when I had handed over ten coupons. Early this morning when I was still in bed Becher came round clutching a minute bottle of scent in one hand and a shiny cane in the other. He thrust the scent into my hand and, after apologising for its shape and size, told me not to mind the odd bottle but it was actually Chanel bought from a black-marketeer. It looked to me as though he had pinched it from his girlfriend.

PQ appeared this morning half a second after the exit of the Horse Thief. Had they met on the stairs or on the doorstep? Or just missed each other? At first I thought it was the Horse Thief returning, that he had forgotten something. The footsteps drew nearer and eventually halted outside the bedroom door, stamped into the bathroom, stamped out again, paused on the landing and then someone switched on the light in the hall; my door was flung open and I was face to face with a puce Quennell. Searching glances round the room in quest of clues. What an insufferably suspicious nature! I must say the bed was in rather a pickle with the bedclothes in disorder and dirty towels strewn about the floor. My pyjama bottom was flung across the room. 'Why was I not wearing them?' 'Why hadn't I telephoned the day before?' 'What did I do?' 'And who with?' I tried to change the subject by pointing to the wine but all he was interested in was to know who had given it to me. He eventually went away apologising.

The Horse Thief's English has improved. Starting with the alphabet I was given a Serbian lesson. We lunched at Prince's and had some excellent meat and then saw a Russian film. Then we went home and drank some tea.

I should have met Becher at the Ritz at five. When I got there he had gone. There were masses of people sitting under the palms and I was looking very shabby; stockings full of holes and woollen socks over them. Becher was waiting on my doorstep, so we had tea at the

Hyde Park. I dined there later wearing my new suit, with Peter. Both in good humour. Went home and polished off the Horse Thief's white wine. I knew it would not be around for long.

Today cleaned up the flat. Scrubbed bath, swept rooms, prepared a stew, ate it with PQ, followed by a blackcurrant tart and a pot of tea. Read books until midnight. It was just like the second year of a marriage.

Next day felt depressed. Lunched Becher Ritz. Felt shabby. Oh! To be smart and rich or something. A party of Yugoslav ministers appeared from behind the palms, we got swept up in their wake. Becher very taken with them. Drinks Ritz; full of homosexuals. Dinner PQ and Becher. The latter laborious and facetious, the former unaccommodating. Home by tube. It was very depressing to see all the homeless lying about in pitiful huddles. Hideous Christmas cards pouring in. Jo Mattli helped me choose two more ties, one for Feliks and one for PQ. Goodness knows why I bother, they will certainly not give me anything. Anyway I am sick to death of both of them.

Arrived at office late and sleepy. Was having an interview at Victoria Labour Exchange. Set telephone in Vlajcic room and proceeded to Victoria. Changed buses several times, then, thinking it unwise to get there late, took a taxi on the last lap. Got to the women's section 11.10 punctually. About ten other women were waiting, factory girls mostly, sitting resignedly on the kitchen chairs. After fifteen minutes I was led into a back room by an examiner, a woman of about fifty. She took me into a corner where I was questioned behind a screen about my schooling and various occupations. As I became more vague she became more official and asked what secretarial qualifications I possessed. 'Did I type?' 'What speed?' 'Did I do shorthand?' In desperation she handed me a list of services to choose from. 'Well, what have you decided?' She looked at her watch. I looked sulkily down at the list and asked if I might think about it. She said for the present she would exempt me, but I was liable to be called again in a few months. The same day I bought some brightly coloured celanese stockings to the knee from

Harrods and changed the red tie that I had bought for Peter. I presented the new one to Feliks and he seemed pleased.

On Christmas Eve Peter took me to dine with Cyril Connolly. Cyril always manages to create a strained atmosphere, which was a pity, as Joan and John Rayner were there, and Mamaine Paget. They were all nice. But it was another of those occasions when I found myself either incapable of speaking or else only in whispers. Self-consciousness being caused by the infrequency of my remarks so that when I felt like saying something was prevented by shyness, thinking everyone would stare. We were given some delicious ham and drank lots of very good wine followed by rum. The other guest, Arthur Waley, was a funny man who talked in high-pitched squeaks as though he were addressing himself. He had tiny rabbity front teeth with dents in them. Whenever he spoke, he had a sneer on his face accompanied by a half-smile, as though to apologise for his malice. On Christmas Day Cyril's girl, Lys,[*] came round to put us off for lunch. I had to talk to her as Peter was in the bath. She makes me feel unnatural and uneasy, but she is really quite sweet. Jo Mattli brought my suit round. Very depressed. I went to have tea with the family. My sister's future husband, the fat boy, was there. A cake for tea. I took them all a present. Brenda a hat Miss Morris had given me! Mummy some face-powder that I couldn't use! And Daddy a tie that I had bought for Peter!

Last night Peter and I dined with Cyril Connolly and Augustus. Cyril seemed more human, as he was not being a host at one of his own dinner parties. He was very sweet with Lys, who was being as tiresome as ever, trying to make the apt reply to everything. Augustus became very drunk; he praised Feliks's talent and described him as being a brilliant draughtsman, but Connolly looked doubtful and said *Horizon* wouldn't print any of his drawings at any price. Augustus swayed a lot and made sweeping gestures with his hands. We ate some very stiff veal which looked as though it had been flattened by a roller, drank whisky, wine, and rum in large quantities, while Lys fussed and flattered Augustus as though he were her property; he asked Cyril, editor of *Horizon*, why

---

[*]Lys Lubbock, who was secretary to *Horizon* magazine.

the magazine didn't print paintings done by real artists like Rembrandt. Cyril said that they preferred, on the whole, to give contemporary artists a chance to make some money, especially now in wartime, and also to give them a chance of making a name. After considerable coaxing, Lys managed to cart Augustus away, although he would obviously have preferred to remain drinking with us in the bar. We couldn't get a taxi so trailed home by tube with me lagging behind all the time grumbling. When we were preparing to go to bed, the front-door bell rang. I sent Peter to see who it was; I heard Feliks's voice booming up the stairs saying, 'May I come in? Is Barbara there?' Back in the bedroom Peter broke into a rage and, picking up a large empty flower vase that was lying beside the bed, held it poised in mid-air, then dramatically and self-consciously let it drop to the ground, having given us ample time to remonstrate with him and prevent the breakage.

What a hideous New Year! What exhaustion, what depression! Peter's idea of affection in an endeavour to cheer one up: 'Oh! Poor thing. Oh! You pretty little thing. You poor dainty pretty.' Ugh!

Mr Cubrilovic, Minister of Food and Supply to the Yugoslav Government in exile, has just come in and wrung me by the hand saying 'Happy New Years'. I went to work in a taxi as I have been arriving so late the last few days. It is so cold getting out of bed that I wait for Peter to get up first and turn on the bath, so that one can dash straight into it. He doesn't have to be at MEW until ten, so it makes me late. Last night we dined with some other Ministry people at the Ritz. The food was quite good, but the waiters seemed terribly clumsy and kept spilling soup down John Rayner's neck. Peter was in a tiresome broody mood. I felt quite sorry for him; he appeared so battered and uninterested in everything, and hopeless generally. There were ghastly lapses at dinner, and long drinkless periods when we all stared gloomily before us. The host insisted on being very difficult over the brandy. He was set on having a certain brand of a certain year which was unprocurable. Each time the waiter produced an alternative, he was sent away with a flea in his ear, and we all became sobered and subdued, restlessly fingering our empty glasses. When the brandy did arrive, the glass contained two sips and even furthered everyone's depression. We eventually crept out into the night undecided and dispirited, and then, after several attempts at getting a taxi, resignedly walked to the Gargoyle. The streets were crowded with drunken revellers, swaying about the pavement or leaning against lamp posts trying to vomit. Sober and bored, we reached the Gargoyle expecting to find scenes of abandoned gaiety, only to see a few dismal drunks propped against the hatstand – Cold Veal among them – and everyone else on the verge of leaving. Augustus John prancing about the dance floor trying to pinch all the women's breasts. John Strachey swayed drunkenly in my direction, but could make no close approach as Peter planted himself between us. John was wearing a corduroy suit similar to my trousers, and was very puce and pocked. Peter and I finished off a bottle of red wine on the table, and sat back hopefully waiting for it to be replaced. There were no cigarettes and no more wine. Augustus's girlfriend Mavis appeared suddenly and drove all the men into a frenzy of excitement. Ivan Moffat[*] and David Tennant rose from their seats in unison and chased her round the floor. After fifteen minutes the band stopped and brought the evening to a close with the National Anthem; everyone staggered to their feet. David rose and, tottering for one second, collapsed head-first across the table, splintering glasses; Ivan reached forward to haul him back, but lost his balance and toppled too. We decided to go home. Still sober and bitterly cold we walked silently through the empty streets back to Brompton Road.

Slept until ten o'clock. Terribly late. I am immediately called into Dimy's office to be reprimanded on behalf of the Finance Minister for being consistently late every day for the last month. I looked penitent. Then a succession of phone calls for me, while the ministers walked disapprovingly through to their rooms. Last night met Monsieur Boris for a drink; he gave me two pounds for a Christmas present. I have no particular feeling for him now.

Great activity at the office. People came and went. Telephone rang nonstop. Peter and Feliks telephoned. Which to choose for the evening? Last night dined at the Normandie with the Horse Thief. Saw Jo Mattli there and Lee Millar looking very slim and well corseted. She swept majestically across the room as though she were balancing a plate. She was very friendly and said how pretty I

---

[*]Son of Iris Tree, daughter of Herbert Beerbohm Tree.

was looking. The Horse Thief told me of his various professions; said at one time he had taught ballroom dancing and even used to act. I left the office early and taxied to the studio with my basket. Wore red stockings and new bootees. Feliks was distressed when he saw bootees, said the whole effect too Christmassy. At eight I met Peter in the pub. He was sitting in a corner in his black trilby, brooding with a large whisky. I told him Miss Morris was departing from Brompton Road so that the flat would be free. He showed no interest. Went to bed with no dinner after drinking three large whiskies. On the last one I remarked cynically and bitterly that, after all, what were we but a pair of opportunists huddling together in a vain attempt to ward off the blows of life.

The Yugoslavs' Christmas Day. Felt dejected and self-pitying. Rang Feliks and arranged to go round to the studio. Went home first, changed into corduroys and collected rations. The previous evening Feliks had inspected my basket and, seeing the liver and leeks that I had intended to cook for Peter, said, 'Lucky man who eats that liver.' He had then hurried away to the Café Royal to meet a woman with one eye. So that, when I reappeared with the same piece of liver and leeks and a bottle of white wine the Horse Thief had given me, he was very pleased, as he is extremely fond of liver. Then, his neighbour, the painter Marik, appeared with the blackout men. Marik drew Feliks, Feliks drew the blackout men and I read Balzac.

A bearded Commander and his wife came to tea. There was a long discussion on beards; the wife said she liked them clipped, and the Commander said he preferred them bushy. She looked a beastly nagger and became increasingly tight-lipped at the mention of the word 'bushy'. They all left after tea, but another Commander came round for drinks with a woman called Mrs Haldane.[*] They were both war-effort conscious and seemed of great national importance. The Commander had just returned from Russia where he had been to tell the Russians about submarines, but he had not been allowed near one the whole time he was there. We all dined at the Ivy. There were many familiar faces. I was particularly silent as I had taken an immense dislike to Mrs Haldane; so when Feliks turned to me and asked what I was brooding about I replied 'Mink

[*]Wife of J B S Haldane.

coats' as I hoped it would shock her. We went home by bus. It was impossible to find a taxi.

Feliks having said to me for days, 'You poor thing you have no shoes; let me buy you a pair,' telephoned today and told me to meet him in the shoe department of Lillywhites. He arrived there at three o'clock and found me already trying on several pairs, but he pulled a face when he saw the ones I had chosen and asked the salesman to bring us the heaviest leather brogues in the shop. We were shown a very pretty pair in tan leather with tongues and yellow lacing. I liked them so much that we decided on them straight away. 'Have you got your coupons?' Feliks said to me. 'Certainly not,' I told him, thinking that was a fine way to give a present. 'Well, take them off,' he said. But, after a considerable fuss, he eventually produced his coupons, at the same time stating that anyway I owed him twelve shillings for Dimy's present, and why should he have to pay for a present for Dimy? Also he thought Peter ought to pay for half the shoes. That meant they each paid twenty-five shillings. Twelve shillings from twenty-five added up to thirteen. So in the end I was paying the whole lot. A jolly nice present. Peter breezed in at eight with the news that he had found a lodger for Brompton Road. Anna Maclaren. I said 'No!' Told him I am determined to move into a bedsitting room. This will be sheer masochism, but I seem to like to manoeuvre myself into unpleasant situations. I resented Peter's attitude. He wants me to be the one to take on any responsibility. 'Baby takes flat on and has lodgers.' When I didn't agree, he said then he might take it on himself. I would have been very pleased if he had offered from the beginning, but not now when it is obviously the only solution. What a hateful pair of responsibility shirkers! Peter is now demanding his typewriter back. We dined at the Speranza bickering. Two large rums at the pub and we went to bed.

Depression and despair. Wore yellow stockings and new shoes. The stockings wrinkled and the shoes slipped up and down. Peter said I looked like a frog and should have been wearing a yellow stomach. Larzo brought me some coffee which made me feel better. Perhaps everything is not as bad as I like to make out. Took shoes back to Lillywhites. Had a fitting for the blue overcoat. The material is going to rub. I trailed out to Warwick Avenue by tube at six and collected my basket. Later met Peter at the pub. Both gloomy. Had a very bad night. The worst nightmare of all. The falling-out-teeth one. Peter said there were bells ringing all night. It was probably Miss Morris locked out again. The night before last we were suddenly awoken at four in the morning by the sound of voices and scuffling noises on the landing; then the door was flung open and a torch flashed round the room. 'Sorry,' said the apologetic voice of a police officer. 'Your door's been broken in.' It took some time to convince him we had done it ourselves. A new coffee brewer has arrived at the office. His name is pronounced Marmoy and spelt Mzehwkov. Mr Litvinne told me that I look a fragile type that needs to be looked after. I told him men are sissies these days and don't wish to look after anybody.

This morning I walked to work in the snow. I should go to see my family, as yesterday the rate demand for Oak Cottage arrived; it had been forwarded on from Cranmer Court with a slip of paper from Mummy saying 'Daddy very ill'. Sidney telephoned and asked me to lunch. Mr Angelinovic shuffled in and fumbled about on my desk looking for any letters. 'Nishta. Nishta,' I told him. A man arrived with the soundproof boarding which is to be put up outside Mr Budisavljic's room. Mr B kept asking me if I felt cold. 'No fire? You cold?' When I said no, he asked 'Why sneeze you?'

The officious BBC woman who came yesterday was Rebecca West. Same type as Mrs Haldane. She wanted material for a broadcast. That pretentious little Chopin came to see me. Sat smoking that beastly pipe in a silly self-conscious way, with a supercilious expression on his face. Peter said he was probably trying to be what the French call '*digne*'. We drank two bottles of wine and then went across to the pub and had some rum. Peter lit a match and showed me the two lions that he had fallen over in the blackout the other night. Jolly sweet they were too, resting their heads on their great paws. Peter's black eye is better. I was awoken in the middle of the night by gurgling noises coming from the tank. Discovered in the morning that there was no water. Both hot and cold taps frozen. This is final. Must move. Especially as the lavatory is blocked. Miss Morris has been ramming brown paper down it. Peter's only comment being 'How like my sister.'

Took my washbag to the office and had a bath there. Felt very depressed. Bitter cold. Where to move to now is the question. Luba's sister Lukey has sent me some raffle tickets at two-shillings-and-sixpence each in aid of comforts for the Russians. She said would I try and dispose of the lot. I have already sold nine but the trouble is the Yugoslavs seem to think I am thrown in with the ticket. Mr Anjelinovic bought two, then whipped out his engagement book and said 'You me dinner?' Everyone screamed for Turkish coffee but Larzo was not to be found. The Minister of Supply called louder than anyone. When I told him 'No Larzo,' he said 'This is pity.' A photographer arrived to take his picture for the *Illustrated London News.* 'Why he take my picture?' he demanded angrily. 'I little man.'

I found the green baize soundproof screen has been put up outside the Minister's door. We experimented by shouting to see if it worked. Saturday Peter took me to see a Veronica Lake film. We dined at the Queen's with Connolly and Lys, joined by the Penroses. Delicious wine and liqueurs tasting of TCP. Then back to the black sheets. The kitchen infested with rats. Found half a Hovis gnawed away with nothing left but the outside crust. Sunday Peter helped me take suitcases home. Find Daddy in bed ill with bronchitis, bolstered up on four mattresses. Felt very sorry for himself and wished to appear half-dead. Got furious with Mummy for saying he was getting much better. Didn't want to get better. Liked to think it would lead to pneumonia. And everybody would say 'Your poor Daddy!' How badly we had treated him and now he is dying like a hero. Later in the evening he crept out of bed and sat huddled in a corner in his dressing-gown.

◇◇◇

Was so sleepy this morning, could hardly get out of bed. Wore my new navy coat, a stuffy affair and tight under the arms. Terrible bedlam today. Cables arrived, telephone pealed, doorbells rang. The Ministers shouted and noisily cleared their throats. The Horse Thief arrived carrying three volumes of gramophone records, behind him Larzo with a friend, both balancing trays on their heads laden with platefuls of sliced onion and sardines and chunks of brown bread. Minister of Food and Supply suddenly rushed out of his room brandishing a cable and crying 'From family in America'. I opened the bathroom door and found the Minister of Social Welfare bending over the seat. I apologised. 'But please, all right,' he said, beckoning me in. None of them are great plug-pullers, the lavatory is invariably full of bubbles or communiqués. Met Freeny in Harrods, she had just bought a large pot of caviar. We went into the restaurant, ordered toast and coffee and opened the caviar. Walked back to work in the snow. The Horse Thief was interviewing some newspaper men; he gave me four onions and a smacking kiss on the cheek, and handing me a pound told me to pay for a couple of fowls that were arriving. He left early with the fowls in a carrier bag and a magnum under each arm.

A lot of snow fell in the night. I sat on top of the bus on my way to work. Everyone stood busily sweeping their doorsteps and soldiers with shovels loitered outside their depots talking in groups. They all looked very hunched up and pink with the cold. The park looked lovely with no railings and everywhere thick snow, in contrast to Park Lane where it had already gone to slush. Had terrible trouble with my eyelashes, the eyeblack refusing to stay on. Shopped at Harrods for the Horse Thief. He annoyed me today strutting about the office like a self-satisfied bull. Miss Morris has now dyed her eyebrows orange. There is something quite obscene about her appearance. With that thin gash of a mouth with lipstick smeared over the edges.

Felt beastly today. Cried last night. Sore eyes. I typed with gloves on this morning it was so cold. The char complained of communiqués stuffed down the lavatory, causing 'blockades'. I am doing very well with the raffle tickets.

Got up without washing. A quiet morning at the office as everyone had gone to a meeting. The Horse Thief came in wearing a new blue pinstripe as he was lunching with Amery. He gave me a lift to Mattli's where I had a fitting for a red dress. Went to Brompton Road and packed. What a day! Moving! Found suitcase not big enough, so crammed the rest of my belongings into paper carriers. Noticed that my last pair of silk stockings had disappeared. Took everything to Cranmer Court in the rain and slush. Have had wet feet for three days. Daddy had risen and was doing the washing up. But, resented it very much. Told me that his doctor had diagnosed his case as bronchial pneumonia. Well! Homeless again! Living out of suitcases! Shall I ever settle? Peter irritating beyond belief. The cold weather makes him terribly snappy. In fact, any time now that his life doesn't run absolutely smoothly he behaves petulantly. And, if it wasn't the 'silly creature' record, it was 'poor little thing'. Now I can see how annoying I must have been when I kept calling Becher a 'goat'.

Had a reconciliation scene with Louise at the Queen's the other night. She kept walking through the restaurant and passing our table to get upstairs to the cloakroom. Each time I said to Peter, 'I hope she doesn't stop and talk.' But, of course, she did, and announced that she was married. 'Whatever made you do it?' I asked. And we laughed about Schoolboy being best man.

Friday night I dined with Peter. Went home first. The family quite bewildered by my frequent visits round six o'clock when I make a quick dash in and out of the bathroom carrying a *douche* can, and then disappear into the night. Met Peter at the Spanish restaurant. He was already on his second course and seemed to be in one of his grumpy good humours. Several of his friends kept coming over and exchanging gossip. Stephen Spender sat with us for a bit. At first he gave the impression of being very casual, vague and untidy, but after a little while even his ill-fitting clothes struck one as having been thought-out. Went back to Drayton Gardens. Cyril was away at Brighton trying to get his voice back and Koestler was installed in the big bedroom. He asked us to have a drink, but then yawned a great deal. He seemed terribly anxious to create a good impression and made a point of letting us know that he rose before eight every morning. I don't think he had much use for Peter, who took him in an early morning cup of tea and found him sitting up in bed wearing a black hairnet. Four times Koestler repeated that he'd cleaned out the bath for us to show what a noble fellow he was.

Met Peter at the Belle Meunière and waited for Feliks who was taking us to a party. In the middle of dinner Videck, Feliks's nephew, appeared in sailor kit with a message from Feliks to say would we join him at a party. We asked Videck what it was like. He heaved a great sigh, sank onto the *banquette* and promptly ordered a *coquille St Jacques* and a partridge. Peter generously plied him with red wine to encourage him to give us an account of it. We gazed at Videck expectantly as he attacked the food. He adopted the attitude of an experienced man-of-the-world by sitting with his palms on his hips and his elbows out, while he appraised each dish as it arrived with a knowing air. But, half way through the partridge, forgot himself and, rolling up his sleeves, attacked it with his hands.

While we were on the third carafe, Feliks strutted in wearing a raincoat which he removed and collapsed next to Videck. Rather discouraged by their combined exhaustion, Peter and I cautiously said that we would just look in on the party for a second, and then go home. Feliks ordered another partridge while Videck started fretting about his mother, who had been left behind. So one more bird was ordered to take away, which the waiter brought to us wrapped in a brown paper bag. Then everybody seemed content, even Peter when he found he was not responsible for the sailor's appetite. We arrived at the party far too frivolous, as it was trying to be a very intellectual affair. We were given a choice of wine or beer. Several deadly people were there including Rodney Phillips and John Chandos, and a tiresome hostess with a running nose, who hung about the icy studio hopping from one foot to the other, clutching her stomach and complaining of the cold. She was wearing a horrible pair of blue rayon pyjamas, which were much too short in the leg, but evidently she fancied herself in them, as, when I suggested that she put on something warmer, she bridled and left me to talk to someone else. Peter and I could be heard at regular intervals clamouring loudly for more wine but, no notice having been taken, we then thrust ourselves on Rodney with our empty glasses. He explained the wine had run out and there was only beer. And, then, a fearful scene was caused by Feliks showing me the way to the lavatory on the fourth floor. I was accused of leaving the room for too long and was led back into the studio by Peter, who immediately attracted attention by screeching at the top of his voice and grabbing hold of my hair. Feliks was then drawn aside by the hostess and asked to take us away. On reaching the street, the sailor walked ahead determined to find someone to fight. But fortunately the streets were deserted. So, pretty disgruntled, we all took a tube. Peter tried to invite himself back to Warwick Avenue, but Feliks was not forthcoming. When we got out at Paddington Station, Peter suggested we put up for the night at the

Terminus Hotel, but it looked grey and depressing. He then disappeared into the public lavatory, telling me to wait for him on the surface. When he was out of sight, I walked away. It was very black outside the station and I found myself in a cobbled courtyard full of wagons. I became frightened, imagining an encounter with a slasher, and ran panting across the yard until I knocked against a policeman, who asked me where I was going. Still running, I continued over the bridge until I reached Warwick Avenue. Feliks and the sailor were calmly sitting downstairs reading *Harper's* magazine. I telephoned Peter next day and attacked him for deserting me. He was very apologetic. We arranged to meet later and all was well.

At eleven this morning the Yugoslavs heard their first siren. Shut up in my dungeon I heard nothing, but seeing the whole place in an uproar I asked the cause. Frantic telephoning ensued. All the extension flaps shot down. Frenzied demands for personal lines. A general call to all Yugoslav wives. Yugoslav wives appeared to be out. No time being lost in making for their respective shelters. The all-clear sounded within five minutes, but no one seemed aware of it, too engrossed in notifying wives.

Mr Fish came bustling in looking pink and purposeful. He seemed to have become more corpulent and prosperous since soap rationing. Some weeks ago, Mr Fish decided to take his family on a holiday to Devonshire on the proceeds of bad red wine. Every precaution was taken before his departure to ensure he had been paid, before the Yugoslavs discovered the quality of the wine. Mr Fish departed rich and happy. Unfortunately his holiday was curtailed. Not three days had elapsed before the sudden announcement of soap cuts. He took the first train back to London and appeared at the office wearing a beige linen shirt and bow tie with small white dots. He was carrying a box marked 'Baby Curd Soap' on its way to the Horse Thief. From out of his hip pocket he took a large bottle of olive oil, which he handed to me; it looked a very strange colour, resembling treacle with small pieces of fluff floating in it. I thanked him and paid him six shillings. Mr Brandy appeared soon after carrying four coat hangers with price labels attached. The competing black marketeers did not acknowledge each other.

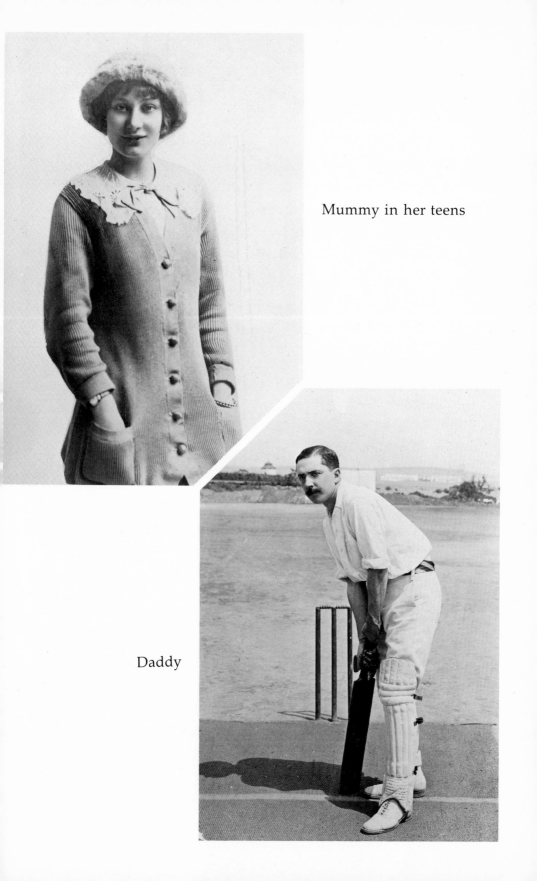

Mummy in her teens

Daddy

Uncle Dudley

Gerda with her Chow

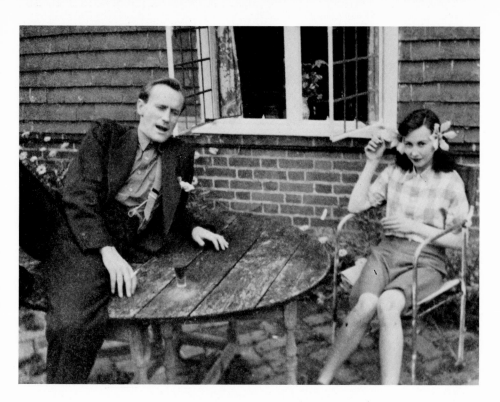

Peter Quennell with Lys Lubbock

Me with Louise

Me at Poona

Charles Langford-Hinde

Feliks Topolski in Russia as a war artist

Feliks in his studio

Lucien Freud

Augustus John

Poppet

Farouk

Me with a guide in Luxor

Feliks in Luxor

Yesterday, met Peter at the Ritz. I arrived early and sat in a corner, drinking a large whisky and soda. My hair had been set on top of my head in a poodle cut with a fringe and I felt very self-conscious. Many of Peter's friends sat about in groups gossiping in loud affected voices. The Queer group was headed by a fat pimply spectacled young man called Spongy who, before the war, had been an interior decorator. Loud-voiced girls in shapeless tweeds wandered idly from group to group and finally formed their own circle in another corner of the bar. Next to them sat a terrifying huddle of women wearing large black hats on the back of their heads and dark glasses (to show they were suffering from bad hangovers). Then there was the usual bar stool group of Queens dressed up as Guards officers. When Peter entered, howls of recognition rose from every quarter and subsided as suddenly as they had risen. Standing hunched in the doorway, Peter waved a limp hand at everyone in turn and then tottered over to my corner; 'And how's baby this evening? Is baby pleased to see Peter?' 'Baby's been sacked,' I said, 'for arriving late at the office every morning for the past two months.'

◇◇◇ Chapter VII ◇◇◇

Egypt

Homeless and jobless, with the threat of being called up, I set about finding a serious war job. One evening in the Café Royal, I ran into the diplomat, Donald Maclean. He suggested I offer my services as a cipher clerk to the Foreign Office and said he would be my sponsor. Though Osbert Lancaster had taken me out to lunch several times and spent an afternoon assiduously chasing me round Gerda's settee, when asked to be a second sponsor, perhaps wisely, he refused. So Ned Grove and Sidney valiantly rallied to the occasion.

After three months training in the bowels of Whitehall, mostly on night shifts, I qualified to serve overseas and was given the choice of being sent to Guatemala, Sweden or Egypt. And one day in July of 1942 I took a train to Liverpool and boarded a ship bound for Lagos.

Diary

We are now passing a long stretch of land rumoured to be either Scotland or the Isle of Man. Nowhere to sit on the ship except in considerable discomfort on one over-crowded deck. The passengers are mainly technicians who congregate in spectacled pale-faced huddles on the jutting planks and tarry coils of rope. Frequent drill practice. One is constantly being jerked out of a deep sleep by the insistent peal of an alarm, then, after scrambling into a life jacket with an exposure suit attached, one runs up two flights to the Captain's bridge where we answer to our names and are then dismissed.

I like listening to the screeching of the gulls and watching them swoop down from the mast, almost brushing one's cheek. Today we passed several trawlers and stray fishing smacks surrounded by gulls, flitting white dots circling about the masts and settling on the water.

The full convoy assembled this morning off the north of Scotland. Clear sky and blazing sun. Going through the minefields each ship followed behind the other in single file. When the file broke up we were the last and had to make a tremendous spurt forward to fall into convoy formation. One could see each ship get into position and with perfect timing turn simultaneously, as after facing due north we veered west. At eleven, there was a short gun practice. As each machine gun fired, the tracer flashes gleamed in the sun and curling puffs of smoke gradually dissolved into the clear blue sky. Except for the constant vibrating of the engines and the lazy bustling of the natives across the decks, with the heat and endless blue sky, one could imagine oneself to be sitting on some secluded beach.

I have now been on the ship two weeks. Have had several days of gloom and persecution, imagining the dried-up officials consider me stuck-up. I resort to the company of the Congolese and have adopted their way of dressing. Blue cricket caps and thick woolly pullovers with their names chalked on the back. It is appallingly hot. Impossible to concentrate on anything. This morning there was a tremendous storm which cleared the air a little. A thick mist and lots of white horses with heavy rain.

We have arrived in Freetown and been stationed in the harbour for two days. Nobody is allowed to go ashore except on some special mission. I commissioned the purser to buy some kirbygrips, cold cream and scent. He returned frightfully pleased with himself, laden with vanishing instead of cold cream and bottles of Soir de Paris, French tart scent. The inevitable amorous complications! Culminating in fisticuffs one night between a young Frenchman sometimes put on duty in the gun turret and a drunk purser. The sight of the Frenchman suspended horizontally across the top rail, about to somersault into the sea, sent me shrieking, with two haircombs missing, to the bridge, where I elicited the help of the Captain. The following day, to my surprise and irritation, I was greeted by my two courters, pacing the deck arm-in-arm. They had come to an agreement, and with solemn faces presented me with an ultimatum. So, taking a coin out of my money box, I tossed, promising to favour the winner. François chose heads, won and looked pleased. The purser slunk gloomily away to have his lunch. I was about to enter my cabin when he caught me up and said he could not possibly abide by the toss. Seeing his unhappy dark face, I felt sorry for him, told him to have his lunch and forget about it. Later I found François sitting in a deck chair in the sun, reading, and confessed what I had done. He immediately rose in a fury and, dragging me off to a remote corner of the ship, banged my head very hard against a spare engine that is being exported to the Congo, threw two of my combs into the sea and then ran as fast as he could in the direction of the kitchen.

Freetown looked green and hilly. There was a mass of ships in the harbour. Oil tankers, corvettes, cargo and troop ships in which men stood naked washing in tubs. Sirens roared and all the passengers lined the decks.

We remained in the harbour four days. Tiny native canoes laden with fruit crept to the side. The natives wanted to exchange fruit for clothing or cigarettes. One passenger dropped a woollen skirt over the side in exchange for some unripe bananas that were drawn up to her level in a worn-out bucket with a hole. I bargained for a dozen bananas for a shilling and was told by a cabin companion to throw them overboard, as they would spread disease. Audrey is a prim girl who wears large sun hats and is continually disinfecting the cabin with 'Flit'. Since we have been stationary there has been a persistent tapping. Groups of natives, wearing large eyeshields and resembling giant grasshoppers, hammer at the steelwork that was eventually repainted bright orange and gave the ship a very gay appearance.

Our cabin has got the reputation of being the most dissolute on the ship. Even Audrey, one of the most irreproachable girls, is suspect.

On entering the dining room, we arouse immense interest, particularly at breakfast, when each of us troops in looking increasingly dishevelled. Joan, a married woman about to join her husband, disappears each night to meet the third officer on the bridge, followed by Sheila who has a standing date with the second officer, while Audrey sits and flits. There are several rather obvious-looking security agents on board who spend their time in the bar drinking tankards of beer and endlessly smoking cigarettes.

I have made friends with a Russian boy, Vladimir, an engineer on his way to the Belgian Congo. We agreed that ship life had a very numbing effect, that we were both lazy, changeable and frivolous. We then discovered we were both Crabs, whereupon we went into the bar and drank several whiskies on the strength of it.

While in the harbour of Freetown, we were able to smoke on deck after dinner; the lights of the town and other ships were reflected on the water and one could hear an occasional launch chug to the side taking officers to shore and back. But, it is a relief to be on the move again, one's nerves were getting into a bad state. When I suggested to the purser that we separate for a day he told me not to speak of it. Didn't I know there were only five more days before we reached Lagos?

The thick cold that developed in the harbour is beginning to clear. When I told Vladimir that I must have caught a chill from getting very hot and then becoming cold, he sniggered in a rather unfriendly way. The purser keeps referring to this diary as my black book and begs to read it. His English is deplorable and he translates hair in the plural, referring to the way I do my 'hairs up', which sounds indecent.

We are in a very fast convoy again and there is speculation as to where the troops can be going. Some say India. I have had two injections for typhoid, resulting in a sore arm, slightly swollen, but no fever as prophesied by the doctor.

I feel sick today. Sat up last night drinking coffee in the nightwatch-man's den and met François on deck at midnight. He interpreted my amiability as encouragement and tried to hurl me against the rails. But he failed to maintain his balance and kept slipping over one of the funnels.

The purser told me that while training for an AB he studied astronomy. I asked him to point out the Great Bear, to which he said, pouting, 'I can show you more than the bears, you know.' He tells me, when I sit in the sun, to please pay attention. Yesterday, the first officer came up and apologised about the hammering. His English being limited, he had difficulty in expressing himself. He has delightful manners; after listening politely to my chatter, he rose abruptly, bowed stiffly and, pronouncing each word with difficulty, said, 'Thank you so much.'

Because of my reputation of belonging to a dissolute cabin, I am now waylaid by middle-aged officials who try to make dates for the evening. The request for a dinner date on a ship seems ludicrous. The intense grumbling on the part of the passengers about the food and ship being Belgian has now generally died down. It is impossible to complain about anything beyond the fact that there are foreigners aboard.

The majority of passengers are so nondescript that even after three weeks one comes across a face that strikes one as new. It is now too hot to remain seated in the sun. I have become very tanned, though, and have hands like the negroes, bronzed on the outside with pink palms. Boat drill is much less frequent. I mislaid my life jacket after the first week and in its place found a fearfully smelly ragged one without an emergency light. There is a monkey on board. It lives in the crew's quarters and runs about with a permanent erection.

This morning while I was drinking a *citron pressé* with the purser, a Dutchman passed and they exchanged greetings in Flemish. When I asked what he had said, the purser thought for a few seconds, and then said, hesitantly, 'In English, I think it means, good morning, you old bastard!'

Two days ago we arrived in Takoradi. The ship steamed right into the harbour and pulled up in the docks. François and I leant against the rail of the lower deck and watched the gathering crowd of negro porters, shouting on the quay. There was one sitting cross-legged wearing a dhoti and an off-white cricket cap. One or two went about draped in yards of native cloth and gym shoes. Some wore tarbooshes and some had bare feet. Several stood in groups of threes wearing shapeless trilbys, torn shirts and black patent shoes, propped against each other smoking long pipes. Two negro policemen in topis stood out prominently in their blue uniforms covered with shining buttons; clusters of white-kneed sailors with caps perched on the backs of their heads, square-necked black braided shirts, black socks and shoes; to complete the picture, masses of smart immigration officers in wide-brimmed cowboy hats. I suddenly thought it would be a good idea to send Becher a message through a pasty-faced moustached man setting off for Accra.

After lunch the purser rushed into my cabin in a great state of excitement. He had arranged for everyone in our cabin to go ashore (strictly forbidden to other passengers) and several passes were faked by the immigration officers.

At 6.30 sharp, the four of us were smuggled down the gangway to a waiting car and taken to a modern bungalow situated on a hill overlooking the harbour. Relays of sandwiches were prepared by two boy servants and passed round with large mugfuls of Scotch. Three out-of-date records, a tango, waltz and quick-step, were repeatedly played over on the gramophone as we were whirled round the floor by Elder Dempster officials as though attached to roller skates. The host took me into the garden to pick a paw-paw and showed me the kitchen quarters, where his negro servant, Mugwub, dressed in a green Jaeger dressing-gown, was bent over a small sink, a cigarette behind his ear, filling sandwiches.

We had just settled down when we were swept off to another shore party in an identical bungalow also on a hill, where we were plied with more sandwiches and drinks. On reaching the fifth bungalow, I had the brilliant idea of taking a hot bath. When I joined the others, they presented me with a large plateful of spam and chips which I took into a corner and ate while reading a collection of *Life* magazines. We were eventually walked back through the harbour surrounded by fireflies and the sound of cicadas rubbing their wings together.

Today, I took a desultory walk round the docks with Vladimir who thought some fresh air might do me good. After trailing along the waterfront for an hour, he led me into a foul dumping yard and, behind a stack of coke, gave me a smacking kiss, whereupon I felt sick and had to be hurried back to the ship to find the purser pacing the corridor; Audrey had twice caught him trying to climb through our porthole, so she threatened to report him to the Captain.

After three days in Takoradi, we joined another convoy. I am feeling very ill, headachey and lethargic. The purser becomes more and more intense, proposes marriage and has several weeping fits. For we are approaching Lagos and a packing panic ensues. The poor man is all the time being disturbed with a request for the keys to the baggage room by anxious trunk owners, when all he wants to do is to weep on my shoulder. I have a great washing morning and hang up rows of pants on the line erected across the top bunks. François, looking pale, wearing minute blue shorts, is seen running with his long skinny legs backwards and forwards to the hold while talking hysterically about films, customs and the future.

After spending a week in Lagos, I boarded one morning at dusk an airport bus with an engine driver and a boat companion, a gentle man with a caved-in mouth, two Ensas and a Polish Rabbi who had been torpedoed off Lagos.

Fearful nostalgia, as we took off over the lagoon. My hut stood out so clearly one could almost see the lizards creeping about the roof. The first day, we flew over vast stretches of flat wild country, with no signs of life except for an occasional cluster of huts like mud bee-hives with a tiny track running toward a river or a forest. The first night was spent with the Resmin of a northern Nigerian outpost. I shared a room with Mrs Ensa, who gave me her entire life history as we lay under our mosquito nets drinking China tea with slices of orange.

The second day we flew over endless stretches of flat red country until gradually all signs of habitation vanished. The earth became rocky, sandy and desolate. We stopped in the Sudan for lunch and it was unbearably hot. Throughout the journey, I shared a mattress with the Rabbi whose remarks were confined to 'You go Cairo? Me go Televiv.' Or, 'Me take mattress now?' He was completely unself-conscious and remained with his trousers unbuttoned as he repeatedly combed out a speckled beard with a very fine dog comb.

We arrived in Cairo at three in the afternoon. The Egyptian officials were rude due to a dispute over my camera. One snatched my handbag and rummaged through it. I was retained at customs by four unshaven officials who stood scratching their heads until I mentioned the word 'Embassy'. There was an excited chorus of 'Wheech?' When I said 'British', the camera was hurled across the barrier. I then joined the others who were sitting silently sweating under their topis in the airport bus.

Cairo was oppressive, dusty and colourless. Trams ran in all directions hooting, limp little donkeys loaded with fruit trailed along the gutters surrounded by horseflies. The pavements were crowded, women with frizzy black hair hurried along on taloned cork sandles, and tarbooshed men shuffled with limp arms or stood picking their noses and spitting into the dust. Gary carts drawn along by bony, glistening horses clopped by full of American soldiers on leave.

We were dumped at the Airways and our luggage flung onto the pavement. Feeling lost and miserable, I rang the Embassy and was put through to the cipher room. An elderly voice told me to get into a taxi but, apparently, I wasn't expected.

The Embassy was grey and deserted. The cipher room was on the ground floor with steel bars across the windows. I was greeted by a skeletal old lady who said it was lucky I had arrived at such an hour, as the room was usually filled with over twenty people. Lipsticky cups of half-drunk tea were scattered about amongst used carbons, despatch books, partly chewed slabs of chocolate and countless cigarette ends. Then, I was put into another taxi and driven to the Continental Hotel where another cipherine showed me to my room. After providing a lot of information with a benevolent half-smile, she went off to work and I observed my surroundings. For one thing, there was a fearful noise outside. My verandah looked onto a square where everything revolved round the statue of a man in a tarboosh, striking an imposing attitude with one arm raised and on one side was a line of gary carts with a taxi rank on the other. The drivers from both ranks congregated in a spitting huddle at the foot of the statue, their whips resting on the big toe. Below my window was a terrace. Moustached men in uniform sat about in basket chairs drinking iced lemonade. On the fringe of the terrace were several Egyptians sleepily eyeing girls' legs as they hurried past. One or two pretty girls sat surrounded by Americans, or in couples with spry Frenchmen in képis. I pulled down the blinds, lay on the bed and stared at the ceiling.

The following morning, I presented myself at the Embassy. Rufus, a red-faced young man with a lisp, wearing an old Etonian tie, a pale blue shirt and white flannels, asked me when I would like to start work. Then, jerking back a strand of red hair that had been obliterating his sight, he moved away and went on sorting papers. Days later, when I strolled in I was put to work with a phenomenally fat ex-naval commander who sat surrounded by tiny dishcloths used to mop the sweat from his eyes. Each day, fresh mops were brought to work in a satchel containing pencils, pens and an India rubber attached to a string. We worked on shifts and got picked up and taken to work in a kind of cattle truck.

The first day, I was taken to lunch at the Gezira Sporting Club, where I was introduced to a bumptious major who became a guide and companion for several weeks until the relationship ended abruptly one night in a taxi.

The second week, Ramadan began. All Arab pursuits were slowed down to an imperceptible pace. The absent-mindedness of the boys at table drove one to despair, so that after watching them standing idly rolling up napkins or picking their teeth, one rose in desperation and, snatching at a fig, hurried off to await the horsebox which became as unreliable as the lunch. There were occasions on the tennis court, when the ball boy stated it was too much of an effort for him to stroll across the court that day.

PC Boot had been left in charge of the cottage. His letters arrived by Bag, and went like this . . .

'How are you, Miss Skelton? PC Boot speaking. Everything at the farm quite OK. So sorry to hear of your dislike of Cairo and nature habits, etc. I had difficulty securing the front door the other day. Only one way out. Go home and get the necessary tools. Lo and behold! who should turn up in the intervening few hours but mother from Hythe. She had another young lady with her. They had come, apparently, for a couple of mirrors and a carpet that were in the sheds, and I was not carrying the keys. I felt a little pleased about that, as I don't like letting anything go without your approval. I despatched two old razors to Mr Quennell but have not heard if he received them. Is Mr Topolski still in London? Give him my respects when you write. All your books are keeping in good condition. That creeper near the house was lifting up tiles so I have eliminated this by cutting offending strips away. The painting of the fat ram still gazes down as you light a fire. I've named him Sir Cuthbert de Mouton. Well, Miss Skelton, I must conclude, hope to see you soon. Best respects from Mrs Boot, baby and myself etc. . . . '

'Dear Miss Skelton – Yours of no date safely to hand. Many thanks same. I have not heard from Mr Quennell. I suppose he got his razors alright. I was pleased to see Mr Topolski in this week's *Picture Post* with our prominent friend Mr Bernard Shaw. Everything at the farm is in good order. The process of moth ball protection etc. and turning off of water is being steadily carried out by Mrs Boot. On Saturday, I noticed a disturbance of the rotted boards that cover the well in the rear of the house. On looking down I saw what appeared to be the body of a squirrel or a cat floating on the water. With the aid of a pole with a couple of nails at the end, I brought it up. It was a weasel measuring nearly two feet. I suppose he had been after rabbits and met his unfortunate end through trespassing. The past few days have seen the farmer very busy with the harvest . . . there is, I suppose, the greatest harvest in history and the least amount of labour to deal with it. However, I expect they will soon be singing in Elmstead Church "All is safely gathered in ere the winter storms begin." The cottage still looks as inviting as ever. So does the shed where Miss Skelton is going to accommodate her cow. By the way, your Elmstead neighbours Mr Moody and Mrs Risdale wish to be remembered to you and hope to see you again one day. The war situation is pleasing to everyone; without undue optimism it does appear that the tide has turned. Oh, before I close, from the 17th August there is an intense tightening re entry into the area. I only mention it so that if anyone intended to visit the cottage the said persons must be in possession of a police permit. So cheerio and kind regards from myself and Mrs Boot. I haven't heard any more from mother. Well, Miss Skelton,

I must conclude as I want to get your jodhpurs in the post. I would like to thank you again for the film you kindly obtained. I was able to let my sister at Blackpool have some excellent snaps of the baby etc. . . .'

'Just a line inquiring if your jodhpurs arrived safely. I mailed them several weeks ago. Everything at the farm is in good order. The exceptional severe weather has called for a little more attention. I've had a good fire going every week. The front door has its funny little ways of refusing to lock but I have put it right. You have a new Vicar at Elmstead, the Rev. Stevens. He is a younger man than his predecessor and takes a much greater interest in the parish. I expect you wonder why the hell I'm telling you all this, but I promised to keep you informed of all the village excitement. A crowd of gypsies recently encamped not far from the cottage and I was unable to move them as the owner of the land gave them permission to be there. A few complaints of poultry stealing etc. came to me . . . However, I used a little diplomacy. I told them I thought it only fair they should know that the lady at Oak Cottage had two very dangerous Bull Terriers. It worked all right . . . they fought very shy all the time they were there . . . Well, Miss Skelton, Mrs Boot wishes to be remembered, so does Mrs Risdale and Mr Moody. Best of luck . . . PC Boot . . .'

Throughout the Cairo era, Peter Quennell was an assiduous letter writer of gossip, sending scraps of information . . . that Cyril, though a Blitz hero, was very buzz-bomb conscious and took refuge under the stairway in Bedford Square . . . that a pink and grey Australian parrot given to him by the *Picture Post* tycoon, Edward Hulton, when let out of its cage, descended on people's heads with raucous guttural squawks . . . that Brian Howard described his new young man as looking like a 'tortured jaguar, my dear . . .' And, at Tickerage, the choleric Major Dick Wyndham had hurled a hammer and murdered one of his geese because it had wandered onto a lettuce bed. Lee Millar wrote, 'Hello honey, what an odd place you've chosen to live . . . say hello to my husband, Aziz Eloui Bey, Club Mohammed . . . All love, Lee . . .'
From the Continental Hotel I moved to Zamalek. When Patrick Balfour* came to take me to a party, he thought the Villa Moskatelli,

---

*Lord Kinross, the celebrated gossip columnist.

where I resided, looked suspiciously *louche*. In fact, it was owned by a respectable Italian family. The daughter of the house brought up breakfast and kept the room free of bedbugs. Though should there be a sandstorm, the sand seeped into everything.

One evening at an embassy party, a smiling dark gentleman approached and introduced himself as 'Freddie, a Copt who had been educated at Oxford and owned a Bentley'. Freddie introduced me to Cairo night-life. Another rich Coptic playboy, Mansour Wassaf Simaika, otherwise known as Victor, had been an international polo player, in the same team as Porfirio Rubirosa.[*] I went riding with Victor and, during one summer leave in Alexandria, he showed me all the class beaches. The lowest grade consisted of nothing but boulders. Victor had a beach hut amongst the wealthy Egyptians who never entered the sea, but were to be seen lunching on the sands under vast parasols, being served by white robed servants. Victor claimed his idea of bliss was to make love to a beautiful woman on a bed of tuber-roses. Now, with frizzy white hair, a carnation in his buttonhole and supported by a cane, he still hobnobs round Parisian café society every summer.

Many old friends turned up in Cairo, including Topolski in his role of war artist. We made a memorable trip to Luxor and had the tombs to ourselves but for a guide who brought along a donkey that I mounted when overcome with fatigue.

Anthony Steele, then a Captain in a Gurka Parachute company, stationed in India, used to fly over on leave. He was a hearty, genial young man using expressions like 'darned sticky' as we lay on the fish slab of the Gezira swimming pool.[†] Then the Bastard turned up on leave. In fact, it was while we were dining at the Auberge des Pyramides that I met Farouk. We had been put at a table next to the Royal entourage; an equerry came over and invited us to join them.

Then, Farouk's permanent companion was a very beautiful Syrian girl whom the Bastard lost no time in whirling round the dance floor. Farouk was in one of his playful moods, flinging coloured pompoms at all the nearby tables; the stuffier the people, the more he enjoyed himself and roared with laughter. But I found his infantile side rather endearing, even this kind of thing . . .

---

[*]The infamous Porfirio Rubirosa first married the daughter of the Dominican dictator, Trujillo, then the actress Danielle Darrieux, the heiress Doris Duke, and Barbara Hutton, of the Woolworth millions.

[†]He later became a film star.

'What does a pullet call for when it's just been hatched? . . . Ma-ma-lade.' Followed by the comment, 'That's a good one, don't you think!'

In fact, Egyptians, in general, were easily amused. One would see the fellaheen enveloped in blankets, huddled in doorways bent double with laughter at the expense of passing Europeans. A few days after dining at the Auberge des Pyramides, an equerry came to the Embassy with an invitation to join a Royal house party in the desert. I was picked up at the Villa Moskatelli by an Italian servant, Antonio Pulli, who became Farouk's eminence grise and was given the title 'Bey'. About twenty of us boarded a private train that ran like a centipede through the desert and on which we were given lunch. When we reached our destination, Farouk was the first person to step out of the train blowing a trumpet to summon us all together. A line of fellaheen stood either side of a track kowtowing and clapping as the convoy of cars drove toward the Summer Palace.

The first night, we were told we all had to sleep on the Palace rooftop where mattresses had been laid. Farouk never stopped chatting in Arabic and laughing with his underlings at his guests' discomfort, as we all trooped onto the roof in our respective nightwear. When I appeared in a green dressing-gown he said I reminded him of a cabbage. At sunrise, we were awoken by the inevitable bugle call. I had a pair of earrings in the shape of curly fish that I had bought in the Moosky. Farouk took them, saying he was going to give me a surprise. One night, I was getting into bed when I found a jewel box tucked under the pillow; the curly fish had been copied in gold with emerald eyes, and a clip to go with them, that I treasured for years until, like anything I ever owned of value, they disappeared.

I was nicknamed 'Kiwi', after the famous boot black, as I always had a shiny face. Sometimes, we'd dine in the Abdin Palace and afterwards watched movies or swam in the vast Palace swimming pool. Farouk always drove me back to the Villa Moskatelli and, as we passed through the Palace gates, I had to duck so as not to be seen by the dozing nightwatchmen.

In spite of the rather dull sycophantic people surrounding the King, I must confess I was never bored. I was always treated with great courtesy and I never felt that I was amongst a 'clique of corrupt lackeys'; 'with a depraved ogre surfeited with sex and gourmandising'; 'a paradigm of cupidity with gross features and bloated figure' or observed that when he ate 'he stoked himself with rich food' and then 'shambled with wobbling jowls' as described in *The Last Pharaoh*. Farouk seemed to prefer rather simple food – he was very fond of chicken carcasses, claiming the parson's nose to be the best part of the bird. He loved oysters and fruit, and wherever we went there were large platters of muscat grapes, figs and mangoes from his own plantation, and those delicious rose pink water melons with huge black pips that taste so good when eaten iced with fresh goat's cheese.

One day I was summoned by the first secretary at the Embassy, Bernard Burrows,[*] who said that if I went on seeing Farouk I would have to leave Egypt. Then Burrows gave me two weeks leave which I spent hitchhiking round the Middle East.

Diary

I am now dining alone in a dim Ismalia hotel. A strange contrast to my dinner of last night with the Monarch! Have just eaten a nasty meal which I tried to disguise with ketchup. It is amusing being alone, people come up and talk as though I were an old friend. I have a room overlooking a railway terminus, trains rumble past the window, there is a screech of children's voices and a clatter of plates from the kitchen below. I am deadly tired and ache all over from a flogging of last night on the steps of the Royal Palace. I would have preferred a splayed cane, but instead had to suffer a dressing-gown cord which created a gentle thudding sound over an interminable period.

The first evening in Jerusalem was spent drinking with a small lecherous Frenchman who had picked me up in a taxi just outside Gaza. Very spry and talkative with many amorous little gestures and references to his bottle of whisky at his *maison*, which made me increasingly anxious to escape. A very bad dinner, rations are very small here. After each meal little men appear with trayloads of assorted nuts. Managed to abandon the Frenchman after a slight

---

[*]Sir Bernard Brocas Burrows, KCMG: he became HM Ambassador to Ankara in 1958.

tussle in the taxi when he received two sharp raps on his head with
my Virginia Woolf.

I am already very fond of Jerusalem. Bells chime continuously.
Donkeys, a tougher breed than the wiry Egyptian ones, pad up and
down the streets loaded with small packs. The women are big and
strong with ruddy complexions, and wear long, loose, flowing
robes with square embroidered fronts. They carry large baskets of
fruit on their heads as opposed to the inevitable Cairo cowpats.
Such relief getting out of Egypt, with its consistent flatness and
colourlessness. 'How did you like the old city?' I asked my cell
companion. 'OOOH!' she said, pulling a face. 'What a good thing
they built that wall round them.' She told me that the Allies had
entered Paris two days ago.

Tiberias seemed to be a popular swimming resort. It is a sweet place
reclining on the slopes overlooking the Sea of Galilee. In its centre is
a motherly old mosque like a Queen Bee. It was deserted but for
two ancient bearded Arabs eating water melons and spitting the
pips into a yard. Carrying his Bible, a bespectacled UNRRA
enthusiast with an SCF (Suffering Children's Friend) on his
uniform took me out in a rowing boat and pointed out all the biblical
landmarks. I joked with the boatman to try and forget his existence.
We dined on the promenade under a flamboyant tree and ate quite
the most disgusting fish, tasting of drains, called *musct*. Rose early,
determined to escape SCF. But there he was, waiting to see me off.
He insisted on getting me breakfast, a stale roll with local jam
wrapped in a newspaper, greatly attractive to flies, that I found
myself carrying around for the rest of the day. Eventually, I left it
behind in a lorry which took me along the shores of the Galilee.
Then, in another lorry, we climbed into the hills, where I ate some
eggs, bacon and real butter. Later, rejoined my luggage to find a
thoughtful driver had carefully lain the discarded fly-blown roll on
top of my suitcase.

At the frontier, after making friends with the Military Police, I
was put into a taxi full of sick women bound for Damascus and
dropped in the main square at one o'clock. Great difficulty in
making myself understood, so in desperation I got someone to take
me to the YWCA (four magic words in the Middle East). They were
helpful and sent me off to the Church Army hostel. Woke up next to

a roomful of sergeants, having been kept awake most of the night by Arab wailing which seemed to come from a mosque on the roof. Had the usual guided tour and made friends with a tiny hunchback corporal, suffering from an idolatrous worship of Monty. He later took me to an Eddie Cantor film, made several attempts to hold my hand, then walked me back to the hostel with the words, 'Pleased to have met you.' The big mosque was like a market square, full of Arabs engaged in every activity bar prayers. Some were sitting cross-legged counting out their money on the mosaic floor, and a great number were just leaning against the pillars spitting and picking their noses. After buying some Syrian silk stockings, I boarded a car loaded with WRENS who never stopped chattering about their mothers' dogs, other WRENS' young men, or dances. The driver and I exchanged desperate glances.

Spent a morning at the Fench Consulate trying to get an exit visa. Then, I took a taxi to the outskirts of the town, and waited on the kerb while a French *gendarme* stood on my luggage and began hailing all the army lorries on their way to Haifa. Suddenly a contractor's lorry halted a few paces away; the gendarme had boarded it in no time, piled in my luggage, hauled me over the bonnet and then jumped into the middle of the road with outstretched palms awaiting a reward. We left him gesticulating and panting after us in his booted uniform. My lorry friends were delightful. We stopped at a beer café on the road, then roared past the Syrian frontier without looking back and later shot past the French frontier leaving a cluster of waving screaming officials in our wake. When our routes differed, they solicitously put me into a fruit truck. The driver drove at a terrific speed without stopping all night until we reached the outskirts of Haifa, where he made an abrupt halt outside a mud hut, out of which roared a family of dirty dark-skinned children who clambered all over the truck with screams of delight, ripping open the sacks and tumbling out their contents into the road. When the driver became aware of me, he rather touchingly offered me a handful of apples and took me to the YWCA.

From then on, I was solely concerned with getting back to base and joined a convoy travelling at a speed of twenty miles an hour, so when it reached a canteen stop on the edge of the desert I got out and ate some eggs and beans. Tried to sunbathe by lying on a wall with my skirt up, but sand kept blowing in my face. Suddenly a very dilapidated bus inscribed with 'ENSA' drew up and out leapt two uniformed Semitic drivers chewing gum. Assuming me to be an ENSA girl, they at once felt responsible and drove me back to Cairo.

◇◇◇ Chapter VIII ◇◇◇

Italy and Greece

On my return, Bernard Burrows announced that once the Germans had retreated over the Greek border, the Embassy in Athens would open up, and Mary Foreman and I had been chosen as the new cipher team. Soon after, to the envy of the other cipherines, we were driven to Alexandria to board a crowded troopship bound for Italy. Also aboard was Michael Spears, son of the General. Small and tubby he bore no resemblance to his famous father, other than in disposition. Finding me in a good humour as we were stepping over the troops lining the crowded decks, Michael jeered, 'You're the sort of person who'd laugh on seeing someone break his neck on a banana skin.'

Mary and I disembarked at Salerno, where we spent the night. It was raining, and sad, as practically the whole of the town had been wiped out. We were then driven to the Palace of Caserta. Built for the King of Naples in the eighteenth-century, the Palace had been transformed into a British and American army headquarters. A miniature Versailles, it was filled with marble statues and massive pillars. Lions leered down from the tops of stairways. The grounds were laid out with terraces and fountains with water cascading over marble statues of the hunting goddess, Diana, with her leaping hounds. The cobbled courtyard abounded in jeeps. Mark Culme-Seymour was stationed there. When he fell ill with tuberculosis, my off duty hours were spent visiting the hospital.

One lunchtime I was on my way to the NAAFI to a menu of *Consommé aux Nouilles, Boeuf à la Vénétienne, Choux fleurs au Bacon* and custard pudding, when I was waylaid by a smiling blue-eyed

American Air Force colonel in a peaked cap, and from then on had access to the American PX, a great blessing, when it was impossible to obtain stockings, hair-kirbies or shampoo. When not flying off on some secret mission to Budapest, he would take me to dine in a villa overlooking the Bay of Naples where American officers spent their leave. They were even more cosseted in a villa on the Island of Capri. The colonel flew me to Rome. He would drive on to Naples air strip and hail a bomber as though it were a taxi.

Then, who should turn up once again but the Bastard. One bitterly cold night we drove north in a jeep in torrential rain, passing through towns reduced to ruins, where the residue of the Italian Army was to be seen camping under canvas in muddy bogs. The Rome shops gave short change, the *femme de ménage* in the hotel emptied out a bottle of Schiaparelli scent and refilled it with water, and overnight the hood of the jeep was ripped off.

Then, in late autumn, Lady Leeper, the wife of the future Ambassador to Athens, Mary and I were driven to the foot of Italy, stopping on the way to picnic in a forest of cork oaks, where most of our lunch was given to a troupe of ragged barefoot children gathering acorns, then a wartime coffee substitute.

The troops boarding the ship bound for Greece had been issued with a booklet which began with the phrase . . . 'You are lucky to be going to Greece . . . it is a country of allies worth having . . .' Then followed a list of DON'TS . . . 'Don't admire the baby the mother might think you have the evil eye . . . Don't pull up vine stumps for firewood . . . Don't rub it in about fleas . . . Don't say you have won the war . . .' and terminated with a security measure to beware of agents and saboteurs.

Many Greek families were travelling back for the first time since the occupation and, long before our arrival, stood hatted and gloved, clutching suitcases, ready to disembark. Everyone seemed apprehensive, imagining untold discomfort.

It was a beautiful autumn day with brilliant sunshine when we came within sight of the Piraeus; there was great excitement as Athens loomed closer and exclamations of delight at the soft clear light. Field glasses were produced, someone pointed out the Acropolis and the Temple of Athena, standing out like a lone tooth on the summit. We remained outside the harbour and were led in slowly next day by a minesweeper to dock some distance from the shore. The ship was immediately surrounded by fishing boats rowed by young men or pretty, flirtatious girls who ogled the troops, begging for cigarettes. But, after reading their booklets, the men seemed very much on their guard. Drachma notes were sprinkled over the sea to indicate their worthlessness.

It took all morning for the troops to disembark in landing barges. During lunch, a considerable stir was caused by the announcement that the Greek Prime Minister, Papandreou, and Sir Rex Leeper, HM Ambassador to Athens, were coming aboard to greet their respective wives. The Ambassador, looking strained but happy, appeared out of a small turret in the rear of the motor launch; behind him was Papandreou followed by the first secretary, Michael Cresswell.[*] Then, we all boarded the launch and made for the shore. A silent crowd stood waving and clapping on the quayside and cameras clicked. Unlike the sallow Italians, the Greeks had fresh brown complexions; there was a smell of pine everywhere, which is not the case now, alas, the pine trees having been replaced by shoddy buildings. From then on, the entire staff remained within the confines of the British Embassy off the Vasileos Konstantinou. From my room, I had a view of a tiny Byzantine church surrounded by cypresses.

When Osbert Lancaster arrived as Press Attaché to do what's known as 'muzzle the press', he had to share a camp bed with one of the Embassy guards. On seeing the fat red and blue Buddhas draped on the walls to brighten my room, he said they reminded him of his old rival, Topolski. We lived on a diet of bully beef and spam. It was forbidden to buy food, but Mary and I would go into the market, buy a cabbage and eat it surreptitiously. What the Greeks seemed to crave were very rich cakes and the town abounded in pastry shops.

Two café society playboys arrived from Cairo and we were taken to a round of parties given by the Greek aristocracy. Michael Cresswell, who considered himself to be a Greek scholar, got hold of an old car and in the evenings we would drive into the country to stop at some wayside taverna. In exchange for tins of bully beef we would be given a delicious dinner of pigeons roasted over a pinewood fire. All the family would join in the feast. Then a turbaned Turk came in with his guitar and sang flamenco.

We were returning full of ouzo and retsina from one of these delightful evenings, when we saw all the young Greeks seated on their doorsteps polishing rifles. Soon after, the civil war broke out.

---

[*]Sir Michael Justin Cresswell, KCMG, later became Ambassador to Buenos Aires and married Baroness thoe Schwartzenberg.

It was a perfectly still day with sunshine streaming through the window when suddenly bullets were whistling all around, while Spitfires flew overhead gunning the area. From then on there was a continual noise as of croquet mallets or cricket bats hitting boundaries. The grenade and mortar shells fired from Hymettus seemed to skim the Embassy roof only to land a short distance away with a tremendous explosion which reverberated because of the surrounding mountains. Women were seen running along the streets crossing themselves in terror as bullets whistled past. The rooftops abounded in snipers. The police would enter a house only to come out with a rifle and a communist KKE badge.

Church bells chimed as a signal to the communist-run Greek Liberation Front to start or cease fire, but as soon as the shooting stopped in one area it started up in another. A constant stream of ambulances and tanks passed along the boulevard, and night and day there was shouting magnified by megaphones coming from various points of the city.

On the first day, eight police stations were captured and over a thousand *gendarmes* killed or wounded by the left-wing Popular Liberation Army. Stray bullets pierced the Embassy windows. Two safe experts arrived. The bars of the cipher cave were filed down and replaced by bars closer together. We were supposed to be protected by guards, otherwise known as The Snoops, who remained on the roof all day taking photographs. There was a curfew at night and for days we were without water; the electricity was then cut and we worked by hurricane lamp. When a column of the Popular Liberation Army was approaching Athens, planes dropped flares all night to show it up and the mountains were lit in a hazy pink glow. When the communist headquarters was finally captured, many German and Bulgarian deserters were found there.

Mail was brought to the Embassy in an armoured tank. My mother had written to say that Aunt Nancie had died. There had been no contact with my uncle since the Poona days, but I wrote him a letter of condolence and received the following blimpish reply . . .

'My dear, I do thank you so much for your lovely letter. Every letter I get about my darling Nan makes me the prouder man. She was such a dear and a darling, and I do miss her so dreadfully . . . she was always so supremely brave, even when swarms of those damned doodles were skidding past her window . . . you sure are passing through an interesting time.

On the BBC, you can hear the fighting from the Acropolis as plainly as if one had been sitting on a balcony of the Grande Bretagne. Aren't they a lot of perishers? What with the Free French, the Belges, the Serbs and now these perishing Greeks. It is hardly worth fighting for them. But how amused Tommy must be to have to stand by and watch them slaughtering each other, and for nothing except some ridiculous political ideology. I shall look forward to you coming to stay. You can have your brekker in bed and everything you like . . .'

Boot had written to say that 2,400 doodlebombs had fallen over Kent alone. Increasingly alarmed and claustrophobic, I wrote to the Foreign Office asking to be recalled, and when Michael Cresswell came into the cipher room and said, haughtily, 'Farewell, CREATURES . . .' before leaving for England, I asked him to use his influence, then ordered two demijohns of retsina, packed my bags and waited.

After Harold Macmillan's brief visit with his secretary, John Wyndham, always referred to by the Embassy staff as 'that delightful chap', we all left together in an armoured tank, and were driven through the Embassy gates into the Boulevard Konstantinou and all the way to the airport. The streets were lined with snipers, but the plane took off without mishap.

The American colonel met me at Naples where I spent some Christmas leave. The plane from Naples touched down in Marseilles to refuel; the airport was embedded in snow. After the arid months in Egypt I felt stimulated by the sight of snow and took a short walk, getting back on the runway to find the plane had taken off with my suitcase and the baskets of retsina. I was wondering what to do when a Marauder landed and out got two pilots who were flying the plane back to England to undergo repairs, and they agreed to give me a lift. From the cockpit, we had a clear view of snow-ridden France and were approaching Paris, when one of the engines froze. I was hoping we might have to land; instead the pilot did a series of nose dives which unfroze the engine, but left us all deaf. We continued over the Channel and landed at an airfield on the south coast, where I underwent an official interrogation, the absence of luggage being considered very suspect.

Nothing had changed on the British railways. With their scruffy packages, the British still looked bombed out. The green carriages reeked of soot. You couldn't tell whether the greyness resulted from the dirt on the panes or the reflection of the sky. Being a

Saturday, each small brick house had a washing line suspended across a dismal plot of garden.

I arrived at Gerda's with nothing but a handbag. The bulk of my luggage had been left in the care of an army major, Hugh Ryder, who was attached to the Embassy as a kind of majordomo. He was a charming man and, as the months went by, we sustained a regular correspondence, his letters beginning, 'Dear Skelters,' and ending 'With all my blessings, dear Barbara and the Best of Luck' – which, in fact, I never had. He had despatched my luggage by train via Italy, so that it shared the same fate as the Schiaparelli scent. This time, for some reason, there was no compensation. All the same, the major went on being joyful. 'Now I do have good news for you,' he wrote, 'your old mackintosh has just been found. I am sending it back by Bag. That way, you're bound to get it. Apologies . . . for so many delays . . . which shows that old Ryder is tired of organising . . .' Yes indeed!

I went on working for the Foreign Office in London, until the war came to an end and they wanted me to proceed to Lisbon. Although London remained sad and drab, for some inexplicable reason I missed the plane and wrote from Cot pleading that I had not had time to obtain a suitcase. The Foreign Office do not sack their employees, they put them on suspension, in which state I remain.

Chapter IX

After the War

'A woman who
has never been hit by a
man has never been
loved.'

Zsa Zsa Gabor

Within a month, I was pushing a trolley of recordings along the
corridors of the BBC, where Louis MacNeice was often seen flitting
in and out of the self-service canteen.

One evening, when dining in the Queen's Restaurant off Sloane
Square, Peter Quennell came through the revolving door escorting
June Osborne,* then a teenage beauty. Only on closer acquaintance
did one perceive the slightly bandy legs and wrestler's arms of a
champion horse-woman.

Peter Quennell offered to put me up in the Park Village East
house he was sharing with George Weidenfeld. The two men must
have been leading very social lives; I never saw either of them until
late one night Peter and I collided in the basement kitchen, when a
spoonful of the chutney I was eating fell on his bedroom slipper.
After the rumpus, I moved to Rossetti House in Flood Street, where
John and Marjorie Davenport were living in dire distress. On sunny
wartime days, John and I used to picnic in Bedford Square Gardens.
Amongst the classics I could never get through that John listed to
improve anyone's mind was Huysmans's *Against Nature* and de
Quincey's *Confessions*. During the war Marjorie had worked for
Lady Wishart whose house in Hove had been transformed into a
club for American officers on leave. One of Marjorie's duties as
hostess was to be whirled round a billiard-cum-ballroom on

---

*June Osborne later married Randolph Churchill.

Saturday evenings, though it is doubtful if that is how she met John. Marjorie was a very likeable girl with long flowing hair. We became close friends. While John haunted the Chelsea pubs with Dylan Thomas and Tommy Earp, Marjorie and I subsisted on the experimental little dishes I took back from a Cordon Bleu cookery course in Sloane Street. When June Osborne tempted me with a sitting room in Cadogan Street, I moved in with her and remained crouched before a tiny gas fire with a slot machine throughout one of England's bitterest winters, with Tony Steele for company, when Tony was a simple rugger player, prior to becoming a filmstar and the husband of Anita Ekberg. In my opinion his most successful film role was that of a Kenya colonial dressed in khaki shorts and topi, leaping smartly in and out of jeeps, a jovial smile on his face, rather as he used to be in everyday life.

I never really appreciated conventional good looks. Eric von Stroheim was my ideal. Also, spare me a whistler or a practical joker – someone who prepares a bath, tells you it's ready and then stands by beaming as you step into ice-cold water. But the frustration I once suffered due to a thwarted passion for a bone surgeon with a harelip! And then, I fell head over heels for a *unijambiste* who was also simpleminded. The anticipation with which I would listen for the tap of his crutch striking the tiles, as he mounted the stairs of the Vieux Auberge de Cagnes, where Augustus John's daughter Poppet and I spent three consecutive *après guerre* winters. Marcel's day was spent lounging with his torso bared in a corner of the Auberge bar. At lunchtime, should Poppet and I be seen dipping into some *oursins*, thumping the bar, he'd cry excitedly, *'Mais non! Mais non! Mais non!'* 'What is it now?' I'd ask Poppet, whose French was more advanced, and she'd reply wearily, 'He says you're a panther and shouldn't be eating fish.'

It was François Villiers who introduced me to Cagnes-sur-Mer. Ever since parting in Lagos, we had been in touch. He and his brother, Jean-Pierre Aumont, owned a villa in Cagnes that they lent me one summer. François was a redhead and such a compulsive whistler, I always imagined him riding a bicycle and named him the 'Paperboy'. His father owned a chain of linen stores, La Maison Blanche, and after the war my first residential visits to Paris were spent in their lugubrious apartment off the Avenue Wagram.

François took me to Claude Dauphin's ravishing little château surrounded by meadows near Tours, and through him I met Iris Clert before she went into the art trade. She was running a handbag shop with her mother in the rue St Honoré and much later, after

76

having her nose job (to look more Greek apparently) she had come to Cot to recuperate, quite suicidal, as she feared the celebrated Archibald McIndoe had snipped off too much.[*]

At the top of Hauts de Cagnes there was a tiny bar where, during the evenings, the village fops and foreigners gathered. You didn't have to squat long on one of Jimmie's bar stools before someone came up, not to offer a drink, unless it be mineral water, but to shuffle you round the *place* to a pick-up. As well as ex-Maquis combatants, there were American art students living on a Guggenheim grant, Swedish and Spanish painters, even a German who had spent the war living clandestinely with an ugly mistress. Jews drifted back from camps and, maybe because they had suffered and Cagnes life was so frivolous, they gave the impression of being rather surly. Not only that, but Parisians with villas in Cagnes remained unabashedly anti-Semitic, as one observed when John Sutro flew down from Paris and we did a tour of the cafés, where John would whistle tunes from famous operas, to the annoyance of the habitués.

The first person to shuffle me round the *place* was an ex-Resistance leader. Pierre Sauvaigo was a big handsome man, then studying for a lawyer's degree, and during the evenings we got into the habit of meeting in a downtown neon-lit bar, where the atmosphere struck me as being strangely romantic on a sultry summer's night, with 'J'ai bu' drooling away on the machine. Pierre became very possessive and went on employing Maquis tactics long after the combat. One afternoon, seeing me basking on the beach in the company of a cheque forger, he sleuthed us back to the villa and, when my companion left, he burst in to the bedroom shouting, 'Garce', and beat me up. He then vented the residue of his rage on the walls with the aid of a knuckle-duster. Terrified, I fled into Cannes, where people were so horrified to see my appalling bruises that they offered to go to Cagnes and beat Pierre up.

Then, the Croisette abounded in jobless war veterans living on black market deals who assembled in the bar of the Carlton. Amongst them was an ex-bomber pilot who owned a twin-engined

---

[*]In her book of memoirs, *Iris-Time* (published by Denoël, 1978), Iris Clert writes: 'François was our mutual friend. Tall, sandy-haired, unselfconscious, amusing, he was worldly and superficial – but madly sympathetic. He'd had his handsome nose broken in a car accident but, in spite of his boxer's head, always found a way of seducing the most beautiful girls. Thanks to him, we were witness to a long procession of the most extraordinary creatures. One of them, Barbara Skelton, was a superb girl with panther's eyes and became my best friend.'

Consul plane that seated about six people. Graham was engaged in smuggling and took me on several trips. He would call up at the last minute and say, 'I'm just off to Tangiers. Would you like to come?' His plane was invariably parked on the outskirts of some airport. The first time, we took off over a herd of cows and then had to make a crash landing. We remained unhurt, but the watches he was carrying sprang out of their wrappings and hopped about the field. Graham's instant reaction to any catastrophe was hysterical laughter. He drank a great deal, his evenings being spent on what he called the 'Toot'. One would try to keep him away from bars as drink made him so aggressive, his rancour seemingly due to the fact he had been awarded the DSO; 'They think that by giving you a medal,' he snarled, 'they can get away with anything.' One time we went on a charter flight with a nightclub owner and his blonde Grosvenor House crooner. When we landed at a small commercial airport outside Paris, Graham got a tremendous ovation. The officials shook his hand and patted him on the back, as though they were all in on some enormous joke – smuggling, in fact.

Then, should you be dropped blindfold in France, you would know where you were from the smell of Gauloises at customs. I used to enjoy smoking 'pot', which could be found in any Tangiers souk. You just had to go into a café and say, 'kif, kif', Arabic for intoxicant, and someone would lead you to a stall where hasheesh was sold in grimy paper sachets. There was one time in Tangiers when I stocked up on sachets to take back to England, stuffing them into my basket. For once, on landing at Cannes airport, the plane was searched. They even took up the floorboards. I went straight into the airport bar and ordered a drink, leaving the basket dangling on a bar stool, then I joined the others to undergo a baggage check. When we were released I went back into the bar, retrieved my basket and we all taxied on to the Carlton. Our last flight over the Alps in a thunderstorm skimming the mountains, with the plane bobbing about like a cork, was so scary that I was unable to fly again for several months, even on a commercial flight.

From the villa I moved to the Vieux Auberge. Half way up the hill the Auberge de Cagnes had a beautiful terrace overlooking the sea where Poppet and I took our meals. It was run by M. and Mme. Delenne who had a son and daughter, and two poodles, Rita and Kiki.

Jeanette was jolly and barrel-shaped. She worked very hard and was always flying into a rage. Jasmin rarely spoke. He remained grooved to the stove, a happy smirk on his face, revelling in his wife's hysterical scenes. Rosa Lewis style, if someone left the bar without paying, the drinks would be put down on some regular lodger's account. Jeanette often worked off her ill humour on some totally innocent victim. One winter, it was a young American writer who aggravated her because he never drank. She was bawling him out and, his French being limited, he kept repeating, 'Mais, Madame Delenne, qu'est ce que j'ai fait?' So, it became his name. Laughing, Jeanette would shout from the bar, 'Have you seen Qu'est ce que j'ai fait aujourd'hui? There's a letter for him.'

Many friends came to Cagnes. But Louise thought Gerda so tough she named her the Iron Girder. And Gerda was aggravated by Poppet's voice, she claimed it was affected. Poppet was always in a good humour. She reminded me of the Chekhov character Olenka in The Darling, who puts her heart and soul into every amorous relationship, and as soon as one husband dies immediately finds another on whom to lavish her devotion, until too old to marry again she adopts a little boy to pamper.

One time Poppet and I decided to lunch in Vence. We took the bus and on arrival made straight for the nearest bar where two coarse fellows plied us with Pernod. After lunch, they suggested we accompany them back to their work, and we found ourselves in an abattoir surrounded by hunks of meat and were entertained by the two butchers until they went home to their wives, each one with a string of offal dangling from the waist.

Poppet never lacked admirers. One had been champion of the Tour de France, when, to my annoyance, the way to her room would be barred by a bicycle. We even followed that dreary sport, if it can be called such, as far as Draguignan and stood in the pouring rain with outstretched arms, administering lumps of sugar as her admirer peddled past.

The last character to appear on the Cagnes scene was a Corsican ex-Maquis friend of Pierre's who came down from Paris to supervise security measures when de Gaulle was to make a speech on the place Masséna. Monsieur le Préfet got into the habit of flying down weekends, which we spent in the Hotel Negresco. But, once, he turned up unexpectedly at the Auberge to find I was out, whereupon he spent hours pacing my room, ripping my clothes and filling all the Arden pots of beauty cream with black cigarette stubs. Soon after, he died of a strange tropical fever.

By then, I was installed in a topfloor flat in Queen Street, where John Sutro and Peter Quennell were frequent visitors, as well as Gargoyle friends like David Sylvester looking very handsome in battledress, Xan Fielding and Jocelyn Baines,[*] so that I had a kind of salon. Xan would accompany me to the cottage. Once, while he was staying, the local parson came to the door with a book of Peter's that he wanted to have signed. Whereupon, Xan quickly obliged him and the parson went happily away under the impression he had obtained the author's signature. Jocelyn Baines then worked for a bookshop off Piccadilly where Sutro had an account, so that sometimes when he came to see me Jocelyn would bring me a book put down on Sutro's account.

The French can be very inventive when it comes to terms of endearment. You can be *ma puce, une colombine, ma reine, mon doux ange, ma fille, bébé, mon mimosa,* or simply, *chérie;* so that when Pierre wrote to say he was coming to see his *'chou-chou chérie, pour te garder pendant huit jours, comme une proie à laquelle personne ne touchera; je ferai de mes bras un prison qui t'isolera du reste du monde anglais'* and I failed to take him at his word, the visit turned out to have grave consequences. I was modelling for Mattli who had a salon in Carlos Place. Pierre would walk me to work. He understood very little English, but one day I left my diary behind and he soon gleaned the sense of 'John Ritz 1.15', 'Jocelyn drinks', and 'PQ Etoile 7.15'. I got back to find all these pages with dates had been carefully dog-eared and from then on I was kept a prisoner and restrained from answering the telephone. Pierre became increasingly violent and showed me a gun he had hidden in his suitcase. When Poppet rang, we agreed to meet her for dinner at the Ambassador's where I told her Pierre had resumed his *Maquis* tactics, whereupon we thought it wise to notify the police.

The following morning, two plain-clothes men rang the bell of Queen Street and how sad I felt when Pierre was politely extradited!

---

[*]Xan Fielding spent the war in the Greek *Maquis* sabotaging the Germans. Jocelyn Baines worked for the publishers Longman, wrote a book on Conrad and committed suicide in the late 1960s.

◇◇◇ Chapter X ◇◇◇

Cyril

It was Natalie Newhouse who initiated a meeting with Cyril Connolly after the war, when he was living with Lys in Sussex Place. Natalie had been a regular correspondent throughout the Cairo era. She was a very pretty, witty girl with green eyes and dark hair worn in a page-boy. Natalie was always falling masochistically in love and doing destructive things like falling through a skylight, breaking a leg and spending months in hospital. Her great love was Ivan Moffat. But, when I got back from Athens, she was living in Tickerage Farm with the actor, Bobby Newton, whom she eventually married. It was then she told me that Cyril was bored with Lys and was seeking someone new; she had titillated his interest, she said, by claiming I had a passion for learning facts, without adding that, once acquired, my memory failed to retain them. She then invited us both to lunch at the Etoile. I had become the proud owner of a red convertible Sunbeam Talbot and my popularity had increased. In fact, one year later, Nancy Mitford was to claim that Cyril had really been captivated not by me but by the Sunbeam.

Peter Quennell was the first person to come on a trip. We drove to France passing through Beauvais to visit the flamboyant Gothic cathedral and join Cyril in Paris for some memorable meals. When I was due to join John Sutro who had booked rooms in the Hotel des Bergues, Cyril decided to follow me on to Geneva and booked into a hotel opposite the Bergues, on the other side of the lake, so that we could signal to each other from our respective rooms.

When Cyril arrived, on the pretext of going to a *coiffeur*, I joined him for tea and caviar on the corner of the street. From then on we would meet every day, when Cyril would consult his guide and tell me where to take Sutro that night for dinner. 'Here's a very good restaurant,' Cyril would say, 'where you can get the best *quenelles* in Europe.' By this time, Chuff, my pet name for Sutro, became increasingly surprised at my being so knowledgeable about Geneva restaurants while remaining 'uncoiffed'. When he flew back to London I drove Cyril sightseeing.

We visited Madame de Staël's château, Rousseau's house outside Chambéry and then drove up three thousand feet to see the Monastery of Chartreuse, only to be confronted by a hoarding announcing the monastery was closed, requesting us not to laugh, sing or smoke, but respect the sanctity and privacy of the monks . . . It was toward the end of this trip that I suffered the first of Cyril's deflating quips. A heavy smoker, I was lighting up during the cheese course, when he said acidly, 'I suppose you think the hollows in the gruyère are there for you to stub out your cigarette.'

By then, he was beginning to pine after Lys and went off to meet her somewhere near Marseilles. We separated in Cannes, where, in a nightclub, I developed a crush on a Parisian lawyer, small and dark with an alluring dyke hairstyle, who came up and asked me to dance. A great *coureur*, wherever we went she invariably picked up some pretty girl in a cloakroom. She excelled in gallantry; no sooner had I pulled out a cigarette than she leant over with a gold lighter with such rapidity that my eyelashes got singed. We travelled back to Paris together. She insisted on driving the Sunbeam and, once there, bombarded my hotel room with bouquets. But her breasts made a mockery of all that masculinity and my enthusiasm abated when she shed her clothes.

When I got back to Queen Street Cyril was living alone in Sussex Place. Although they met practically every day, he had made a final break with Lys who had taken on a lover.

Diary

March 9, 1950 Queen Street
Chuff, having said for weeks he would give a party for Peter's forty-fifth birthday, had, when the day arrived, forgotten to ask anyone. Xan Fielding came round for a drink, very spry and sweet, said Chuff's new magazine, *Vista*, was going to be a great success and already saw himself as a future Hulton! When Peter arrived, he

read out passages from *Palinurus* and said to me, 'Has Baby read her *Palinurus* yet?' I replied, 'Why should I read it, when I live it every day?' Chuff eventually got Pauline and Sylvester Gates to dine. I arrived at the Caprice feeling very tipsy, having drunk a lot of champagne. Had a gay and pleasant dinner until Pauline suddenly turned to Chuff, after giving me an arch look, and said, 'Seen much of Cyril lately?' After dinner, we went to a party. Cyril, who had done his best to make me jealous by saying that he was taking out a glamour-puss, turned up with a large dumpling.

Last night Jocelyn Baines came to see me. I had the most appalling *cafard*. We played chess and won a game each, which put me in a better humour. We were having a very agreeable evening until Cyril rang up in a terribly self-pitying state. How could I have been so beastly as to send him back to his cold empty house? Was it because of Baines? That I was a selfish bitch. Why did I play chess with Baines and not with him? That he had no money, and Lys, who had said earlier she had 'flu, had now gone out to dinner and it was all my fault. So, I packed my basket and trekked off to Sussex Place, expecting to find him in a terrible state of gloom, but he was prancing about the bedroom barefoot, very pleased with himself, feeling he'd scored off Baines, said he was pleased to see me, whipped off his dressing-gown, sprang into bed and was asleep in no time.

July 13
Cyril rang up early this morning. Said he had not slept all night, and was still brooding on the last two days and what I might have been doing. Said he had spent the greater part of the night allotting marks to all the women of his circus, according to their suitability as wives. I, of course, got fewer than any of them for spirituality, but top score for sex appeal, followed by Sonia Orwell, who had tremendous appeal in a blowsy way when blotto. Lys and Joan (Rayner)[*] got top marks for loyalty and giving a sense of security.

Chuff had a tough time getting through on the buzzer. He had been told about a luncheon party given by Cyril at the Ritz. Waugh, who had been invited, had complained of the food, adding that he had the impression Cyril had asked a lot of people to lunch, forgetting he no longer had Lys as a cook. Later, I rang Cyril and

[*]Formerly Joan Eyres-Monsell. She married John Rayner and then Paddy Leigh-Fermor.

said had his lunch been a flop? Very hurt, he replied, 'But it went on until four . . .' This evening Jocelyn came round with another book put down on Chuff's account. When I said Chuff was broke, adding, of course, not broke as we know it, he kept repeating, 'Oh, you are sweet, really.' Then, the old mystic, Ned Grove, came round looking as absurd as ever with his lined India rubber face, eyeglass, sticking-out snout, bowler hat and brolly. He said, 'I see you are very nervous tonight. We must give you a lot to drink.' I knew quite well what he had on his mind. He never stopped talking about the god Pan and referring to a little black devil at the back of his head that manifested itself always when he was with me. He harped a lot on the imagination. How one should have more faith in the imagination than any medium, such as one's sight. After all, he claimed, this tablecloth appears white to us now, but turn out the lights and what do you see!

We had a very good dinner at the Etoile. When we got back to the flat, Ned became dreamy and sentimental. Did I remember the story of Miss Skelton's onion? During the war, on one of my visits to Great Eastwards, when onions were almost impossible to procure, I managed to get hold of one, and kept it on the windowsill of Hertford Street, until one day it disappeared. A search was made, but the onion was never traced and from then a blight was cast over the house, until it was hit by an incendiary bomb. That kind of whimsy had great appeal to him.

Rise early. Cyril had to return to Sussex Place to shave and collect suitcase. Reappears in Queen Street two hours later. Departure delayed. Halt at Maidstone for a cold lunch during which I said I was feeling dejected and sick of life . . . What with the old circus round, and nothing but futility. 'You ought to marry Jocelyn,' he says. 'I would rather join Patrick Henderson in Canada.' C appeared quite troubled and said, 'Has he asked you to?' So I pretended that he had. The pork pie Cyril was eating got pushed aside. 'Unfortunately, we can't possibly marry,' he said, with a trapped look, 'as we don't get on at all well when things go wrong and you couldn't bear being poor. After all, it's not as though anyone is likely to leave you any money we can count on.'

Have been twice to Wimbledon. Once with Patrick and once with Cyril. It was the first time Cyril had been. The Queen being there, he spent the whole time looking over at the Royal box, where Ali Forbes was sitting, and felt he was getting some of the reflected glory. As far as the tennis was concerned, he was only interested to know which of the women players I thought had the most sex appeal.

July 27
Wake up with terrible gloom. No char. Spend all the morning cleaning while Cyril soaks in the bath. He is obsessed with arranging a luncheon party for tomorrow, has asked Nika Hulton, but could not find any other guests who were not already lunching. Takes each refusal as a slight, even on telephoning someone and finding them out. Goes off to dine with Angelica Weldon.* I feel rather peeved at not being asked. Mooch about the flat, do washing.

Cyril telephoned at midnight to say how much he has missed me and pretended his dinner with Angelica was a great embarrassment, saying she became maudlin and sentimental, cooed over her dog and kept saying what beautiful legs she used to have. When Cyril took her home, she produced Mounsey's rubber bone and made it into the shape of a cock, saying, 'What do you think of that?' Cyril just whistled! We decided she had definitely made a pass.

Went down to the cottage for the second weekend running. Cyril very active in the garden, rolled up his sleeves and, bare-footed, clipped the hedge. Said the air is very good for him there. He is always telling me of the number of women he nearly went to bed with and when I say, 'Why didn't you?', he says their scent put him off.

July 28
The bell rings very early in Queen Street and Xan (Fielding) appears with a suitcase. Says he is on his way to catch a train and wants to borrow my typewriter, as he has just got a temporary job typing out the memoirs of an Egyptian staying at the Hyde Park Hotel. Finds the unmade bed inviting and immediately tries to get into it. Seems very worried about money, as usual. I said that Daphne Bath

---

*Angelica Weldon was an American girl inclined to alcoholism.

should find some work for him on her farm, but he thought that a very comic idea. Actually, Xan dislikes any form of work more than most. What a pity he can't be kept by the state for doin' nothin'. As soon as he had gone, Chuff appeared with a letter in longhand that he wanted typed to a Mr Money. 'You won't have trouble spelling him!' he said. He enjoyed dictating the letter and kept saying, 'We should do this more often. If I had you to type my letters, I should get a lot more work done.' Another writ arrived from the Canterbury Telephone Service. Being in a happy generous frame of mind, Chuff wrote out two cheques, one for the writ and one for me. Then Cyril arrived in a taxi laden with food and drink. We reached Sussex Place as the first guest arrived. State of panic. Lys, having been over-zealous in tidying up on her last visit, had hidden the key to the cellar and all the corkscrews. An amiable lunch. Cyril fussed. Nika and Henry Yorke[*] talked nonsense, Henry's wife Dig made prattling noises, remaining throughout in a large black straw sunhat, as though attending a garden party.

The lunch upset the plans for the weekend. We came back to Queen Street and had an hysterical quarrel as I wanted to go to the country and Cyril didn't. He kept sneaking out to telephone Lys while I went downstairs to have a drink with my neighbour, the streetwalker, who showed me photographs – 'Mon amour! My doggie!' – and made me admire her flat all over again. Then C and I went to see a film starring Joseph Cotten, whom Cyril feels sentimental about, as Cotten once made a pass at him. Went back to Sussex Place and cooked some chops. Then as a joke I suggested Cyril put on his diving apparatus and flippers, which he dutifully did.

The weekend in the country passed without any rupture until Monday, when we went for a long excursion to find Grove Ferry Hotel set in very pretty country beside the River Stour, but the menu was disappointing, so we decided to return to our haddock. We were both delighted with the country round Upper Hardes and were admiring the cottages in that area, when I caused C to take the wrong turning and we found ourselves on a long strip of road leading back to Canterbury. 'Really, you have the brain of a feather!' 'With all your brain, you can't even drive a car!' I

---

[*]The writer Henry Green.

responded. And once more we were a couple of battling kangaroos. 'I'm not going to be shouted at any more,' Cyril said, and scrambling out of the car hovered about the bonnet before deciding to demonstrate his independence by walking away. I had driven about two miles when I felt guilty and returned to pick him up. He was nowhere to be found. Searched all the pubs and, in a great state of fret, drove back to the cottage. At one in the morning, I heard the click of the gate and a jaunty beaming Pungle appeared. 'The air suits me very well here,' was all he said, and 'What is there to eat?'

August 15   Cottage
After preparing some *tomates provençales*, the calor gas ran out. The builders said they had no staff to send to repair the stove. So we went to dine at the Smugglers which pleased Cyril. He discovered it on his nine-mile walk and considers it a welcoming port in a storm; he can also buy cigars there. We ate a very dull mixed grill. A red-faced, check-coated man came in and exclaimed joyfully, 'This place reminds me of the Old Trout at Oxford.' Cyril said disparagingly, 'What do they know of Oxford!' When we got back, still feeling hungry, I cooked the tomatoes on the bonfire which was still smouldering.

August 16
We had to leave early as Cyril had arranged a lunch with Peter Watson.[*] A great state of fret, as I insisted on taking the mowing machine into Hythe on the way, which seemed unreasonable even to me. It had been lying in the garage for years. Each ironmonger took one look at it and hurriedly said they were overworked. When we arrived in London, I was complimented on my driving, as Cyril had got to his lunch on time. He suggested I join them, but I was unwashed and in trousers. Chuff came to see me at six, still in a financial flap. Said his two weeks in Paris had been spent reading the *Continental Mail* and working out figures.

Cyril has another luncheon party. Stephen Tennant, a strange Frenchman, Janetta, Tony Bower and a friend of Sonia. Stephen: 'I hear you know Cairo well?' Me: 'Oh, do I?' 'But you were there?'

---

[*]Peter Watson's main interests were modern painting and music, and he financed *Horizon* from 1939 to 1949.

'Oh yes.' 'Were you there for long?' 'Eighteen months.' 'Then you do know it well!' Long pause. Sonia's friend: 'I hear you like swimming?' Me: 'Well, I like the sun.' Apart from answering everyone's questions, the Frenchman hardly spoke either. There was a conversation about jewellery. To bring him out, Cyril asked, 'And what stones do you like the most?' The Frenchman said dourly, *'J'aime les cailloux.'*

August 17
Lunched with Cyril at Sussex Place. At my suggestion, he had prepared a table in the garden, but as soon as we went out the sun disappeared. The lunch was not a success, the garden being overlooked by workmen, and the food was cold. C very solicitous as he is going to Scotland. Talks of our living together, preparatory to marriage, when he gets back. He said that, if two people who live together don't marry within the first year, they never will. He can't live alone at Sussex Place and that if he doesn't marry me he will marry someone else. Half an hour later, says he thinks he has been in a married state too much in his life.

August 18
Cyril was dining with Clarissa (Churchill) and told me in such a way that it was meant to arouse jealousy, so I arranged to see Jocelyn, who came round with a book on French cathedrals put down on Chuff's account.

Sidney visits me in the morning. Appears to be in better health. Moaned a great deal about financial problems. When I told him my debts amounted to £200, he said that if it had been for less he might have been able to help. I wonder why he likes these short morning visits.

August 19   Queen Street
All the papers full of Farouk's visit to Deauville. Both the tarts from downstairs flown over there! C has arranged to lunch with Tony Bower. I spend the day with Poppet, but rush off to have an abortive interview with Chuff's bank manager about getting an overdraft. Manager asks me how I intend paying it off. Did I have any income? I said, 'None whatsoever.' Told him I could always pay off overdraft with my jewellery. He said he wouldn't like me to have to do that as it was probably a family legacy. I didn't tell him it

was mostly unpaid for and that Chuff still owed Cartier £100. Returned to Poppet and whined about Chuff sending me off to such an unhelpful interview. She agreed. Gossipped. Went off to see Cyril. Tried to justify his visit to Scotland with Clarissa by saying he thought about me more when I wasn't there. Said they dressed for dinner and, after packing his dinner jacket, asked what other suit he ought to take, so I suggested he took a pinstripe, if it was that kind of house. On the way to the station tried to justify his departure once more by saying he always managed to write so well at Glen. And, anyway, I wouldn't be missing him as I would be spending my time with some other man. I said he couldn't reproach me for that, as he always seemed to need the company of other women and was, in fact, going to stay with one now. Then he became indignant, said there would be a large house party. In that case, I told him, it doesn't seem you will be doing all this writing you mentioned. In order to reassure me further, he then stated he had quite made up his mind not to take Lys back and that he had told Joan very firmly he had no intention of going abroad with her again.

Cottage
Start feeling more adapted to my own company. Have no desire to see anyone. The char, Mrs Willett, comes round to clean and helps me carry the desk upstairs. Clear the outhouse and give her an old racket and broken down baby chair. Tell her how nice I think her husband is. She says everyone tells her that, but she finds him difficult as he never argues, so she cannot pick a quarrel. Cigarettes arrive in the post. Sent by Chuff. Do a lot of sickling and build up a bonfire. Heavy rain in the evening. Go and eat at The Smugglers. Talk to the proprietor. Tells me he has a snack bar at the Elephant and Castle, and a beach bar in Folkestone, but cannot make either place pay. In London he is cheated by his manager and at Folkestone the weather is bad. Very proud of all the notables who have visited the Smugglers, in particular the actress Martha Ray. While at the bar, he said, she did more acts in half an hour than in all her films. He gives me some gardening hints. Pour boiling water on weeds and you will never see them again.

A very satisfactory day. Early morning, a lot of sun. Take all the empty wine bottles into Tappendens, useful for bottling vinegar, they said. Go into Wye and buy a dozen eggs and visit the builders.

Find them most helpful. Hands me over a plumber who was about to have his dinner. Brings his sandwiches with him and sets to work on the stove. Spends three hours here. Tells me that he gets six pounds fifteen shillings a week, is not allowed to work overtime because of the unions and has to spend twenty-three shillings on renting a house. He was a very nice man. Took great trouble over the stove. Said he would like to come and do the garden. Then it poured with rain. I discovered the advantages of forking and dug up all the nettles. Visited the farmer and asked if he'd mind a hole being made in his hedge to let in a tractor. 'Don't want no holes in my hedge,' he said firmly, but laughing. Some more cigarettes arrive in the post. Chuff rang to say perhaps it would have been more sensible if he had sent me a bird. Took a boiling bath and went to bed aching.

Go over to Hythe. Mummy completely exhausted from looking after Brenda's children. When I timidly suggest she lent me Tina the dog for the night, she took great pride in saying she was not going to let anything entrusted to her out of her sight and treated me as though I were attempting to rob her of a bag of gold. Before leaving I told her I had met the Barenlays in the lane. She said, 'You ought to call on them, they would be useful people to know.' 'But they must be so dull,' I said. 'Of course not!' Mummy was most indignant. 'How can they be dull, she worked with you at Schiaparelli.' I then realised whom she meant. 'A rather pretty girl, a similar type to Auntie Vera, with large fishy dead eyes,' I said. My mother became quite excited, as though she had caught me out. 'You mean to say you think Auntie Vera has fishy dead eyes?' And, when I tried to reword the sentence, I could see she already visualised herself repeating the slander to the whole family. Got back to the cottage at eight, feeling very lonely. Cooked a nasty meal but there is no pleasure in cooking for oneself, even if you feel hungry. Slept better. Chuff telephoned at nine.

Queen Street
Last night, I had a strange call from Paris Plage. A voice said, 'I wonder if you remember me?' I said, 'Who are you?' It was Farouk. 'It would be nice to see you again,' he said, 'why don't you come out and join us?' I told him I would have to think about it and asked him to call me next day. The two men of letters, PQ and Cyril, were in the flat at the time. Pungle guessed at once, and went into the

bathroom to lie and soak and brood on it. An hour later, to my surprise, he said, 'I think you ought to go. After all, a King's a King.' He then jokingly ordered me to have us both invited to Egypt this winter. Get myself a beaver coat. And extract enough francs for us to spend a week in Biarritz. Say you need it for a honeymoon. I was quite surprised on hearing these instructions, not wanting to go a bit. Had a confirmation call this morning. Cyril more enthusiastic then ever, almost wanted to speak for me, to make it quite clear I was accepting.

Cyril saw me off, very attentively buys a bundle of newspapers and then forgets to give them to me. A clear blue sky, as the plane flew up over the damp haze surrounding England. At Le Bourget airport, I ran into Robert Capa, the photographer, who had just arrived from Germany. We sat in the airport café drinking and reminiscing about our initial meeting, sitting in a hammock at a diplomatic garden party during the war. Am met at La Baule by Freddie, the Copt, who is now married. The royal party consisted of about twenty guests, including Freddie and his wife, Farouk's doctor, barber and bodyguard, and took up two floors of the Hermitage Hotel. I am introduced to Monsieur et Madame Kahil. 'What does Monsieur Kahil do?' I ask. Farouk laughs. 'In England, I think you'd call him a drone.' They had all come on from Le Touquet, where there had not been any pretty girls, but Farouk added, 'In Deauville there were plenty, professionals, too. They cost me a packet.' I said, 'Your doctor says I look run-down.' 'It's after your journey. We all looked run-down when we got here.' He tweaked my ear, and turning to the Kahils said, 'She's a real minx, this one.'

At this time Farouk resembled a huge sawdust teddy bear badly sewn at the joints. Wherever we went, we were surrounded by people screaming 'Vive le Roi'. Every evening we dressed up and after dinner trooped into the Casino where I was given a thousand francs to play roulette and, when that was lost, I remained seated beside Farouk as a kind of mascot. After I had lost everything at a roulette table three nights running, the King's doctor, a rather taciturn, sympathetic man, knowing I did not have much money, persuaded me to keep some chips aside and cash them in as we were leaving. The Casino in La Baule is small and, if it was not full, Farouk would say, 'Not enough suckers here tonight.'

Members of his bodyguard haunted the hotel corridors. Mornings, I would be summoned by one of them to join the King for breakfast, then his barber appeared to curl his moustache, when we would be told the plans for day. Farouk had a mania for cleanliness. One time, in a star restaurant they brought in a cracked soup tureen, whereupon he strode into the restaurant kitchen and proceeded to break all the cracked crockery he could see, splitting them into two with his hands. Should one ask what he was joking about with his Arab staff, he said simply, 'I like to have cheerful people about me. None of your English poker faces around for me.'

The *Daily Mail* had commissioned Cyril to do an article on him. Farouk had a horror of journalists. To him writers and journalists were synonymous: when Cyril arrived in La Baule Farouk refused to see him but we would meet for drinks. When Farouk announced that we were proceeding to Biarritz and would be 'hitting the road' the following morning, black berets were meted out and we were told we would have to wear them. Still hoping to be included in the trip, Cyril bought himself a black beret and told me he would be sitting drinking coffee in the last café outside the town on the route to Biarritz. A French bus stacked with luggage went on ahead of us that we kept overtaking all along the route. As the convoy of cars left La Baule, with Farouk and me in our berets in the lead and a police car in the rear, the streets were lined with people excitedly shouting and waving, for as we know the French are mad about royalty, no matter whose. Sure enough, there was Cyril wearing a black beret, reading *Le Monde*, seated at an outside table at the last café, a suitcase beside him. But no pleading on my part would induce Farouk to pick him up. The journey from La Baule to Biarritz took ten hours. When I complimented Farouk on his driving, he said, 'A compliment from you is a rarity, I'll take it.' We stopped for a late breakfast, and then at four o'clock trooped into the Chapon Fin. Innocuous souvenirs like labels were steamed off bottles and the accumulation sent back to Egypt, and crates of mangoes accompanied us everywhere. Once more, we took up two floors of the Palace Hotel in Biarritz. Before allotting us our rooms, Farouk strode into his suite saying, 'Let's get everything shipshape in here,' and proceeded to move all the furniture around. When shown the specially large bed he had commanded in advance, he expressed his satisfaction and jokingly said to the manager, 'Now, I'll be able to have some fine *partouse*.'

In Biarritz we were pursued by journalists wanting to interview the English Mystery Woman. I went on losing at the roulette table but managed to put enough aside to give Cyril some cufflinks and provide for our eventual trip back.

While we were lunching one day, Farouk said he wanted to see my eternity rings, one of sapphires, one of rubies and one of diamonds, that I'd had for years. Stupidly I took them off and never saw them again. Having confiscated my rings, he summoned the manager of Boucheron. I was later given a ring with emerald chips, a gold cigarette holder and a large vulgar clip inlaid with multi-coloured stones that was pinned onto my evening dress like some badge of merit. Madame Kahil, who had a reputation for being an envious troublemaker, tried to persuade me to ask him for some earrings to go with the clip, but all I wanted was to have my eternity rings back.

The time came for the entourage to proceed to Cannes. My suitcase was returned to London by Bag and Cyril and I travelled back leisurely through the Dordogne. When I went to the Egyptian Embassy to collect the suitcase, with it was a crate of mangoes, a present to Cyril, as I had said he loved them so. Later, we read in a newspaper that, in the Cannes Casino, one of Farouk's opponents had dropped down dead at the chemmy table.

◇◇◇ Chapter XI ◇◇◇

Marriage

Diary

October 5, 1950

After a year's talk of marriage, we have decided that this is to be the day. Cyril, very slow in getting up, has even talked of putting it off, on the pretext of having time to find another witness. I tell him that, if he does, he shouldn't go on living in Queen Street, as it puts me in a false position with Chuff who, after all, has been paying my rent. 'An ultimatum!' C says. Later, tells me I am nagging him into it. We have to pick up PC Boot, who is to be the main witness, and as soon as we leave the house we immediately start quarrelling. C insists on telling me the way to Elham, as though I am new to the district. He studies maps and forgets to direct me at the crossroads. Then says to me, 'I thought you knew the way.' I say, 'I thought you were directing me.' We find Boot dressed in civvies, waiting on the kerb outside his house. He has a very solemn air, especially for the occasion. Cyril makes an effort to be friendly and asks him about the animals getting their winter coats, as Boot has told me the badgers are growing extra thick fur which indicates a hard winter. We arrive late at the Registry. Announce ourselves, then Cyril suddenly disappears. 'Is he a nervous type?' Boot asks. A clerk comes in and presumes Boot to be the future husband. Very pleased, Boot says, 'If I weren't a married man, I'd take his place readily.' Cyril reappears looking harassed, laden with glasses, a bottle of champagne and a second witness he has picked up in the street. We are all taken into a room with bare walls except for an

94

enormous warning about the penalties of making a false statement. Boot points it out to me and grins. I am reminded of *Huis Clos* and feel like giggling. The woman official starts her dissertation. 'Do you take this woman . . .' Cyril is asked to repeat the necessary words which he does with great solemnity. – 'Do you take this man . . .' and I after him have to say the same words . . . Towards the end of my recitation I get terrible giggles and can barely complete the sentence. Am reprimanded by the woman wedder. Feel furious at being ticked off and forget my hysteria.

Then follows a long silence, but for the clerk scratching away on a sheet of paper. We are both asked to sign away our freedom. When PC Boot has to sign, the clerk says, 'Your initials are N N?' 'No sir, W W . . .' 'And they stand for?' 'William Wellington,' says Boot proudly. We discuss whether or not to drink the champagne there but decide to go off to a pub. Stop just outside Elham. Boot hailed by everyone in the saloon. They all get a matey welcome. Cyril having stated that his father belonged to a Yorkshire Light Infantry Regiment, Boot points to a dreary-looking soak in the corner and says, ' 'E come from Yorkshire, Gov.' C very shocked that I couldn't remember my father's regiment. Cross words exchanged all the way back. C insists on trying out a new route which meant taking narrow winding lanes and backing into car tracks to enable cars to pass, so I arrive late for a dentist's appointment. A cold lunch in sullen silence in Maidstone.

October 8   Queen Street
Still fearing there might be headlines on the front page, 'Writer Weds Friend of Farouk', Cyril goes downstairs to get the newspapers, but rather disappointed to find no reference at all. Puts on kettle. When I suggest he makes the toast he says, 'Don't know how to make toast.' Makes tea, drinks half a cup and sinks back into the bed like a dying goose, still in his dressing-gown. 'What is it, bright spark? . . .' 'I have a swollen stomach,' he says, 'and feel sick.' Sinks further into the pillows and closes his eyes, with an expression of resigned suffering. Later, I ask how he feels. 'On the defensive,' he says. And, when I ask why, puts it down to a feeling of guilt. 'Guilt about what?' 'Not making the toast when you asked.' I read the paper. An article on flying saucers. I take a bath, thinking what a slothful husband I've hooked! An hour later, I go into the bedroom, Cyril is lying with his eyes closed. 'Picture of a man with a future,' I say. He rings up Sonia and complains of his health. Says he thinks he has a bad appendix. After the conversa-

tion, seems in a better humour. Asks me to sit beside him and be more sympathetic. Tells me that Sonia had spent the evening with Lucien Freud, who had said how much he worshipped Cyril, that he was the nicest man he knew.

October 10
C collects the newspaper and makes the tea. Has a long session in the bath while I do the laundry. Go into the bedroom later to find him standing naked in an attitude of despair staring into space. Take my bath, return to bedroom and find C still gazing into space. Go into the sitting room, to write a letter, return to bedroom, C still with his back to the room propped against the window ledge. I ask, 'What is the matter?' 'It's marriage,' he says. 'I feel trapped.'

Feel very restive and dissatisfied, saddled with a slothful whale of a husband who spends his time soaking in the bath and then plods despondently to White's where he studies the racing form. He is later seen by PQ wearisomely dragging himself round the expensive *antiquaries* in Mayfair. Today he went and bought himself a silver coffee set and sat gazing at it enraptured all evening. 'Who's going to clean them?' I asked. 'I am,' Cyril said, and proceeded half-heartedly to rub a duster over them. 'I can see us setting up as housekeeper and butler,' he said.

An enormous basket of exotic plants arrived today sent by Farouk, with congratulations on my marriage. Pungle returns from White's looking particularly glum. Ask him why. Goes over his movements of the morning and says he thinks it must be after reading an article on Tasmanian Devils. 'What was so depressing about that?' 'Well, they're becoming extinct.' Also said he'd seen Peter Q in the street looking terribly red-faced and ugly, which had depressed him even more.

I had a drink at the Ritz with Peter who was very interested in the Pungle news. I said I was in despair, he seemed so apathetic and gloomy. Peter said he might be pining after Lys. I told him that at the moment, to buck herself up, Lys was consulting five specialists. A psychoanalyst, deportment crank, gland specialist, gynaecoloist and a beautician. Peter was concerned about the expense, as indeed we all are. I told him she was trying to inflict as much guilt as possible. Peter said he had seen Pungle first at White's, where he had not dared approach him for fear of being snubbed, and later plodding up Bond Street lethargically raising his trunk at all the *antiquaires*.

I got back to find the dear boy lying on the divan. Said he wished he were dead, that anyway he didn't think he'd live to survive fifty. I looked at the three-piece coffee set which had been so tenderly polished earlier and felt quite touched. Tremendous arguments and discussions about Sussex Place. I say I refuse to live there in its present state of wreckage, that it needs redecorating.

'What you don't realise,' I am told, 'is that it's like that because its chief adornment has gone.' When I enquire what that was, he says, 'Lys.'

November 4
Further discussions on Sussex Place. I suggest we live on the top floor and let the rest of the house. Pungle not at all pleased with the idea, hankering after all the large rooms, and suggests splitting the house into three. A heated discussion until we are screaming at each other. Feliks telephones and I tell him about the house problem. Says he sees Cyril's point of view, that I should move in and let him keep all the large rooms. 'You'd like us to move into the attic and have it oak-beamed,' Cyril says to me. Then, decides he would rather sell the house as otherwise the Adornment Lys might take up residence with her young man, or might start demanding her premium back. He mellows in the bath. Later, we go into the market for the rations. Pungle insists on buying some Dublin Bay prawns at one and sixpence each. He carries the basket and plods after me. I leave him in Heywood Hill cashing a cheque. Later, appears laden with books on gardening, having become a great enthusiast, has plans for planting a selection of rare exotic tropical creepers at the cottage. Expresses desire to visit Kew again to see some rare specimens. Toot rings up and asks if I'd like to leave for Cairo as he has bought a new plane. I ask how many engines it's got. Tells me it's a one-engined Beachcraft but a nice BIG engine. 'You'll have to get a few more to tempt me,' I say.

First Married Christmas 1950
Pungle took me to stay with Heber-Percy (Mad Boy). We both travelled with a trunk apiece as though for an extensive visit. Left late on Saturday to avoid all other journeying Christmassers. Jowly Pungle effusively greeted at Swindon station. I slunk into the back seat of the car unobserved. Met by Garth at the house who acted as hostess and said, 'Pleased to meet you again.' He poured us out a

delicious iced gin cocktail sugared round the edge. The house was very centrally heated, a strong smell of incense that Garth said was smouldering rosemary they'd put on the fire. The rest of the house-party did not appear until dinner. Clarissa Churchill had not changed, as I had been made to, for she had no evening dress with her. There were two other queens. A very pretty American who didn't say much but seemed intelligent and kept pursing up his mouth; a blue-eyed airman called Ken, snobbish and self-assured who never stopped talking, anxious to be a social success. The whole weekend I found a strain. Lengthy meal sessions, messy food with little wine and a row of watchful eyes with everyone making guarded statements or listening to Pungle holding forth. We had dinner with Sir Oswald and Lady Mosley. The host talking politics without drawing breath: it was like listening in to Radio Luxembourg. I kept switching off and tuning in, depending on whether or not I made any headway with the American on my right who talked about his mother. During the fruit course one of the table flaps collapsed and all the port decanters crashed in a heap. I was accused of kicking it loose because no one was paying me any attention. After dinner Hubby inspected all the rare pieces of ornamental china in their sitting room and, after tilting them upside down, declared each one in turn to be a fake.

Got some dirty looks from Cyril when I barged into Mosley's smoking den and disturbed the men drinking port during the segregation of the sexes. The following day we dined with the Betjemans and had the best meal over the whole of Christmas, and a great wine tasting session. I suddenly turned on Hubby when he was talking with Clarissa, at the further end of the table, and screamed, 'My God, you are a bore with your shrub talk all the time.' Everyone stopped talking and looked very shocked. Then there was a poet guessing game which Hubby got right every time and even I managed to spot a Spender, and felt extremely proud.

January 1, 1951   Queen Street
Am trying to cut down on cigarettes, have managed to reduce them to ten a day. Imagine I feel much better, less cotton wool in the head. Both wake at noon. Screams for food from Hubby who has put on an inch of jowl since Christmas. Tell him he must go on an orange juice diet, but I produce some eggs and bacon. Then he says he has devious things to do. Reappears at six, when I ask what he has been up to, says he won't tell me as he will be scolded. Catch

him furtively eyeing all the empty wall space. 'You've been looking at those antique desks again,' and he chuckled. I ask him where he thinks he will find the money. But all he was interested in was explaining them all in detail. He hasn't been muttering so much lately. On bad guilt days, he remains in the bath and groans, dense steam seeps from under the door and spreads round the flat, and I hear an ectoplasmic voice crying, 'A million miles from here,' pause, 'A million miles from here,' or, 'I wish I were dead.'

Robert Kee came round in the evening, popping dexedrines and benzedrines into his mouth as though they were boiled sweets. He jokingly asked if I was prepared to do any pill swops. He eventually went off to a Milner Street party. Poppet reported next day it had been absolute hell. When she arrived, one drunk woman was being carried out and several people wandering up and down the stairs gripping the bannister. Xan was pouring gin down his throat. While one woman stripped, other women were sprawled on sofas combing their hair.

January 3
Wake up late with a sore throat and no energy.

In the evening, Cyril suddenly announces he is off to have a drink with Janetta. I telephone the Bastard and go round to see him. When I return C is in the throes of packing a suitcase, but after enclosing two shirts says weakly, 'You can finish it for me. I shall cook myself a sole,' and with a martyred look begins to consult a cookery book. 'I'd rather you packed your suitcase, and I cooked the sole,' I tell him, but it ends in us both reading our respective books.

Natalie having installed herself at Sussex Place rings up from Pungle's bed, comatosed by drugs, and suggests she rents Sussex Place for three months at ten guineas a week. Pungle goes round to discuss it and finds her well dug in surrounded by dregs of tea and half-eaten scraps of food. Pretends that, by lying in his bed and thinking about him, she is in a permanent state of sexual excitement. Pungle flees nervously saying he must not keep the taxi waiting. The actor Bobby Newton rings us up next day asking where we have hidden his 'darling little wife'.

We are both hibernating like dormice, sometimes sleeping on until past noon, hardly ever going out, as it is so bitterly cold. Have had Janetta and Derek Jackson to dinner. I spent two days and nights fretting over a piece of meat that the newspapers claim is three-year-old refrigerated string. Had it stewing the whole of Sunday and took great pains over a wine sauce. A special selection of wines were fetched from Hubby's cellar, a Margaux 1900 and a Château Latour 1924. Just before the guests arrived Hubby and I had a squabble as he claimed the vintages are far too good to waste on sauces. We polish off with a fine assortment of cheese including a *fromage Monsieur*. Joan rings up next day and asks Pop how he liked Derek. Cyril thinks him a jolly nice Cuss; 'He really does have a great feeling for claret.'

February

Had a glimpse of Augustus (John) today looking very arty, wearing his beret about the house and puffing at his pipe. Poppet tells me he wears his beret night and day, as he says it keeps out the draughts, and that she went into his room the other morning with some coffee to find him fast asleep with the beret lying beside his head on the pillow, but when he woke up he very firmly placed it back on his head. And, this morning, Dodo (his wife) went into his room when he was out and discovered a half-drunk glass of Irish whisky. So when he came in she ticked him off and asked him what he was doing drinking whisky on the sly. He looked very sheepish and said that he had felt very low that morning and he needed a pick-me-up. I asked Poppet if there had been signs of high spirits as a result (had she heard him humming?) but she said the only sound coming from his room was coughs and grunts. He has been kept on a wine regime after the Bogomoletz injections,[*] as otherwise his hand gets too shaky to paint. He is very deaf now and has the radio blaring away all the time, but is otherwise very quiet about the house. Poppet is getting much too keen on Robert Kee – it will only lead to disaster. Cyril is going through a pining-after-Lys phase. They have had secret meetings every afternoon this week. Cyril compares her to a juke-box. She says how wonderful her lover Andrew is and how Cyril would like him, because everything is dust and ashes to Andrew, and how once he came into the room and, 'What do you think, Cyril, he said? "Kiss me Lys," and I kissed him, and what do you think happened, Cyril? We fell into a trance.' 'You mean you were unconscious?' Cyril asked. 'We fell into a complete trance for twenty minutes.' So Cyril asked her why she

---

[*] A rejuvenating treatment.

didn't marry him, but she complained he was too narrow-chested. And, another time Andrew came into the room and said, "Everything is dust and ashes to me," and then Cyril, what do you think he did? He rushed out of the room and beat his head against the wall.' Apparently, I am the most ruthless homebreaker! And all Cyril's friends think he must have gone mad to marry me.

Lys has become the toast of White's – the toasters, it seems, being two elderly gentlemen with sportscars. 'But the trouble with me is, Cyril, I just don't care about money.'

Last night we dined with the Slaters. Had a tremendous stuff, as for two weeks there has not been any money, except when Chuff has given me some, and sometimes I don't own up to having any, as then it goes on lavatory paper. We had several helpings of duck and then played a boring horse game that Humphrey had invented which, he kept stressing, required a great deal of skill. The only skill, as far as I could see, was being able to count up to seven.

Cyril has gone out early to meet his mother who is arriving from South Africa. Our char, Mrs Munro, is very stern about Cyril and thinks he is a selfish, lazy man but he looks kind, she says. That was when she first came to clean; now she states that, if she were me, she'd wring his neck in a week! When I told her that at the end of March we would be leaving Queen Street because it was too expensive, she said, 'Oh dear! Mrs Connolly, you won't like being stuck out in the country, will you?' When I pointed out that Mr Connolly would like it even less, she said in surprised tones, 'Oh! So he's punishing himself as well!' She always has a drip on the end of her nose and, whenever she brings me the yoghurt in the morning, I can barely eat it. I find being penniless one appreciates things much more. Tea with Chuff at the Ritz now is an enormous treat. All the sandwiches taste particularly delicious, whereas we used to think they were quite disgusting.

January 9
Terrible hangover. An oppressive headache. Took potion at the chemist but to no avail. Hubby has a boil on his leg and a bad stye, full of pus which he squeezes in the bath. Both go out late afternoon to buy food. I am anxious to try a new recipe for Dublin Bay prawns but can only get scallops. Hubby brings back latest Hemingway book. Now have quite an assortment of reading matter, an André Simon wine book, the Bible, two books on psychology, Socrates

and several new cook books. Chuff comes round at six looking rosy, restless and clean for a change. Gillian Sutro always manages to spruce him up. Did a great deal of pawing and butting, though. I then experimented with scallops and made a rich sauce. Cyril not at all appreciative. Tell him I won't bother to cook anything special again, he can just eat bread and cheese.

Both wake up at noon. I lunch with Poppet. She tells me she has a new beau, Lord Hambleden of Hambleden Hall, Hambleden. Says she is teaching him a thing or two. Meet Hubby at Sussex Place roaming round admiring all his possessions. Inspect Janetta's quarters with a view to living in the lower part in order to be self-contained, but the whole house is in such a bad state of disrepair, it would take too much money to put it right. We cart away a lot of books. Meet Derek Jackson and Sonia for dinner at the Etoile. Sonia, subdued and on her guard for fear of provoking Hubby, hardly dares smoke a cigarette; a great wine ceremony as usual and vintage talk with the waiter. Sonia ironically pulls a face. She and Cyril always have a great showing off act, almost as bad as Xan Fielding and Paddy Leigh-Fermor with their Greek turn. Sonia soon gains assurance, and they both try and talk each other down. Went back to Derek's room at the Dorchester and drank a lot of brandy. Sonia and Cyril start lashing into Peter de Polnay, saying how malicious and boring he is. Sonia and I are asked if we can imagine Christ with a penis. I say yes, but he never used it. Sonia said yes, but he did use it, and the men's view was that he had been a bugger anyway. Then the Virgin Mary went through it. Sonia visualised her with a cunt, with lesbian tendencies. Sonia and Derek became very excited over the Russian novelists. Hubby only likes Turgenev and we decide to go home. The day before we had seen *Samson and Delilah* and so have become Bible conscious. I now insist on Bible sessions every night. I wonder how long that will last.

January 16
Spent the weekend with Mary and Robin Campbell. Nearly missed the train. A lot of loafing about and then last-minute panic. Had to collect some claret from the cellar of Sussex Place. Met at station by Mary with over-rouged dairy-maid cheeks, in a tiny four-seater box. She was squeezed into a pair of tight sailor's breeches and looked as though she had come straight from milking. Found them

delightful people to stay with. Easy, informal and no heckling in the mornings to get us out of bed. Saturday, lunched with Sylvester and Pauline Gates. A lot of Natalie talk. Drank a bottle of Fumé and Fusé white wine. Hubby complained bitterly at having to drink such young wines which were far too acid-forming. Also, thought the lunch nasty, as he had been given a bad egg with the *hors d'oeuvre*. Had a sleepless night in a too-narrow bed with Hubby heaving about like a giant seal.

◇◇◇ Chapter XII ◇◇◇

Kupy

The first time I ever saw a coati-mundi was in the small mammal house at the zoo. On her plaque was inscribed 'DIANE'. She was very fat and sat humped against the bars of the cage, hoping someone would come along and scratch her. She seemed to be such a charming animal that I asked Sutro, who was about to visit Uraguay, to bring me back a coati. It travelled on the rack on the plane and, apparently, created such havoc that the other passengers wanted the stewardess to get it flung overboard.

I was not in London when Sutro returned and he deposited the animal at the zoo. When I went to collect it, the keeper produced a nice wooden box. He said it would grow to four times its present size. At the cottage, the baby coati lived in the dining room, but could always be coaxed back into its box with grapes. It slept rolled into a ball with its snout clasped between its paws. It fancied a varied diet, one memorable meal being half a pound of black grapes, two live worms, a raw egg, some lumps of sugar and, finally, a raw chicken leg. As for drink, it was partial to milk and water in which it afterwards washed its paws. When tame, the coati became a great show-off, swinging from beam to beam with its long ringed tail erect or it would tear round the room at a tremendous pace making excited squeaking noises.

Diary

Monday, April 23, 1951
The first good signs of spring. A ravishing hot day, 'the best England can do,' said Mrs Willett the char, on arriving, 'not a breath

of wind.' We have the coati out of doors all day without mishaps. It has no inclination to roam away from where we are sitting and spends a lot of time snuffling around for worms, biting off twigs and wrestling with the branches, or clambering up the elder tree that Cyril despises so much. It increases in charm each week, has developed a passion for tugging at my hair, leaps onto one's back and takes small nips at the nape of the neck . . . 'Kupy kupy kupy' is the usual cry. When hungry it runs at our heels like a kitten, and when excited lets out birdlike yelps and springs into the air on all fours. We have had one or two scares. Once it escaped into the field and we had a hard time getting it back. Eventually, I had to be quite ruthless and grab hold of its tail. Occasionally, it gets too destructive with Cyril's new shrubs by taking sprigs in its paws and swinging on them. I don't know what we would have done without the coati and its enchanting ways. Such a relief to the monotony and poverty of our existence at the moment, always running out of money, and Cyril just sitting brooding like a furious fallen emperor.

Monday we went into Hythe and bought a mass of new shrubs and rock plants for the new wall. The gardener comes twice a week, works very hard, has dug up a large bed in the front preparatory to planting flowers, and is getting the back dug up for vegetables and mixed fruit trees to be arranged in circular fashion at the end of the so-called lawn. Pop is *obsessed* with planting, is a great bud inspector and dusk waterer, slobbering water all over the kitchen floor as he carries saucepan after brimming saucepan into the garden. When he sees me he scowls and scurries in the opposite direction, as I am always finding fault – comparing him to my mother. For instance, he puts plants into the ground keeling over, being too lazy to dig deep enough so that mounds have to be piled up afterwards to cover their roots.

Still delicious blazing hot weather. Cyril has a lunch in London, so I take him into Ashford to catch the train. As usual, the stove is blocked and not drawing sufficiently to make hot water. Have to boil kettles to add to bath. A few drops of boiling water fell onto scowl-jowl-face's Chinese coolie legs which he had dangling over the side of the bath; fearful abuse. Both part at the station delighted to see the last of each other.

April 28

Icy cold, snow, frost and bleak grey sky, sunless, windy. Merry
England. Whereas no sign of any leaves on anything when we left
the country three days ago, we now see all the tiny buds have
blossomed out. Instantly make a tour of inspection and find all the
new plants doing well. Cyril tells me he has a better offer than the
New Statesman, that the *Sunday Times* want him on their permanent
staff of reviewers, doing an article every fortnight with almost
double the money and less words. It looks as though we might be
able to keep ourselves in lavatory paper now instead of having to
resort to magazine covers. Mrs Munro came to Queen Street
bringing the material she had made for the kidney dressing table.
Hatted, with dripping nose, her legs bandied with age in concer-
tinaed lisle stockings, she was carrying a battered old fish basket.
'And how are you, Mrs Connolly?' she asked, in her usual high-
pitched squeak. 'Not very well . . .' 'I thought not,' she said, as
though that meant that everything was all right. She then made
confidential enquiries after Chuff. As she was leaving she said with a
deep sigh of contentment, 'Now that I've seen you, Mrs Connolly, I
feel ten years younger,' and tottered off down the stairs.

Saw Peter for a pub lunch. He was looking very clean and spruce.
'No frayed edges about you these days,' I said. He had his usual
stock of malicious stories. One, passed on from Waugh. Apparently, Cyril had told him our telephone was cut off, whereupon
Waugh said to Peter that it looked as though our water had been cut
off too.

I had the coati in bed for the night. It remained curled up on my
back and only got up once to shit in its box. Its snout is beginning to
fill out. I do hope it won't resemble that mangy Diane at the zoo
with its short scrub of bristly fur like a worn-out bottle brush. Kupy,
although the colour of verdigris, is quite silky to touch.

Today we washed the coati. It made a fearful fuss with its head well
back and shark's snout wide open emitting a continuous squeak.
Apart from the initial shock of encountering water, it rather liked
the warm tap trickling onto its back.

◇◇◇

Cyril has just come back from Bath, where he spent two days with his mother. We have resumed relations with quite a resurgence of affection. I had two days of Chuff. We went to the second day of the Festival. Earlier, I ran into an old modelling friend, Marcia, in Oxford Street, as I was slouching along in the pouring rain with a bag of sawdust under my arm, bought from a fishmonger for the coati cupboard. Marcia asked me to her flat. She talked all the time of her infidelities, referring to her husband as 'that boring old basket'. After two gin cocktails, I left her sewing pink ribbon bows onto all her underwear and so was late for Chuff. A fret rush to the Festival concert. Patrick Balfour was there in a dinner jacket, looking very cadaverous but dignified with frayed edges to his collar. The concert was disappointing with Sargent conducting, except for the choir singing the National Anthem.

May 7
Cyril jealous of coati because I was teasing it and making it squeak. He said, 'You are completely obsessed with that animal. All your mothering instincts go on it instead of on me.' He then stumped up to bed at 9.15. I went up half an hour later taking the coati as it was so silky and clean. Being a cold night, I thought it could have a treat and sleep with us. Scaly Skin had kept his filthy shirt on, a check rancher's affair, very rough to touch. 'Take that beastly shirt off,' I said, but he didn't want to get scratched, turned his back and indicated that he was generally not at all pleased at having the coati in bed; the other night in London, though, he was very cross with me because I would not allow it to spend the night in his room. I was called 'Ajealousbitchgetout!'

When I told Peter that Cyril had been bitten by a lemur in the zoo (a reincarnation of his first wife Jeannie, as he ironically put it) Peter expressed surprise and commented that it was usually the 'Man of Pleasure' who bit the hand that fed him.

May 12   Sussex Place
Sunny day but cold. I suggest we catch the early train. Pop in agreement but potters. Have great difficulty in getting the coati into its box, such squeals result from my persistence that I am accused of sadism and working off aggression, and Pop rushes out of the house in a fury, slamming doors and saying he is off to Camden Town in search of a cat basket. Go to Shepherd's Market to collect month's rations, stop in Marylebone High Street and have some coffee and an omelette at Sagné's. Get back to find Pop in throes of

trying to get coati into cat basket. I don't admit to having eaten when asked, for fear of resulting ill humour. Catch late train. Garden disappointing. The gardener spends his time digging and hoeing the future vegetable patch, although it's getting too late to put in any vegetables. Pop tells me we are going to spend the weekend visiting private gardens which are open to the public, there being two on view on Sunday and one on Monday. Weather bad – so cold all the fires have to be lit.

Pop is in a very good humour almost all the time now – so pleased about the *Sunday Times* articles. We went to London on Tuesday to go to a Freddie Ayer party, very strong cocktails. Isabelle Lambert is upset as Pop, unaware of her second marriage to Constant Lambert, introduces her to someone as Mrs Sefton Delmer. Awkward silence, winks and smirks. I get stuck with a bore in a corner. Someone asks if I am going to the Pen Club meeting in Lausanne. Humphrey (Slater) agrees that the Festival is nothing but taste with no imagination, like an elaborate shop window dressing with nothing in the shop. Freddie asked us to dinner afterwards with an Australian dandy and Freddie's pixie-looking Australian girlfriend Jocelyn Rickards and Angelica Weldon senti-mentally drunk. Pauline Tennant with her theatrical chatter and thickened 'chops' (as Humphrey describes her jaw) aping her father, David. She repeated one funny thing David had said, when talking of Xan, who we all agreed had become impossibly self-confident these days, even to the extent of criticising Pauline's hat. Apparently, Xan was standing up to David one night at the Gargoyle, when David turned to him and said, 'Really, Xan, what are you but a *tiny wasp* attacking a rather *good fruit*?' After dinner, the whole party trooped back to Sussex Place where we did our best to keep them entertained by introducing the coati. Suddenly, there was the sound of someone battering down the front door and, going into the hall, Cyril was confronted by Donald Maclean quite soberly drunk, by which I mean he had got over his aggression and just wanted a bed. I tried to work him up into a state at the sight of Freddie, but he simply disappeared into the hall and crept under a pile of coats. Later Cyril put him to bed and took him up some Alka Seltzer, which is more than he would do for me! On Wednesday, I lunched with Angelica and Johnny Maclaren, for whom I do not have a great liking. Joined Humph and Cyril and went to a book exhibition. Thursday lunched with Janetta and Derek Jackson at Claridge's. They seem real lovebirds. Janetta looking so trim these days, camel-coated with new shoes, skirt and pullover, and Derek less excitable and absurd. Drank a delicious Château Margaux '39. Derek made one of his typical shock remarks saying that he thought E Waugh such a likeable fellow, if only he didn't write such dreadful books. It was only made amusing by the vehemence with which it was said.

Robert Kee back from the South of France, courting an old deb of forty-five in a mink coat and spending nights at Claridge's two doors away from Derek and Janetta.

There is an occasional sheep's cough in the morning; it might be Philip's (Toynbee) who has been in London for two nights without his wife, Sally. He makes a fearful noise now when he goes to bed, every ten minutes there being a series of dull thuds followed by door slamming.

Had tea with Poppet who is just back from the south bubbling over with accounts of her sexual activities with the locals and a phoney Baron. They apparently took it in turns to seduce all the Midi labourers.

Through Cyril dilly-dallying we missed the train at Charing Cross. Bad temper all round and a fifteen shilling taxi fare, which means we have less money for food. A cold bleak weekend. Visit an azalea and rhododendron garden at Hythe; on the way back, go into Saltwood cemetery to see if I can find my father's tomb.

Arrive back at Sussex Place and find earrings missing. Search all drawers, bags and suitcases. Inform Pop who instantly informs the police. Next three days spent surmising. A pound left for the char had also disappeared. Robert is in Germany. Insurance man notified. Locks changed on outside door. Discover a party was given on the Saturday and Pop's wine glasses used, as usual. We pump Mark (Culme-Seymour) for the names of the guests. All seem of irreproachable character. Mrs Mooney, the char, finds human excrement lying next to the bins outside the back door. Find Michael Law and girlfriend have moved into Robert's quarters. Feel Micky Luke will be installed any minute. They go to bed around three in the morning making a fearful noise. I have become a terribly crabby killjoy and each time storm upstairs rapping on all the doors and complaining. Go to a Film Award party. Seated next to James Pope-Hennessy. Tony Steele was there, very modestly pleased to have been offered a role in a film with Bette Davis.

May 26

Nearly missed the train again yesterday, jumped into the guard's van as the train was moving, porters yelling after us as we ran. Were locked in the van and had to attract attention by shrieking through the keyhole at the passengers the other side. It was essential to get out, as the main object in catching the train was to dine in the restaurant car. The guard eventually came to our rescue. A gusty weekend and very cold. Went to Sandling and saw the Hardy garden. Were taken round by the boss himself who pointed out all the special rhodi 'trusses', as he called them.

Had dinner twice last week with the Maurice Richardsons. Told Robert Kee that I had had a bit of an overdose and he said I ought to live in a cupboard like the coati. More pawning had to be done to get us through the week.

June 2

Nude sunbathing for the first time this year. Pop looking pink. Tried a new harness on the coati. Great dream plans of buying the house at the back and becoming a beech as opposed to an oak. Spend hours planning how we would furnish it with our combined junk. Pop doesn't think the house has sufficient grandeur. No walled garden, old yew trees or orchard. Spent the whole of today snooping about their back yard and peering into the windows. Their gardener, Godly, was painting and pointed out all the defects, said it was being ruined by ivy which had thrust its way through the brickwork. Said he wouldn't have it at any price when we were caught by the owner pacing his lawn and had to think up a pretext for being there . . . Pop unshaven in white shorts hanging well below the knees exposing even whiter coolie legs.

◇◇◇ Chapter XIII ◇◇◇

Life at the Cottage

Cyril was never altogether happy living in the cottage. He went on pining for a more spacious house. We were always visiting agents and studying lists of other properties for sale. Oak Cottage was indeed very small. It was only because we loved each other that it was possible to live there at all. And, no doubt, it was partly due to our cramped living conditions that we squabbled so much, so that Cyril maintained we resembled a couple of battling kangeroos.

The cottage had four rooms. On the left as you entered was a sitting room with an open fireplace, on either side of which were built-in cupboards. There was a wall-to-wall Axminster, a chintz-covered settee, bookshelves and a rosewood table. A bathroom had been built on off the sitting room. The dining room on the right had a pretty oak dresser, a refectory table and four highbacked seventeenth-century chairs. There was a strip of kitchen with a door leading into the back garden and an outside privy that we transformed into a coati hut. We were heated by an anthracite stove in the kitchen and the house was lit by Aladdin lamps that had to be filled with oil all the time. Any leftovers were kept in an outside hutch we always referred to as the beehive, often frequented by earwigs. Upstairs were two small bedrooms. To get from one to the other, you had to duck under a beam. There was a garage and a wooden outhouse where intrepid guests could spend the night. Angus Wilson slept in it once and seemed none the worse for wear. When Rosamund Lehmann came down bringing a small suitcase, she seemed to enjoy gathering blackberries from the hedge opposite, but after dinner suddenly recollected she had a breakfast appointment and insisted on taking the last train back to London. Cecil Beaton seemed appalled by our living conditions. He was even more shocked when I appeared in carpet slippers to be snapped standing beside Cyril in the porch. So, although, in its fashion, Cot remained a *clos de bonheur*, Cyril dubbed her 'Oak Coffin', the village Elmstead became 'Elmdeath', and the nearest town, Ashford, was relegated to 'Ashcan'.

Diary

August 15
Had quite a keen couple to visit the cottage. We are convinced it's sold and a lot of mortgage talk kept us happy all evening. The whole of the next day was spent studying maps of the surrounding country and discussing which houses to visit, the ones described as 'Manors' or 'Priories' being of the greatest interest to Pop. I don't know where he thinks the money is coming from. We visited the Appledore farm again, and he stood in raptures in front of the wheat field for almost an hour, visualising a thriving cherry orchard to be carefully nurtured by me. The owner seemed most anxious to get rid of it and talked about lowering the price. When we left, Pop was experiencing to the full the feeling of complete ownership and had already furnished all the rooms with his Regency furniture and built on wings to furnish his books.

We then visited a large manor house complete with music room and swimming pool. After the gloom and squalor of an over-crowded lower-class household, the spectacle of a comfortable middle-class one was even more depressing, with the owner apologising for the aroma of a roasting chicken, and dim spotty grown-up sons and daughters disappearing behind doors. With great pride, the owner took us into a hay field which they planned to turn into a tennis court! On the way back, we ran out of petrol, but both of us managed to restrain ourselves, with no word of blame. I fretted about getting back to cook a duck and complained that these excursions kept us out so late, as I had to cook in the dark. But, when we reached the cottage, we opened up some bubbly and the duck was delicious with an onion stuffing and apple sauce.

The forecast for Monday was rain, but it turned out to be a lovely day, so I sunbathed surrounded by wasps and flies and read Maupassant. Pop studied maps. In the evening, he became slasher-minded and disappeared into the dump to cut down the ivy stumps that were strangling all the trees. He refused, though, to give me any support with the sickle to cut down the grass. Then, removing all his clothing, even his espadrilles, he built up a large bonfire, using most of the available dry wood which would have made excellent kindling.

The beginning of September, I gave up smoking, comparatively easily, by first lighting a cigarette and after a few puffs stubbing it out, then relighting the same stub and once more putting it out. In this way I cut down from thirty to ten a day. Then, by giving up the habit of always keeping a packet in reserve, from the smoker's dread of being without, I gradually became less obsessed. I now moralise when I see chainsmokers and feel very smug. When in London, I smoke other people's; it is one of my town treats.

A month ago Angelica gave a party where I met the Moynihans. Very attracted to Rodrigo. Later I told Sonia that five years ago I used to follow him down the King's Road. 'I've heard the same thing from him,' she said, 'but he is under the impression he was following you!'

I had a letter from my mother this week saying grandma had had a stroke and was lying paralysed. I rushed down to Hythe expecting a death-bed scene but she seemed to have recovered. When my fifty-year-old aunts had visited her that morning, she had greeted them by saying she was going to give each one a penny that day, she saw them all as children. When my mother went to see her, she said, 'Is that Evie? Is Barbara looking after Brenda all right?' They seemed to welcome my appearance as it took their minds off the gravity of the situation. Grandpa was very fretful and asked if I had settled down all right. He gave me some broad beans which he said must be planted straight away.

November 15
Sussex Place sold at a considerable loss, the money gained just covering back rent and other expenses like outside painting of the house. Cyril found it almost unendurable being parted from his possessions. He wants to cram every beloved object possible into

113

Oak Coffin. As a result Mr Maggs, the builder, was called in and commissioned to build each room out six inches! Then I was persuaded to sell a greater part of my furniture to make way for Cyril's, admittedly things that I was not very attached to. The builders remained here three weeks. The whole of the roof was re-battened. We learnt to recognise a valley tile from a hip; as there was a warm sunny spell of good weather, Cyril ordered himself a deck chair from Tip-Top-Taps and spent each day sitting in the garden watching the workmen. If they were laying bricks at the back he would place his deck chair a few feet away from them and sit with his legs crossed and a book in his lap questioning everything they did; his uncombed hair shot in wisps all over his face and when I passed him from behind I could see the beginnings of a bald patch gleam in the sunlight. If there were three builders working in the front and three at the back, he would stroll from one group to the other, usually in carpet slippers and sometimes wearing a dressing-gown, till quite late in the day. 'Having a good brood?' I would say to him and when he saw me he would glare and move to another part of the garden. We had calor gas lighting put in the kitchen and sitting room. A great improvement. A new boiler installed. In fact, everything was made very snug indeed.

Now, every two weeks we go to London and stay with Sonia. Twenty pounds spent in two days; giving people bad meals at the Etoile. 'Keeping in touch,' it is known as. And two sleepless nights are spent tossing and turning in Sonia's bed which dipped in the centre and sloped so much at the sides that one has to cling to the outer rim of the mattress to avoid being sandwiched.

November 17
Cyril keeps me awake by muttering in a stage whisper all through the night, 'Poor Cyril!' over and over while lying sprawled on his back with one eye open to see if I have heard all right! So I insist he moves into the other bedroom.

This morning I heard strange groans coming from the next room and then what sounded to me like 'links' or 'minx' accompanied by a deep stage sigh. Was he sighing for his cufflinks in pawn? Was I the minx? Then it came again five minutes later: 'links . . . links . . .' More yearning this time and a deeper sigh. I went into his room quite soon after to announce that there was going to be a high breakfast . . . kippers, eggs, and ham for those who wished. I thought the sound of food would cheer him up, but he just looked at me with hangdog eyes and said, 'I had a wonderful dream about

Cyril with a goose

Kupy

Cot houseparty:
Cyril with Ali Forbes

Cot houseparty: Spider, Peter Quennell's wife at the time

Peter Quennell

Ann Fleming

Ian Fleming

Evelyn Waugh

Noël Coward

Paddy Leigh-Fermor

Joan Rayner with 'Birdie'

The Bill Davises at La Consula

Cyril being bored by a guide in Greece

Neighbour Eric Wood lunching in his conservatory

Cyril at lunch with Eric Wood

In the south of France

Lys last night.' 'How nice for you,' I said, 'I hope your dream comes true.' 'Why did you entice me away from Lys when all you wanted to do was to push me out of your bed?' He wouldn't come down to breakfast but lay in his bed sucking the sheet ends, which is always a bad sign. He sometimes lies for an hour with folds of sheet pouring from his mouth like ectoplasm. At twelve o'clock I got him out of bed with promises of a bath; he lay in it for an hour and through two closed doors I could hear groans and the word 'Pooey', which means he is in a very bad state of mind.

We have not been out of the house for five days. Cyril has been as far as the garage twice. Restlessness and boredom make one cigarette-minded. Last Sunday we motored to Tonbridge to have lunch with Sir Harry and Lady d'Avigdor-Goldmids. I had been on an orange diet for forty-eight hours. 'I hope you will break your fast at lunch today,' Cyril had said to me before leaving. 'I know the Goldsmids will lay on quite a spread and Harry will be offended if you're not eating.' It took us two hours to get there. We arrived at 1.40 to find the whole family seated at table already on their second course. No apologies, except from Cyril. All through lunch Cyril and Harry talked across at each other to the accompaniment of Rosie's voice telling her child how to eat. I have never met a family so united in confidence. One felt they had not a single vulnerable spot. Rosie said she was trying to slim before having some photographs taken by Baron. I said, 'But he is such a bad photographer.' 'Oh well,' she said, 'I have seen some photographs of someone he took which were very good.' 'You mean the Queen,' I said, and she giggled. 'Darling, would you like some butter?' she asked Cyril. He was busy talking and made no reply the first, second, third and fourth times. But she persevered until he eventually replied weakly, 'Yes.' She had won. I wish I could do that. When not eating Rosie had a cigarette dangling out of her mouth the whole time we were there. The house stood wing upon wing at the top of a steep hill and looked like a vast fortress. I was very impressed with the lavatory. I spent half an hour reading the *New Yorkers* stacked there, surrounded by amber mirrors so that you could see yourself from every angle, while one's feet nestled on turquoise-blue six-inch pile carpet, and facing one was a cigarette box stacked with gold-tipped cigarettes.

November 23
This morning I woke to be told, 'Why don't you drop down dead? That's all I wish, that you'd drop down dead.' He was lying half naked on the bed. 'Is there anything you want?' 'That you will drop

down dead.' Writs arrive by almost every post. Cyril remains in his bed, sucking the sheet. The Waugh article has been abandoned. The Third Programme has made suggestions. C just potters about the house in carpet slippers dusting his first editions and cluttering up the tables with cracked Sèvres and chipped faience.

December 2
The winter drags on apace. The really ice-cold weather has started. Very seldom is the open fire lit but the house keeps warm from the heat of the boiler. The new hot pipe in the sitting room is a great improvement. Went to London Wednesday. A Rothermere party. Before it, the Hultons took us to a Tennessee Williams play. Then a big fuss as Cyril was to be seated next to Princess Margaret. He had spent his day in preparation having nose-trims, haircuts and all his ear whiskers removed. After being ushered into the Rothermere drawing room, we all get split up, and then in a long slow procession troop down the stairs to the supper room, the women clinging to the balustrade, the men nervously eyeing the trains of the dresses that were tripping them up. I was the last in the queue and, on reaching the room where the supper tables were laid, I have the folding doors shut in my face by a swarm of butlers. Find myself in an adjoining room which has been turned into a bar where about four well-behaved couples have gathered and are quietly sipping champagne. They look at me, as much as to say, we got it too, but we're pretending to like it in here. A waiter serving champagne offers me soup. I see Cyril at the far end of the hall trying not to catch my eye. Peter Q comes in and looks the other way; he is talking to an elderly woman covered in sparklers and doesn't want to be interrupted. I rush up to Cyril who is being hustled away to the Royal Dwarf's table by Diana Cooper and I scream, 'It's no good turning your back on me.' But he disappears through the magic doors and from the throwout's foyer I see him eating a hearty supper and beaming across at the Royal Dwarf. I stand fuming in a corner when Lucien Freud comes in. He tries to avoid catching my eye, but I am determined and, pushing my way through the huddle of throwouts, try to engage him in conversation. He makes no response, is looking peagreen and smarmed down with sticking-out ears. Suddenly, Ann Rothermere, spotting him from her dais at the Royal table, beckons frantically and, shouting at Lucien, 'There's a place for another GENTLEMAN here,' comes across and drags him away. I find a chair and sitting down with a glass in my hand say aloud, 'There's only one thing to

do. Get drunk.' The Feddens appear. I pinion Mrs Fedden to the bar and talk at her for a solid hour, when with a look of desperation she asks Robin for a taxi fare. I ask Robin what is the matter. ' . . . She doesn't like you, my dear.' Cyril reappears well-supped and beaming, followed by the rest of the privileged suppers. They all emerge with a healthy tan, the acclaimed heroes of a Shackleton expedition, and mingle with the throwouts. I turn on Cyril, but we are interrupted by Orson Welles, so I try to be offensive to him but he doesn't notice. Cyril says he's going home and leaves me. Mark Culme-Seymour sits with me and we hear a waiter saying as he passes, 'Fill her up.' We go upstairs and have a short dance, there is a fearful crash and looking over my shoulder I see an enormous china vase in pieces on the floor. Mark says he doesn't think we did it. I then want to go home but realise I have no money. I take a last look into the bar in case Cyril is still there but it is empty except for Liz Hofmannsthal* seated on a couch. Peter lies sprawled at her feet in a Byronic attitude which he is now too corpulent to carry off, his puce-tinted face was trying to express ardency, but he seemed to me to be just a dreary old zombi putting on airs.

January 1952
Beginning of New Year. Several good omens. Cyril received a cheque for £5 from his mother. He has an obliging letter from his bank allowing him an extra overdraft, and finally to our immense surprise and pleasure a C & A van stops at the gate. We are immediately guilt-ridden and anticipate bill trouble, as we owe £35, but the van man presents us with a parcel of rare plants that were ordered months ago and forgotten. We straightaway put them to ground, while Kupy gets in our way, thinking we are doing the spadework for her to uncover slugs.

What a miserable Christmas. We see no one, barely each other. New Year worse. Cyril glued to Baudelaire, never looks up from his book, only occasionally peering over the rim of his specs to make a note of the amount of gin I am drinking.

Visit Pop for a few minutes this morning in his pokehole and find him standing before an open sketchbook crammed full on one page

---

*In fact, Lady Elizabeth Hofmannsthal, daughter-in-law of the Austrian poet and dramatist, Hugo von Hofmannsthal.

with his neat handwriting and dates carefully written in the margin.
He tells me it is his current diary, he says that if he didn't keep one
posterity would only have my view of our married bliss. We have
been surrounded by thick snow for several days combined with a log
shortage. I complain that if only I was given a housekeeping
allowance things would be better organised. A great many bills are
paid off but we are always short of money; fruitless trips to London
cost a fortune. The new *Go* magazine arrived this morning and we
discover to our joy that Mrs Edith Munro has won the literary prize of
£25, (a competition Cyril had gone in for in the name of the old char).
We have had three visits to London spent at Sonia's, but she is so
morose and irritable I have vowed never to go there again. I cannot
feel sorry for her, though she is obviously in a low frame of mind.

I reach Poppet's at teatime to find her in a great state of excitement.
Am not past the hall before she blurts out that she is about to be
married to someone she met at Fryern a week ago, a Dutch painter
from Bali, a Glamour Tom aged forty-seven with a stomach ulcer.
Robert Kee arrives, incurring fresh excitement, and when he hears
the glad tidings rushes out to buy a bottle of bubbly. He is looking at
his most attractive, with that misleading air of violence. Then the
future husband is admitted. He strikes me as being a charmer
needing security, but physically pleasing.

Cyril and I dine with the Hamiltons – John Russell (a budding art
critic), Rosamund Lehmann and the Hultons. Nika comes to life on
the subject of bad breath, sex, body odours, pubic hair and
deformities. She looked pinch-toed in over-high heels giving her a
tilting forward stance, and in the excessively tight skirts she
squeezes into, when standing she gives the impression she is about
to topple forward. A lot of *Billy Budd* talk when the Hultons have
left. Yvonne Hamilton became hysterical because of John Russell's
enthusiasm. Next day we see the Francis Bacon exhibition. We are
baffled by the paintings, but like them just the same. Next day, we
read a good article written by David Sylvester explaining Bacon's
attempts to capture the momentary effect of a snapshot, hence the
rather monochromatic colouring.

On January 22 we go to London for an outing with the Jacksons.
Arrive at Poppet's at teatime to find the future husband installed.
Never see Poppet alone for a second except when I catch her sitting

on the bidet. There is now a permanent booze tray in Percy Street and one is offered a drink at all times. Get to Claridge's and on entering Derek's suite find Sonia installed in a large wing armchair looking very much at home, clutching a whisky and soda with a black-gloved hand. Cyril and I are so disappointed to find Janetta replaced by Sonia that we exchange agonised glances. But, as always, as soon as one is confronted by Sonia with her polite feet, neatly crossed in black Lillywhite shoes with bows, all the appalling things one has thought about her vanish. We have an excellent dinner at the White Tower with Sonia taking the credit. She is always having to show off by over-amiability with people like builders or restaurateurs. No snobbery about me, you see; it seems to mean at the same time her whole manner is one of extreme condescension.

February 11   The Morning Routine
Sleep late each morning now and wake up feeling exhausted; we compare anxiety dreams; in my nightmare I am always in a train about to arrive at a station and unable to find the compartment where I put my luggage. I discover one suitcase which with great difficulty, unaided, I tug onto the platform when the train begins to move, so I leap onto it again frantically searching for the rest and get taken on to the next station, all the time fretting about the suitcase left on the platform.

Last night I dreamt of a dead male nude torso of wax-like hue which followed me round a garden. The head was firmly attached but the legs were folded up behind, so that it moved from the trunk only. Then I became aware of being tripped up by obstacles rolling about my feet and realised the torso was rotting and shedding ears and fingers. The final horror was a decapitated cock.

Whenever Cyril has a nightmare, it is usually the same one of me entering White's Club dressed as a man. 'Dressed as a man?' I repeat. 'Yes,' he says. 'How am I dressed?' 'In Eton clothes. With an Eton jacket. Come to humiliate me.' 'How can you tell I'm a man?' 'Your bottom sticks out.' 'You can't convince me that I have a large behind.' 'Last night, it was you and Diana,'* he said, 'who both stormed White's seeking me out on the top floor. I must identify you as the naggers in my life. And, when I begged you to leave, you said, "But this is only a low-class brothel anyway." And, sure

---

*My predecessor in Cyril's affections.

enough, when I got downstairs, there were a lot of *louche* couples sitting about half-dressed.'

Once out of bed, I put on a dirty blue dressing-gown covered in stains and head for the kitchen, the first chore being to stoke the stove, which is either burnt out or shows a faint red glow but too blocked with clinker to draw; having raked it out I put on the kettle. Then I visit Kupy Kupy. She greets me with gentle nips on the wrist. The tea made, I shout up to Pop 'breakfast's ready'. He takes a long time getting up, so several times over I have to scream 'BREAKFAST's ready' accentuating the 'FAST'.

Our day never begins before the post has arrived; sometimes the postman calls before we are up, which is an incentive to get out of bed. If Cyril gets up for the letters, I think, 'That's fine, *he's* out,' or 'Maybe now he'll make the tea,' but he invariably goes straight back to bed taking the letters with him. Often the postman has to knock as the package is too bulky to get through the letter box, and then we shout down, 'Leave it in the porch.' This morning we remain in the dining room reading a long time, awaiting the post, but when Cyril telephones the bank to warn them of some post-dated cheques which will not be met, we discover it to be 12.30. Then I check the hot tank. There is no wind today, only a steady fine snow drizzle, but the flakes dissolve before touching the ground. We throw out bread ends for the birds and watch the blue tits, robins, thrushes and an occasional magpie pecking them up; all the robins are big swollen well-stuffed birds, greedy bullies with watchful beady eyes; the blue tits chirrup away as they peck.

Cyril's morning chore is to empty the chamber pot for the clinker and fill up the coal bucket; this he does very dutifully in his dressing-gown and slippers, leaving the back door open as he goes out, so that Kupy Kupy darts into the kitchen without our noticing her and then creates havoc; today she bolted into the bathroom and scrabbled away at the soap leaving it covered in claw marks, put her snout into my cold cream and left black claw marks. Still no *ST* cheque.

Sunday, we have an early alarm call, as we are setting off to lunch with Harry d'Avigdor-Goldsmid. To Cyril, having said would I wear my black suit, I said, 'Are you crazy?' and put on my hideous pleated brown tweed with new red pullover. We caught the train at Wye, changing at Ashford, and bought the Sunday newspapers (a great treat) and read Harold Nicolson's review of Flaubert. Cyril annoyed because he repeatedly described Flaubert as being 'Not a nice man' which had no bearing on his being a genius. There was a profile on Farouk in the *Observer* which was not too antipathetic but didn't like giving him the benefit of the doubt; as to being a teetotaller, it stated simply that he was not known to drink in public, implying that he probably did in private, and that he had black hair, whereas it is, in fact, mouse.

We arrive at the Goldsmid mansion an hour early but find to our delight we are the only guests. The host very charming, just having returned from the States. I noticed how unswept the floors were, though the house was swarming with butlers (Madame being away). We had been looking forward to a delicious lunch, but eggs came overcooked on slightly rancid ham followed by overcooked beef with a vinegary salad, but we drank a delicious bottle of '23 claret. The whole meal was very rushed, as though we were at the mercy of the servants, all three butlers aching to get off, so that we were served canteen style – on with the next dish. Harry bolted each course watching our plates and as one was on the last mouthful said, 'Have some more,' as he pressed the bell with his foot. A stoneless cherry tart. I thought how vapid meals must be with all the cores removed and everything pared to nothing; port followed with three kinds of cheese, tumblers of brandy and then we were hustled into the sitting room which was dotted about with piles of magazines. Cyril remarked on a Gainsborough-like portrait, saying, 'I don't remember seeing that portrait before, Harry,' almost adding 'old boy'. Then, we did a round of the greenhouses, that were crammed with the dullest plants, all neatly pruned and arranged with tabs. The only exciting plant was a climbing camellia, partially in flower with glowing rosetted blooms of firm crimson petals and tight virgin buds. When we returned, there was three-course tea, buttered bread, scones and cakes. We caught the seven o'clock train back to reality.

Last Wednesday, we went to London taking a taxi to the station, as the car is so draughty, the main incentive being a dinner given by Joan Rayner. Caught an early train and went straight to the massage place where they greeted me by saying, 'Have you heard the strange news? It's about the King,' and then, while I was under the cage, someone came and told me he was dead. A stream of clichés followed. 'How dreadful for the Queen.' 'What bad luck for Elizabeth.' It took all my sweating capacity away. All the mourning horrors were enlarged on with satisfaction, black-edged newspapers, everything shut, no trains running, stricken faces, but when I left the building everything was carrying on in a normal fashion. I rush to the Etoile late for lunch with Peter Quennell who is amiable and restrained in his questioning. Manages to hold out until the liqueur stage before getting me into the witness box, when the inevitable cross-examination started. How was my sex life? As I was in a loyal state of mind he was quite pleased to terminate the meeting. He said there was very little social life in London and now that Ann Rothermere was marrying Ian (Fleming),[*] the breed of party-givers was almost extinct. He was leading a conjugal existence with Mrs U . . . , a pug dog and a pair of parakeets, and when I asked if they talked, he said they made a noise like two stones being rubbed together. Cyril picked me up to go to Joan's. We were introduced to a glaring middle-aged Greek lady wrapped up in a fox tippet, her husband a continental charmer, very popular with the Joan group as he was considered to be a splendid poet. He was anxious to meet Cyril and pinioned him the whole evening and, since Joan's brother, Graham, was the other diner and rarely spoke, we were a pretty dismal gathering. Then, to my horror, when we were on the cheese course, that woman from downstairs (Mary Hutchinson) appeared, and with her arch manner and aging lewd face said, coyly, 'Perhaps I should come later.' When Cyril began reading lengthy passages of George Moore, I behaved badly and started barracking. Then John Russell arrived looking conspicuously clean, as usual, with his concave nails and sandy hair plastered down with 'white lotion'. I asked him which rung of the ladder he had got onto and when he thought he would reach the top; he asked after the coati. Robin Ironside was the next to appear and also asked after the coati. Cyril's friends are firmly convinced I am a moron and the coati my sole interest. Then John Russell and Cyril disappeared into the lavatory to talk about Delacroix. Next day, I was told that when I'd gone James Pope-Hennessy and Alan Pryce-Jones arrived. Cyril said all those people make one feel we are all part of a dead civilisation. Poppet gives a cocktail party in the evening. She and Pol[†] are both very nervous and fear nobody will come so that any chance ringer-up is invited round. As I have travelled to London in trousers with no change of clothing, I am included with a certain misgiving. Mark Culme-Seymour is the first to arrive. Poppet is wearing one of her home-made black dresses

---

[*]Ann and Ian Fleming were married in 1952 in the Caribbean with Noël Coward as witness.
[†]Her future husband, a Dutch painter.

with some chunky ornament round her neck and earrings to match. When she comes into the room, carefully *guêpiered*, Pol says, enraptured, 'You look *wonderful*', and Poppet beams. Mark collapses onto the settee, groaning and, covering his face with his hands, says, 'I feel like nothing on earth.' Then Freddie Ayer frisked in followed by Jocelyn and the Angelica-Maclaren group. The Dutch contingent came in pairs; all the men wore black ties and looked like undertakers; their wives wore black dresses and were beautifully 'coiffed'. The Angelica-Maclaren *milieu* regard Cyril and me as rival camps. One of them occasionally sidles up and whispers, 'I'm on your side, you know.' I should have liked to stay until the end but was dragged away by Cyril to dine with Sonia and Peter Watson. All four of us sat eyeing each other with suspicion and hate, the food uneatable, and the wine had been heated to such an extent that it actually tasted of warm vinegar. We decided never to go to the White Tower again.

March 12
Have had a very bad cold, five days of it, starting off with an oppressive headache, making reading impossible. Instead of remaining in bed I have a prolonged battle with Kupy, who has found a way of escaping out of her hut leaving no trace behind her of the means; like the tunnel burrowers of prisoners' camps. Each time she gets out she starts rattling the front door latch, trying to get into the house, which makes me fretful, especially as I know that when she is loose now she has taken to uprooting all the rock plants. So, eventually, in a fury I shut her up in her travelling basket, strapping it down, but not before I had made several journeys in my dressing-gown into the garden to catch her, which aggravated my throat. I am accused of extreme cruelty, so in the end, out of guilt, I have her to sleep in my bed, but she coughs up the tail piece of a worm in the night. I decide I cannot support her much longer and that she must go to the zoo for a bit; also, she is moulting and one finds coarse sandy-black hairs on one's clothes, the oven, the washing-up mop. Mrs Durnford offers to bring us a new cleaner on appro, a Mrs Lea, who she says can come every day. We are very excited and sit in wait for her to come for an interview. She turns out to be a very familiar figure who passes the gate at least twice a day followed by a pair of dogs, one that she calls Bessie. She is always dressed in Wellingtons and a green beret, and behind a pair of spectacles gleam two beady disapproving eyes. 'She makes me feel I'm not nice to know,' Cyril said. My heart sinks when I see

123

her but we employ her just the same. She is brought along by Mrs Durnford next morning who shows her the ropes, and she is not as disagreeable as she looks, but she talks to herself all the time, particularly when fussed. 'Bloody dark,' she kept muttering as Cyril showed her round the house. The following day she comes on her own and leaves the house much dirtier than she finds it, and then we realise that, as well as being deaf, she is almost totally blind. Oh, the disillusion! Our lives are made intolerable here without a servant. Loud crashes can be heard in the kitchen every few minutes, so that when she has gone Cyril starts checking up on the plates to see which are missing and I search the bucket for chips, but all I find are Cyril's gold cufflinks which have been emptied out with the dust. He says he is sick to death of seeing nothing but crows and sheep from his bedroom window, or gulls that fly in from the sea indicating stormy weather; they swoop down on the field opposite as though it provided them with something very delectable. The butcher delivered two trotters this morning. 'Good morning, Mrs Lea,' I heard the boy saying. She appears to be a well-known character round here. It makes it all cosier even if she is inefficient. *Elle a soixant-six ans après tout.* She lives in a caravan and says she knew this cottage before the First World War.

When she had gone, I went round the house inspecting all the dust-pockets. I am horribly neurotic about dirt. Cyril considers me insane on that point, says I need to be psychoanalysed. I notice every speck of dust not only in this house but in other people's. 'You always gather aged eccentrics about you,' he tells me, referring to Mrs Lea and Mrs Munro. The old boy cross today. Furious when I laugh at the hunt going by. 'You must realise,' he says, 'it is pure eighteenth-century.' He received a fan-letter from a man in Connecticut. He says all fan-letters of more than one page are written by lunatics. This one had eight!

March 5

Poppet's marriage day. Cyril and I go to London on a day ticket. We catch the twelve o'clock train and, when we arrive, lunch at Wheelers in complete silence. Cyril hardly ever speaks now when we are alone except to correct something I have said. 'Not *LauristinA, LauristinUS.*'[*] 'Madame de Pompadour, if you don't mind.' 'Not SORUS but SAW . . . US.' 'Guardsman, not guardee!'

---

[*]A winter evergreen flowering shrub.

He is my father-figure in the form of a pedantic schoolmaster. I then rush off to have a manicure and a hair trim. Chuff picks me up at Charm in Curzon Street; he guides me into a Rolls. Poppet was in the doorway wearing a new green suit, hatted and graciously receiving her guests. She thanked me for the strawberry skin-foods and looked blissfully happy.

I found myself next to Vivien, (Poppet's sister, daughter of Augustus John), and we talked at cross-purposes for a long time. I like her very much. The painter Matthew-Smith arrived chuckling and heaving whispery sighs. Molly was bulging out of her blouse and skirt, and had very clipped, frizzy, towy hair framing a deep puce face. 'Look at all the women jockeying for position,' she said to me and, when I asked her to explain, she replied irritably, 'You must know what I mean, MY DEAR.' Then Sir Philip Dunne came up and said, 'Who is that blowsy-looking woman? . . .' 'Do you mean Pauline Gates?' I said, as she was standing next to Molly. 'Talking of Poppet and Pol,' he said, 'I expect you will be joining them soon to give him a change!' Later Molly became very aggressive and threatened to kick Cyril in the balls, as a result of a conversation on her rumoured forthcoming marriage. 'You, my dear Cyril,' she said, 'would be the *last* person I should tell if I were going to marry anyone!' She then took Chuff aside and said to him, 'I don't know whether you can be trusted to be discreet, MY DEAR, but tell Barbara she is invited to stay any time . . . without *him*,' pointing at Cyril. 'I've quite given up drinking,' she told me as she firmly gripped her glass of bubbly. 'I've given up smoking,' I said puffing away at a Balkan Sobranie. Henry Yorke went through his usual repertoire. He repeats everything Kitty Freud, (Lucien's first wife), says and brings her name into every conversation. Mavis was very drunk and looked immensely tall, like a giantess. She rushed up to Chuff and me, grabbed hold of both of us and breathing alcohol snarled, 'You're married now, aren't you?' Then, glaring and pushing her face up close to Chuff's, she said, 'Any children?' But then she caught sight of Cyril, 'You're just the man I'm looking for,' she hissed.

Goronwy Rees kept bobbing up at my side and tried to persuade me to dine with him. The only pleasant conversation I had was with Sylvester Gates. Angelica was very quiet and sober. Rodrigo Moynihan appeared in the doorway for an instant. Chuff, Cyril and I dined at Wiltons. Catch the 9.15.

March 20

Mrs Munro comes for the night. We go to Ashford early to meet her. First of all we have an exciting shopping hour at Dicksons and buy a hose, a hard broom, curtain rings, a pyrex dish, a saw and a whole spray outfit. Mrs Munro seems very ancient and decrepit. She spent nine hours here sewing and told me she had been married for twelve years to a wig-maker. 'When he died,' she said defiantly, 'I looked into the fire and vowed never again.' And talking of her dead child she said, 'To think one had to go through all that because of a man.' I almost had to carry her to bed after giving her some gin and a glass of bubbly. The following day we all went to London on the lunch train.

March 25

Warm and drizzle, but snow is forecast. Cyril walks about the house in his ginger overcoat, glowering; says he is frozen (it is quite mild) and indicates by a scowling face that it is all my fault. He has the usual succession of boils and styes, and his face is flushed and blotchy which he says is due to sinus. I tell him it looks more like a butter rash to me. A fresh batch of shrubs and hedging arrives from Duruz nurseries. A frantic telegram is sent to the gardener Coombes to come and plant them. He comes to our rescue immediately, looking ashen in the face and shrivelled-up like a nut, complains he never has any appetite and is suffering from nervous indigestion, and that his mate, Harry, is ill with a growth on his nostril. When Coombes is here, Cyril perks up and I hear him whistling as he potters about the wet soil in his bedroom slippers supervising the 'placement' of all his rarities. I only go out to nag when I see him trampling on all the daffodil buds, which are just coming through; seeing me, he looks furious and flees to another part of the garden. Kupy follows suit, doing as much damage as she can in her own small way.

April 5   Grand National Day

I back 'Overshadow' and 'Wot No Sun?' – ten shillings each way. 'Wot No Sun?' comes in third, so I win three pounds ten shillings. Dirty mounds of snow still lie about the roads where the sun has not penetrated. There is a large mound slumped against the hedge opposite which is the first thing one sees on looking out of the window. A small bit all round thaws each day, symbolising the stagnation and boredom of country life. Have just had a pleasant weekend with the Campbells, who are friendly and hospitable, and every meal quite delicious on scanty ingredients that seemed to be portioned round to the last potato. I remained immersed in Paul Bowles's new book *Let It Come Down*, reliving Tangiers, while snowflakes beat against the panes. On the way back we stopped a night in London, staying with the Hultons. We were given twin beds in the servants' quarters. We are offered champagne by the butler. We accept and two quarter bottles of non-vintage instantly arrive.

Excellent service. Nika's facial twitch now expresses itself through her hands and she never stops flapping them about like a penguin. It is usually accompanied by a boast, 'How if they lived to be a hundred they wouldn't know what to do with all Teddy's wealth.' She is trying to persuade Cyril to give his name to a prestige magazine (she suggested it should be called *The Connolly Magazine*) – The CONNOLLY MAG! I expect she would like Cyril to do all the dirty work while she remains the editoress. We go to see a Rattigan play, *The Deep Blue Sea*, which, apart from Peggy Ashcroft, is banal and boring. The dinner split up into Nika and her two stooges (Cyril and Robin Ironside) squeezed together on one side of the table and myself and John Russell who talked in awed whispers.

April 7
The snow has thawed opposite the gate. It is a grey, cold, bleak day with a violent south-west wind. We have a fire. Last night we motored over to St Margaret's Bay to see the newly-weds who have just returned from Jamaica. Ian Fleming, tanned, fretful and thinner. Ann, greyer, older, happier and obviously pregnant. We drive there and back in a thick sea mist and drizzle, but they are both so vitalised and pleasant that it is a successful visit. They were more lovebirdy than ever and kept putting their heads together to inspect the holes in their carpet, and then nesting chirrupy noises would follow as to whether it should be sent to be repaired now or when they were next in Jamaica.

We ate roast chicken served by a new butler who handed the dishes round the wrong way. Ann had redecorated the house; the sitting room was immensely improved by the absence of the two Noël Coward pianos which used to squat in their respective corners like a pair of reproachful giants.

End of April
There is a blustery wind tearing off the blossoms; the grass is green and needs mowing. Kupy is sitting on my knee with icy cold paws

and keeps trying to nuzzle under my pullover. We are very overdrawn, unable to cash any cheques. The two Chinese goslings are double the size of a week ago, the guinea fowl have not started laying yet, and today we heard the cuckoo. C is absolutely obsessed with house-hunting. Every time we go into a town, he puts the cottage into some agent's hands and every house that comes onto the market he buys in his imagination. Stone Hall, the house behind a high wall opposite The George, was for sale a fortnight ago. It had always symbolised a prison to me and for the last ten years, every time I passed, I accelerated. I was eventually persuaded to go over it. The garden was well kept up, and they only wanted £4,750 but it lacks any magic or charm. The rooms are built in the Georgian style, symmetrical and dull. Now, every day, I am made to drive Cyril within walking radius of this prison and leave him to prowl round on his own, so that in the end the dog has got to know him and always runs out when he approaches. The last time we went up to the house in the car and stood gaping from the roadway, whereupon the dog ran out barking followed by its mistress, who was furious when she saw us and demanded to know what we wanted, as though we didn't have any right to be wandering along a public highway. She then snapped that the house had been withdrawn from the market. Was I relieved.

The day after, Pop developed a passion for Knock Farm overlooking the marshes – very bleak and completely ramshackle with beams, sloping floors and no modern conveniences. Now, he never stops going on about Knock and what he wouldn't do to the garden.

May 18
Today has been a most satisfactory day. Coombes the gardener came, although as soon as he arrived one could see he regretted it and was trying to sneak away. Having leapt out of bed the instant I heard his small Austin car pull up in the drive, I ran out in my ragged sky-blue dressing-gown and fluffy red slippers, and accosted him on his way to the vegetable patch, shouting, 'Shall I tell you what we want done?' and pointed; 'the wiring must be moved to the side there to pen in the geese.' 'Ooow! I thought you just wanted it pulled down.' 'I wrote and told you I wanted it moved, Mr Coombes, so that you could bring the correct tools.' 'Ooow! I 'aven't got the tools for that job. 'Ow about Saturday?' He was back-stepping into the car. 'Never mind about doing it properly. Just do it temporarily,' I said, tugging him toward the

goose patch. In the end it was done. 'Can you clip the hedge today? . . .' 'Saturday . . .' 'Will you spray the roses as I asked? . . .' 'Kill 'em to do it now. Too early . . .' 'But, the greenfly are already there. You mean it's too cold? . . .' 'Burn 'em up . . .' 'Did you bring the grass seed? . . .' 'Nope.' He looked dreamily into the distance. 'You want a thorough downpour for that job . . .' 'Well, we won't get it now . . .' 'Nope.' I could hear him banging away at the pegs in a fury.

My lucky day. It drizzles all the time. I expected him to down tools at any moment. 'If only I can keep Coombes here until twelve I shall have achieved something,' I say to Cyril. Coombes packs up at 11.30 without saying a word . . . But the soft broom has been mended. The raspberry jelly has set. The goose patch has been cleared. The old hen coop broken up, the pieces stacked in the garage. Then, C rings up Costa asking him to lunch on Sunday. Costa says he has no car; would we go there? I am reluctant to go, for some reason, and produce the excuse that our car is being repaired. But we accept. Then, on Sunday, we both wake up ill-tempered and when C catches me finishing off some dregs of soup in the kitchen he gets very cross. 'Weren't you going to offer me any?' he says. We depart at midday in a taxi. Neither of us speaks all the way to Ashford. A cold, windy, rainy day. As we leave these hills, the countryside is much greener, fresher and less bleak; fruit trees everywhere in bloom. At Ashford garage we pick up the car. There is a long list on the windscreen of the things that need doing, like decarbonising, so I start driving at a snail's pace as though the car were an ailing invalid. 'You mean to say it won't go any faster?' Cyril says. 'Come along, Baby. You can do better than that.' 'I am driving safely, for a change,' I say, 'and which way now?' Cyril directs me wrongly so that we go seven miles out of our way. 'Subconsciously, neither of us wants to go to this lunch,' Cyril says. We stop right outside the Smarden cider works to ask the way. 'Are you ever going to order some more cider?' I say, thinking if I'd known we were coming this way I'd have brought the cider flask. We arrive on time. Me surprised, C knowing it. Costa talks all the time about India. How they have no culture any more. No art. No writing. Apathy. They miss the British. Would like to have them back. We both comment afterwards on his striking appearance. He was wearing a long-sleeved dove-blue angora pullover matching his bright blue eyes, his white hair almost entirely bald from the rear. 'Look at his head,' Cyril says to me, 'tonsured like a monk.' So circular is the bald patch that it might have been drawn. Over the

129

dove-blue pullover he wore a jacket of small black and white check. His woollen socks were a letdown, rugger team type in large crude stripes. I noticed how capable his hands looked. He was very tanned, hawkish, birdlike and really stylish. 'I am sure he studies all that,' Cyril said. 'He just wants to be admired and is quite content with his life. No sense of wasted talent, having none. His narcissism prevents any emotional entanglements.' Costa is explicit and informative about places, there being hardly any country that he has not visited. I felt we must have been very unresponsive. He gave me a little Afghanistan cap. Princess Anne-Marie Callimachi looking better and less like a boiled monkey after a severe operation. She nearly choked when Costa opened the bottle of Taittinger '43. After all, a bottle of champagne for four is always a letdown. The last five days have been blissfully hot. A lot of work done in the garden. Everything looks promising until one catches a glimpse of the peach-curl on the nectarines; it is like realising one has produced a deformed child; after seeing those blotchy scalded leaves one gets a real understanding of the word 'diseased'.

Raymond Mortimer is back from India, so Cyril has been told to resume only 'fortnightly' reviews. He complains of a pain in his right side and thinks he has a rotting appendix, is slightly sunburnt but on the surface of the brown skin scurfy scales have appeared, so I call him scale-face.

The hedge is full of birds' nests, mainly mistlethrush. One contains four tiny speckled blue eggs.

◇◇◇ Chapter XIV ◇◇◇

Waugh's Visit

Diary

June 8

Start having guilt about Kupy. She has been in the zoo for three weeks as we have just spent two weeks in Paris at the expense of a cultural congress financed by a Mr Fleichman, an American millionaire. Cyril enjoyed mooching about the bookstalls, his pockets stuffed with francs, privileged, with nothing to do but present himself at the conferences and listen to other people's speeches. The most conspicuous pair at the Deux Magots, Sonia and Tony Bower. Two 'memorable' incidents. One, when Cyril took me sightseeing on the Left Bank. It was a very hot day. After tramping about for hours, me trailing several paces behind the great man, both of us quite silent, I expressed a desire to eat. 'Stick it out a little longer, Baby,' says Cyril, 'I have a surprise for you.' We walked on through narrow streets, the gutters strewn with spittle, passing many restaurants with check tablecloths, and my imagination got to work on the lovely lunch I was going to be given by that clever Popple who knew his way round Paris so well! Suddenly, he darted into a doorway, giving me a beckoning thumb gesture and led me up a steep stairway, into a pitch-dark room empty except for a gathering of waiters. I looked forlornly out at the street below bathed in sunlight. 'Could we open the window? . . .' 'Don't look so glum,' says Cyril, 'don't you realise this is LAPÉROUSE?' I ordered a tomato salad, *grenouilles* and coffee. The portions were minute. No one else came into the restaurant. Neither of us spoke while Cyril read *Les Temps Modernes*; all I said was, 'I felt like eating Midi food.'

The second disappointment was a dinner with Pauline Potter,[*] whom we had run into during a performance of *Billy Budd*. 'Wear a little frock,' she said to me, as though she were addressing a *midinette*. So, in defiance, I wore my black suit. When we arrived at her house on the Isle St Louis, she was in semi-evening dress and looked me up and down with great disapproval. '*Comme elle est borne,*' said Philippe de Rothschild and as a punishment I was made to sit on a chair much higher than the others, causing great discomfort. The other dinner guests were Glenway Wescott, his daughter, as well as a lesbian gossip writer, and Tony Bower served up with the desert.

Cyril is sitting in a deck chair in the garden. I am about to weed. 'Have you seen my fucking gloves anywhere?' 'Your fucking gloves are about as common out here as loving fucks,' he says.

His latest million pound lament.

'A million pounds was made and spent, and then another million came and went, and then there came a million more, and then a million as before . . .'

June 26   My birthday
No adequate fuss made. Left to stew with the geese all day while C has lunch with Jack Lambert.[†] I lunch with PQ. Hottest day of the year. Peter carries an umbrella. We go to Wimbledon as I have been given tickets. Never sheds his trilby, complains of the heat, prods the crowds with his brolly and begs to leave every fifteen minutes. I try to distract him by pointing out all the pretty girls; he pronounces them all as being 'common', but takes a great interest in the royal box, until he spots Mr Attlee in a deep sleep. Return to the country in the evening. Cyril and I not speaking.

September 5
This morning I go into Cyril's room with a cup of tea and see a fresh

---

[*]An American who worked on *Vogue* until she married Philippe de Rothschild.
[†]Literary editor of the *Sunday Times*.

packet of biscuits lying beside the bed. A secret eater! I say, 'Where did you get them? Cookes?' He nods, his mouth full. I say, 'You're like the greedy girl in the Stafford story who always kept a hoard of sweet food in her drawers.' 'I shall be having a charcoal grill up here next,' he says, very pleased with himself. He has invented four categories of fart. The 'dry goose', 'wet goose', 'chicken fart' and 'phosgene'; we remark on how frequently we both fart and put it down to boredom. 'Do you think other people fart as much as us?' I ask. C says no.

I was preparing some rhubarb the other day when C said, 'Wouldn't it be improved with some lemon peel?' Me: 'I dare say, but it's not going to get it. It's a question of lump it or leave it.' Seeing some red wine all over his face, I say, 'What have you got all over your face?' 'Hate,' says Cyril. I hardly ever cook now, bored stiff with the whole practice. I say we are economising. We have not had to order any household goods for weeks. The Tide lasts longer and the Vim; the onions remain in the box for ages.

Cyril is lying in the bath brooding on Caligula who liked to pile all his gold coins into a heap and paddle in them with bare feet. We are on bad terms again. I hear him in his room murmuring at night, 'A million . . . Two million' or, simply, 'Just a million.' Yesterday my sister and her family came to tea. She was looking very young and pretty, but the whole effect spoilt by hideous black open sandals and fat legs. Everyone on their best behaviour. Cyril put in an appearance and made conversation. Vivien did his best to be responsive by making a series of obvious remarks. The two children rather dull. Angela looks as though she is going to be sulky. Jo plump and sweet-natured.

We are very worried about the quackers; they are suffering from diarrhoea and loss of appetite. I suddenly feel extremely sorry for them and wonder if I am starving them to death; they are not allowed bread as a rule, as their function is to keep down the grass. I decide to love them up a bit. The hen has lost all her tail feathers and looks absurd. Can't wait to turn her into a good broth.

Have spent nearly the whole day retyping the Waugh portrait that Cyril is doing for *Time* magazine. He compares it to a Max Beerbohm drawing. It is terribly good. While I am typing, he prepares the lunch just when the rates man arrives, so the eggs are overcooked. The man said he had read all Cyril's reviews, adding, 'They're a bit above me. Your husband seems quite happy with them, though.' I can now make perfect *oeufs en cocotte à la crème* and almost perfect *pommes Anna*. Tell Cyril I will soon beat all his circus at their own game, Joan with her cooking, Sonia for her know-allness. Mrs Lea has suddenly arrived with an enormous basket of freshly gathered mushrooms, the first of the season. *Elle est bien gentille* and a great plum, apple and blackberry provider.

Saturday was the gayest day of the week. We would get into the little bus and tear into Folkestone, with Cyril doing witty impersonations all the way, he was so pleased to have finished writing his weekly review, the idea being to get to Jacksons to stock up on Romary biscuits, pumpernickel bread and oat cakes before the shop closed. Then we would head for the Grand Hotel for our usual Saturday lunch. To avoid getting something disgusting, we always stuck to the same menu. Smoked salmon, plain grilled sole, strawberry ice cream and a kind of *Coupe Jacques* of mixed fruit.

After lunch we usually had a row. 'Am I getting any money for the shopping by any chance?' Then I shopped. Not for food but for some weed, slug or ant killer. Then we would go to the cinema. On our way home, we stopped off for dinner at The Rose and Crown in Elham. It was run by Mr and Mrs Millen. She did the cooking while her husband stood behind the bar polishing the glasses. There, too, we stuck to the same menu. Soup, roast chicken, sausage, bread sauce, roast potatoes, then tipsy cake. Another row. Then home.

One night while we were dining there, a man at the next table engaged us in conversation. Eric Wood lived at the White House, Alkham, and from then we often met. He became our neighbourhood friend. Cyril enjoyed going to his pretty house that you entered through a large conservatory with a climbing mimosa. Eric had rosy cheeks and was rather a toper. Although not an intellectual, he was interested in painting and china. He lived alone with a cat, had charming manners and a housekeeper who cooked. At weekends, he might have one of his old boyfriends to stay. Eric always seemed to be so pleased to see us, and we grew very fond of him.

September 24
Sunday, we went over to see the Flemings. I complained of a sore throat and made it a pretext for not driving there in the little open bus, so Cyril rang Crouch's garage and ordered a car and chauffeur. We had the usual mediocre Fleming meal. Why is it the rich always have such bad cooks? C mused. Ian disappeared after the first

course to play golf. Peter Quennell was wearing that ugly brown cabman's waistcoat in leather which stretched across the stomach and tied at the back.

Nothing *but* Burgess and Maclean talk now all the time. Cyril's piece a great success, it has given him an excuse to see a lot of people who could provide information. Expensive restaurants, caviar, champagne dinners and endless long distance telephone calls. Joan's drawl and Sonia's gush came through today. Wrote a bread-and-butter letter to Raymond Mortimer thanking him for our visit last weekend. We played croquet, ate good food, slept in comfortable beds with eiderdowns and listened to classical music.

November 5
We have been hibernating here for a fortnight. Me reading and trying to concentrate on my drivel (*A Young Girl's Touch*) to such an extent that I have a permanent headache and eyes like pinpoints. A succession of dirty grey days and every morning the monotonous cry of Mrs Lea outside Cyril's boxroom, 'Are you getting up today, sir?'; and then her subconscious mutter of 'slovenly bugger'. Every few days we drink a bottle of champagne to fortify us for the winter. Cyril is getting on apace with his thriller.

November 24
Caroline Blackwood telephones. In a state about Lucien Freud who is stuck in Paris unable to pay the hotel. A concerted drive from Ann Fleming, Caroline and Lucien to get Cyril to buy Lucien's latest portrait of Caroline. Cyril feels paternal toward them both and is keen on Caroline. I say it is not worth putting himself in a state of debt for the whole of the next year. A dirty grey pall hangs over the ground, the grass browned-up as a result of the nitrate of soda. The hen keeps clucking at the back door for food and I have to rush out and throw brooms.

Now on to Virginia Woolf's *Diaries*. She regarded reading as a kind of duty. Cyril telephones Ann Fleming about Lucien's painting. They talk for ten minutes of her party last week. Evelyn Waugh being rude to everybody, pretending he didn't know who Rosamund Lehmann was when she rushed up to greet him with open arms. Waugh criticised Alan Ross's beard and, when Cecil

Beaton approached him when he was sitting on the sofa with Jennifer Ross, Waugh exclaimed, 'Here's someone who can tell us all about buggery!' He then had to be carried into a taxi at three in the morning.

Saturday, we had lunch at the Grand Hotel in Folkestone, and invited Eric Wood, who bored Cyril by talking about his visit to London and describing all the drinks he had. They talked about how brave all the buggers were during the war. Eric had been in camouflage and was clearly proud of it.

November 1952
Ann Fleming has Joan and Paddy Leigh-Fermor, the Duff Coopers and Evelyn Waugh to stay. She rings up and suggests to Cyril they come over for tea. After getting his silver teapot out of pawn, especially for the occasion, Cyril spends all afternoon arranging the table. It is a cold and bleak day, almost dark when they get here. I am in the kitchen when the car is heard backing up the garage path. The next thing they are all trooping through the dining room. They pass me in the kitchen, all bent, it seems, on seeing Kupy. So dark, they peer squinting into her outdoor hut. Waugh dressed in a black and white check suit. He has a check waistcoat and cap to match, and a ginger tweed overcoat, a flabby bulging stomach and a small aggressive gingerbread moustache. 'Is she carnivorous?' he asks me, having heard that Kupy is a penis-eater. Kupy is cold and refuses to come out of her hut. Joan whines and sighs, indicating disappointment. Lady Diana Cooper, dressed in a luxurious creamy mahogany mink coat, and a Hermès scarf tied round her head, asks me what Kupy likes eating. I reply to their questions as best I can. They all sit down to tea, a fire has been lit in the dining room by Cyril. Lady Diana remains in mink coat throughout visit. Waugh removes his cap and coat. Paddy is wearing a thick navy fisherman's sweater with threads hanging and an occasional hole; it suits him and he looks quite attractive for once. I think it is because of the polo collar. They talk about animals in the zoo, mentioning several one has never heard of. Paddy says he spent an afternoon once in the reptile house mesmerising a serpent. Lucien is discussed, as usual. Waugh pulls a face. Peter Watson is mentioned. Waugh pulls a face again. He tries to be pleasant to me, looking down at my shabby grey checks and saying, 'You have trousers like mine.' 'Mine are baggier,' I reply, returning the amiability. As Paddy is leaving, he says, pointing to Kupy's hut, 'Isn't Kupy lonely out there?' 'Well, aren't we all?' I say. A few days

later reports of the visit drift back. They were all disappointed (a) they had expected our surroundings to have been far more squalid, (b) because Kupy had not come out of her hut and bitten someone's penis and (c) because I had not been thoroughly rude to everyone. But Waugh said he had enjoyed his tea, the new bread, the farm butter, the bought but home-made honey and the China tea out of the fluted silver teapot. Though, he had hoped to find me more exotic, a glamorous 'Lady of the Town' so to speak.

December
Thursday and Friday Cyril spent most of the time on the buzzer as a result of John Lehmann's loss of status in the publishing world. All the envious wolves ready to pounce. Weidenfeld already planning to snatch up any floating contributors. Cyril anxious to further his aim, to ingratiate himself, but secretly rejoicing at the Lehmann downfall. Middlemen John Russell and John Hayward[*] (for the sake of culture line) are sending a round robin letter to *The Times*. They wish to include Pop's signature. Pop not anxious to lend signature, says he doesn't want to be part of the 'dying old liberal phalanx'. I ask him why they are so keen to have his signature; he says they probably require another heterosexual name on their list. '*La vie est plus grave que ça*,' Cyril says and that they ought to include a photograph of John Lehmann's house, to show what can be acquired on the proceeds of publishing.

Saturday a nice mild day. Pop and I in merry mood, the thousand dollars having been sent from America for the Waugh article.

Weekend with the Flemings. Arrive at the White Cliffs for late tea. Find Colin Tennant[†] there, like a spry whippet. Grace Radziwill, an amiable retriever, and Ann. Ian not back, his plane from New York being held up because of fog. Ann fretful. Conversation. Dukes, duchesses and ghosts in castles as seen by Colin Tennant; china, silver and paintings, relegated to a boasting match, each

---

[*]John Hayward was a scholar. He had multiple-sclerosis and was always to be seen in a wheelchair. He once said to me, 'Why waste your time writing a book? You'd make more money gambling on the stock market.'

[†]Lord Glenconner, married to Lady Anne. He was Stephen and David Tennant's nephew.

one's interest being confined to the objects in their possession. Cyril indignant on the subject of ghosts. 'Who has ever boasted of seeing a middle-class ghost?' No sleep due to fog siren going all night. After spending ten days in New York, Ian arrives lunchtime Sunday and relates a long boring story about two women biting each other at a party. He has written a thriller which is very competent and readable.

December 20

Christmas is upon us. Poppet just back from France. Telephoned her this morning. Her voice seemed to me to have lost its usual bell-like vitality. In the course of five minutes she had used the following terms: 'Can you afford it?', 'Much too hard up', 'Must economise', and 'Far too expensive'.

Cyril is standing on the stairs looking out of the window. Me (from the bath): 'What's that noise? . . .' 'Kupy after the guinea fowl. She's chased them to the middle of the goose patch . . .' 'What's she doing now? . . .' 'Rootling about the ground. The geese are standing either side of her with outstretched necks, hissing. Kupy takes no notice. Now Kupy moves, the guinea fowl are at the far end of the goose patch, the geese close in on Kupy. Now they attack her, one goose bites her tail . . .' 'What does Kupy do? . . .' 'She runs. The geese are running after her . . .' 'What are the guinea fowl doing? . . .' 'They are running too . . .' 'Is anyone hurt? . . .' 'No . . .' 'What's the noise then? . . .' 'Kupy after the guinea fowl.' This is where we came in.

Christmas 1952

Two days ago, Denton Welch's friend Eric Oliver arrived on a motorbike with bicycle clips attached to his ankles. He has a very pleasing appearance, a brown complexion, well-shaped mouth, very white teeth and labourer's hands. I did not sense the ruthless quality he is reputed to have. He seemed to be very shy, listening attentively and nodding to everything Cyril had to say, and would then ask a question, indicating he hadn't understood anything. Cyril mulled some cheap red wine. We had a delicious lunch of pheasant with bread sauce and brussels sprouts. Cyril said that the bird had been sent by Osbert Sitwell, so it was apt that Eric should be eating it with us. Having entrusted all of Denton Welch's furniture to the care of John Lehmann, Eric said he was having the greatest difficulty in getting it back. He had even put himself at John Lehmann's disposal, thereby incurring the jealousy of a ballet dancer in John's attic. Feeling his smooth chin, Cyril remarked on how clean and spruce we all looked, as sometimes he went for days without shaving. 'But today I shaved for you.' Whereupon, Eric turned to me and said, 'And I shaved for you.' Cyril laughed, and added, 'Barbara, as you see, washed her hair for you.'

Christmas Eve, I was taken to a midnight service by Mrs Lea. 'You never go out,' she said, 'and it will be a change for you.' I grumble about it all day and wonder how I will keep awake. She collected me at 11.30 all dressed up in a new sky-blue beret, new fawn gloves and new tweedy overcoat, and turned out to be the smartest person in the church. She and the vicar greeted each other like long-lost lovers. We arrived as the warden was still busying about the aisles. A large furnace blazed away with red-hot coals and the church was lit by double-burner lamps. There were about twenty other parishioners. Mrs Lea asked if I would like a hymnbook and went across to get me one. Although unable to hear or read herself, she goes to every service and knew some of the hymns by heart. When she didn't know a verse, she'd make up for it with an impromptu noise at the back of the throat. The turning of the wafer into Christ's body and the port wine into blood took an interminable time. Three times the vicar curled himself into a white ball on the ground, muttering to himself and, resuming his normal stature, held his arms before the altar and we all trooped up. Awaiting our turn in the queue, I carefully observed Mrs Lea, as I had forgotten the formality. She insisted on seeing me back as she had a torch and Pop was waiting with the remains of the mulled wine, having drunk most of it himself.

December 25
It was a delicious sunny crisp morning and we enjoyed the drive to the Flemings. Arrived on time for once. Everything very Christmassy. There was a holly wreath covered in red berries hanging on the front door; in the hall, an enormous Christmas tree decorated with coloured Bethlehem globes and presents. Everyone very subdued when we entered the sitting room. The Duchess of Westminster, wearing a black suit with gold flecks, was sitting alone in a far corner. Peter Q came up and talked. He was wearing that horrible cabman's outfit that makes him look so corpulent. He asked me what I thought of his weight. 'Your middle-age spread has come to stay,' I told him, 'and there's no point in worrying about it.' They all appeared smug, confident and spiritless. We

139

listened to the Queen's speech. Someone said how middle-class the Royal family were. Cyril told me afterwards that it's the chic thing to say. The Queen Mother, they said, was the most middle-class of the lot. The Duchess of W put on a special voice when talking of the lower classes, implying riffraff or rabble. Once more, she said of somebody, 'What does he do for potatoes?' And Cyril answered tartly, 'That seems to be an *idée fixe* of yours.'

A good turkey, with a nasty sausagemeat stuffing and soggy brussels sprouts. But the Christmas pudding was good with a rich brandy butter sauce. Ian distributed a collection of sexy mottoes and a dummy Lucky Strike carton he'd brought from the States; when holding it up to the light and turning a small lever one could see a succession of nude girls. Peter of course likes the nude girls, couldn't stop looking at them, said they had almost prevented him from getting out of bed that morning. During lunch, the inevitable topic . . . Lucien Freud. Caroline was severely criticised for looking dirty. 'She needs a damned good scrub all over,' Ian said, in his blokey manner. And Peter thought '*les attaches fines*' so important, he couldn't bear to see bitten-down fingernails. Cyril then glanced across the table, focusing pointedly on Peter's hands, as they are not his best feature. Then they talked about a party being given by Maureen Dufferin to which Lucien had not been invited but was determined to go to because of Caroline.

After tea, presents were given – always an embarrassment. Peter gave me a nice book, rather like the one Cyril had given me in the morning (the Berenson book[*]). From Ann a box of Floris soap, talcum powder and eau-de-Cologne. From Ian, a used pencil, a used lighter and a dirty motto. And then we had to admire other people's presents. We left them playing canasta.

We reached Eric Wood at about eight. When we entered the sitting room, someone rose from the couch, holding a book, and gave the impression he would have been happier if there had not been anyone coming. Our host made everything all right, greeting us effusively and offering drinks. He was wearing a shabby grey flannel suit and looked tousled, and explained they had both slept after lunch. They took it in turns to disappear and change into neat blue suits. There was a strong smell of fish soup and I asked if he was preparing a delicious *bisque*. We had a very good supper. After the fish soup there was ham sent from the States, mashed potatoes

---

[*]*Italian Painters of the Renaissance.*

and endive salad, and a pudding which had been made by his housekeeper. We talked about the delinquent Craig, who had shot a policeman, and the Denton Welch journals – how Denton only noticed the unpleasant things in life and how nasty all his meals sounded. I defended Eric Oliver when they suggested he was ruthless. Cyril admired the Larou painting in the dining room. I was offered a cigar with the brandy and we were once more shown round the house. Cyril has been dreaming of it ever since.

December 29
We have just had the Bastard to stay. He rang up the day before he was due to suggest I meet him on Boxing Night fifteen miles away in a house of some friends of his, the Dobsons, living near Leeds Castle. 'You will find it quite easily,' he ended by saying. 'They are giving a party. I expect it will be rather a grand house with a lot of cars outside.' I said it was too far, as I would have driven to St Margaret's Bay the day before. So B said he would telephone from the party. Seven pm, Boxing Day, he calls sounding very subdued, says should he wait for me. When I say no, he disconsolately says, 'Oh, well! I just wondered. My host has kindly offered to drive me over to you.' He arrives one hour later brought by Dobson Junior, and comes swinging up the path with swaying shoulders and fixed grin that stretches from ear to ear, exposing gleaming white teeth. He was wearing cream, stovepipe, whipcord trousers, an off-white flannel waistcoat with gold buttons, a striped city tie and a dark grey worsted jacket of herring-bone design, with solid black leather shoes. The young Dobson was less showily dressed, though they both had a certain similarity with their thick, curly, almost frizzy hair, coarse faces and the confidence of middlebrow philistines. It turned out there had not been a party. Dobson immediately stated that he had met Cyril before on a Chelsea barge. 'Who can he be mistaking me for?' Cyril said, as we brewed some mulled wine in the kitchen. 'Davenport?' Dobson then began quoting some form of torture (rats gnawing away at a victim's face while he is powerless to get away, which I had already heard Koestler gloating over) from a book, Dobson said, 'called 1982, by that chap who died a short while ago'. B corrected him rather sharply, 'You mean 1984,' and looked annoyed, as though he were being let down.

When Dobson had gone, B immediately told us how fabulously rich the Dobsons were. 'I can't bear his reverential tone when he speaks of money,' Cyril confided later.

B boasted about a luncheon he had attended on Christmas Day

given by the Bevans; the other guests included Humphrey Slater with a girlfriend, David Sylvester, Mickey Luke and, I think, Jocelyn Baines. Afterwards, Cyril said how awful it sounded and how it typified the mire of London. B flatters Cyril all the time, treating him as a great man. Cyril says he can only support him so long as he does all the chores. When talking of his firm, B says, 'We' and 'Our policy' and 'We employ so many thousand bureaucrats . . .' 'Do you know so-and-so?' he kept on saying to Cyril, who would grunt and go on reading.

B and I took Kupy for a walk to the Foxhole pub. She was a great success; came into the bar and was given some sweet biscuits. 'I think she's just lovely,' the pub owner kept saying. 'I think you will soon have to release Cyril from the confines of the country,' B said. 'He should live in London and form the core of the literary world. He needs it and people need him.' 'Who are these people?' I ask. B thought hard. 'Well, Alan Pryce-Jones for one.' 'That radio prattler. He can see him any time.' 'Well, he is the editor of the *TLS*.'

Saturday, December 27

Noël Coward *Diaries*:

Gave dinner party for Annie, Ian, Loelia, * *the Cyril Connollys, Fionn and Peter Quennell. Played 'the game'. Great fun.*

In the evening, before motoring over to Noël Coward, I am worried about what to wear. I try on various skirts. B inspects me and pronounces them all to be ugly. So I keep on my utility check trousers and a pale blue polo neck pullover. We stop in Brabourne for petrol and B starts a conversation with the *garagiste*, complimenting him on his window display. 'I'm in the petrol business myself,' B says proudly. We drive on and I can sense Cyril wincing in the back seat. Noël Coward had said, 'Wear your oldest clothes'; we arrive to find Ann Fleming in a low-cut, flared grey satin evening dress, the Duchess of Westminster ditto and covered in sparklers. A glass of champagne all round and then presents. I was given yet another box of Floris soap. Cyril was given a signed copy of Coward's *Quadrille*. When I said to Coward that I would like a copy, too, he replied, 'You can read Cyril's.' The two bachelors, PQ and Michael Renshaw,[†] who were lying sprawled on the floor at

---

*The Duke of Westminster's third wife, now Lady Lindsay.

[†]He had a house in Cyprus which was overrun by Turks. After the Cyprus War he returned to live in London.

Ann's feet like a pair of privileged, sacred dogs, were given egg-boiling gadgets with tight screw-lids and did not seem pleased.

The entire house party had a depressed air, the only one with vitality being the Duchess, who enjoyed steering everyone about. Noël Coward and his friend were both dressed in very new-looking Tyrolean clothes. The house was like an oven, so that soon people's eyes began to puff and close. We ate a cold supper of dry chicken, tomato salad tasting of fertilisers, peas like pellets and lettuce with brown edges. Afterwards we played games. Peter and I groaned when we learnt our fate. Luckily, it didn't turn out to be so frightening as it sounded. I had to convey the book title *The Naked and the Dead* which, according to Cyril, I did with GRACEFUL hand movements and, the second time it was *Darkness at Noon*, artfully chosen by Peter, who knew I had recently been lunching with Koestler. B had a conversation with the Duchess. I saw him wriggling about on his chair and putting on an attentive face indicating rapt servility. But I think he sensed he was not having much success. Later he told me that someone like that could put him off sex for life, in which case she would be doing him a great service, and us, too, I consider. For, on the way back, there he was going on about his new girl again. 'I have her from the back, that's what I like.' 'Does she?' 'Well, I have to play with her first. She gives me some of the best orgasms of my life . . .' etcetera.

I wake up with a feeling of dread, wonder why and then remember we have to go to London. Mrs Lea brings up breakfast. I get up soon after, fuss over kitchen stove, put out clothes I am going to wear, feed Kupy, throwing in a stock to keep her plenished for thirty-nine hours. Run bath and nag Cyril to get up. Catch train from Folkestone in a rush. No time to buy *Picture Post*, *Listener* and *Daily Mail*. Make for restaurant car. Smile at familiar-faced waiter who used to be on the 7.15 dining car. Asks us whether we would like tea or coffee. I say perhaps tea is safer as the coffee tastes of salt. He says in this restaurant car the steward never uses salt. We order toast and marmalade, complain when coffee is brought in plastic cups and fling one onto the table knowing it cannot break. People at next table look up. The waiter takes away plastic cups and brings us the usual dun pottery marked *GWR* in black. Arriving at Charing Cross, as I pass through, am screeched at by the ticket collector as Cyril is close behind with the tickets. We both get into a taxi, I drop Cyril off at White's and go on to massage. Miss Fontaine says everybody has been complaining about their dull Christmas. Go to have fitting with François. We talk about old faces at Schiaparelli. He knows my figure and where to pinch it in and let it out. Go on to Duke's Hotel. Find Cyril installed in a grim two-bedded room, modern stained furniture, a bathroom. Tony Bower for a drink. Toeing the carpet, his eyes fixed on the ground, in an affected drawl, carefully choosing his words, he holds forth on Spain. I noticed how his ears stuck out and, with his tiny head, he looked like a tame rodent. His eyes were tired bulges, glazed and colourless. But his metallic energy kept us amused. He described the life at the Davises in Madrid, almost putting us off accepting their invitation – how ugly the house was, how much Bill drank, the fights he had and how he thought Bill must spend most of his time in brothels, as otherwise he couldn't see what he did all day. Tony asked us if we knew of a good place for winter sports. Cyril suggested Breitmoos. I described the life there, the heavy four course meals with caraway soup, meat and pudding, the dim lighting so that one could never read and, night and day, the clopping of ski-boots. Then, in trepidation, I prepared myself for dinner with the Hamish Hamiltons. The other guests; Robin Ironside, the Duchess of W again, Isaiah Berlin and the comic Connollys.

Robin had a set of new teeth paid for by the Hultons which gave his face a dead appearance. He told me he had been reading a book on tropical fish that lived on human blood extracted through the penis. I said that must be a rare treat; he said, on the contrary, natives were being sucked dry all the time. Isaiah Berlin talked about the nineteenth-century, said he thought the best time to have lived would have been between 1840 and 1860. Cyril said that it was essential to have survived another thirty years to have read Flaubert and Baudelaire, and that he would have preferred to have been a child throughout the revolution and thereby escaped the guillotine. IB said in that case one might have been too old to appreciate reading F and B. Everyone talked a great deal and we had an excellent dinner, *sauce tartare* with scampi (which was sole cut up to look like prawns), followed by a toad-in-the-hole served hot with a sauce, sautéed potatoes and a delicious lettuce salad. (Yvonne explained afterwards that all their salads were good since using garlic vinegar.) Last of all, mince pies with cream. I talked to the Duchess about Christmas Day and Fulco's jewellery that I think so vulgar. Then we played musical chairs; people sat about in pairs and, as soon as one seat was vacated, someone came and sat in it.

As we were leaving I said to Jamie Hamilton, 'Do you do this kind of thing often?' and he laughed. 'Where was the ten pounds worth of good conversation?' I said to Cyril later (ten pounds being the cost of a visit to London).

Have a bad night; it is very quiet, but I feel the airlessness of a stuffy town room. On the way out Cyril asks to pay the bill. They refuse to take a cheque, although they remember him from before. Cyril says we might as well have stayed at the Ritz – it is far more comfortable and only a little extra. I get cross and say, 'Waste of money.' 'We don't enjoy the same things,' Cyril says angrily. The talk about hotels has put us in a bad humour, so that when we reach Jaegars in Frith Street, an open row begins and, after ordering a baking tin, an earthenware casserole dish and a copper saucepan, Cyril cancels the lot. The salesman smirks, enjoying the scene. We leave the shop in a fearful huff. I meet Tony Bower at the Ritz. Drink gin and peppermint. No sign of Cyril. Eventually, he walks into the bar around one, furious; why are we sitting there? – when I usually sit in the entrance in one of the wing armchairs. I explain Tony has been to look for him twice. Tell Tony I'm pleased that he's also in disgrace. Taxi to Angelica, having debated whether or not to take her something to eat or drink, but since Tony has said her liver is in such a bad state, she can neither eat nor drink, I go empty-handed. John Maclaren there. Angelica indignant when I tell her Tony's verdict . . . She has cooked a roast chicken with creamy mashed potatoes and broccoli. We drink red wine. I drop Angelica off at the hairdresser's. She tells me they are going to a fancy-dress ball, everyone wearing Russian costume; she, though, will go in evening dress wearing false eyelashes and carrying a long cigarette holder. 'Let others make fools of themselves,' she says. Famous last words!

Rather tipsy and uncertain what I'm at, I go to Fortnum's to buy Cyril a belated Christmas present of a canvas bag for carrying books. I know he won't like it, but it will be useful. After buying the bag, I telephone Jocelyn Baines and meet him for a quick drink. Talk about his Denton Welch review. He has filled out a bit and looks less invertebrate. I feel he has contempt for me and wonder why. I think him a silly arse, of course, but I was prepared to enjoy seeing him. Kill time and catch the 7.15. Gave Cyril his present. He did seem rather disappointed but pretended to like it to please me.

It is always a pleasure getting back to one's own surroundings after an absence of a couple of days, to go into the kitchen to see a freshly trussed turkey ready for the oven, the gizzards beside it on a plate. Mrs Lea had also left a slice of cake on a plate, but it was not as good as the one Aunty Greta made when I took them the cider on Christmas Eve.

To celebrate the New Year, we listened to the radio. At eleven, Cyril opened the Hulton champagne. It was a very good pre-war year. We drink each other's health. Cyril goes to bed at midnight leaving an unfinished glass of bubbly. I dance round the room to a rhumba band *à la Glur*, or sit and mope, dressed in my skunk stole. Go to bed feeling frustrated.

On Sunday, at a moment's notice, we had Eric Oliver and Jocelyn Brooke to lunch. There was no time to cook the turkey, so we made a *sept heures* beef, adding a tin of pimentoes and the dregs of the decanted red wine. The beef had been stewed in butter and the whole thing was delicious, described by Jocelyn as being a 'fine *ragoût*'. Cyril opened two good bottles of twenties claret that the French gourmet André Simon had given him. We started with *foie gras*, a present from the Flemings. 'Why is it people never give caviar?' Cyril commented. 'It's only another ten shillings.' The *ragoût* was followed by a Scandinavian cream cheese with Romary biscuits and then fudge that Aunty Greta had made, and finally, we christened the Cona coffee machine. Jocelyn and Cyril talked books nonstop. They left early, as Eric had borrowed an army greatcoat from a friend and had to return it that night. We were all very profuse on their departure and many suggestions were made for the future. I even invited Eric to stay, as I thought he might be a good person to help in the garden. He has promised to give me a Staffordshire figure to add to my collection. It's called Flora and belonged to Denton Welch.

January 4, 1953
Had the Flemings to lunch which meant there was no time to concentrate on anything else the whole morning. I heard Mrs Lea bring the cream about eleven and then sneak away. Cyril said how nice it would be if she just made up the fire without being asked. They arrived at about two o'clock by which time the cottage was lying under a thick bed of snow. Looking into the gilt convex mirror over the fireplace, I thought how broad, flat and Mongolian I

looked beside Ann Fleming's elongated features. She really is very handsome and well-bred, but no sex appeal. Why does she always rouge her cheeks like a painted doll? Ian's eyes are too close together and I don't fancy his raw beef complexion. Nothing of the slightest interest said during lunch. It makes one feel what a terrible waste of time people are. And there they are immediately after, tearing off in the sleeting snow to see more people thirty miles away. But they are amiable. 'Had any rows lately?' Ian said to me aggressively when he arrived. 'Not since yesterday.' I was rather waspish when I spoke. We drank a 1929 claret given to Cyril by Derek Jackson and the Bastard's brandy with the coffee. I did not think they praised the meal enough but, as Cyril says, my inferiority is such that I just don't hear praise when it's given. I felt complacent about not smoking and counted all the stubs left on their plates. 'How many stubs do you think?' I say to Cyril in a shocked voice. Ann asks about my book. I say how monstrous of Peter to have mentioned it. As soon as one tells him anything, he has to go beating the drums.

On Saturday, we dined at The Rose and Crown with Eric Wood, and drank champagne. Tomato soup, grilled chicken with roast potatoes and runner beans. They had obviously taken trouble, as we had not been there for some time. Mr Millen, the proprietor, gets very familiar when he has had a few drinks, giving me funny furtive little glances between his puffy lids as he polishes the glasses, and calls me Barbara, as though trying it out to see how I'll take it. When we were leaving, he came and buttoned up my sheepskin coat so well, as I normally never do, that I said, 'I won't be able to get out of it now.' Only Cyril laughed. Mr Millen told us about the number of dud cheques he had been given in his life; one man he had known for twenty years borrowed a pound. 'He never paid me back and I never saw him again.' 'All for a pound, isn't that rather touching?' I said. 'I think it's the limit, don't you?' he added, trying to enlist Cyril's sympathy.

Eric Wood was very amiable and at his best (undrunk). He always gives the impression he is so pleased to see us. We talked about Staffordshire china and Cyril said that I had become a rival collector. Everyone agreed it was an expensive disease to have. I told him that one of my figures was of an old woman in a bonnet holding a trayload of mice and Eric said, no, he had never seen one like that. 'Do you think it's a fake, then?' 'Well, you never know,' he said. But he was more interested to know if we had listened to a 'wonderful programme on the radio. They call themselves the "Lollypops". They're so good, you must listen.' He said he had definitely decided to give up his house. 'Although I know, my dear, that I have missed the market, yes, my dear, I know that. But, I'm sick of living alone. And I went up to London the other night and saw Dicky off to America . . .' 'Who's Dicky?' Cyril immediately said. 'You know, the fashion photographer! One of the best,' said Eric, pursing up his lips as he pronounced BEST. 'He has so much talent. Well, I saw him off in his Rolls to the airport, an ancient Rolls, my dear, but a Rolls, nonetheless, and he said to me, Eric, what you must do is to sell your house and open an antique shop.' Cyril, who had been very bored up till then, came to life. 'What are you going to call it?' 'Aspidistra,' said Eric, firmly. He then told us a long story of how he had wanted to borrow money on a Sunday; the hotel wouldn't change a cheque, so he went to the police and, when he asked if they would cash him a cheque, the police said no. 'But, my good man,' Eric said, 'look at my new car, I've just had it made with a special body.' Then they asked to see his papers. 'How do we know these are your papers?' the police asked. 'My good man, if I have an accident in the street and you ask to see my papers, you don't then say, "go away, how do I know these are your papers?"'

March 10
The first day of spring. Several minutes of warm sun. Pop got as far as putting out the deck chairs, sat in one for ten minutes and went in. I hosed out Kupy's cage. She is getting very fierce and aggressive. She attacked Pop this morning and broke an eight-eenth-century piece of china. He had such a deep gash on his foot that, after disinfecting it with dentifrice gargle, I covered it with elastoplast.

◇◇◇ Chapter XV ◇◇◇

Driving through Spain

Diary

Have been back from Spain for a week. February 6 we caught the train for Victoria. Pop slept at his club and I stayed with the Churchills. A bad night due to an excess of brandy after dinner. June picks a quarrel with Randolph over their daughter, Anabella. I am accused of taking sides. My door blown open during the night by Randolph's snores (he is across the passage). June roams the house at six in the morning.

We had a private cabin on the boat, as Cyril says it's the only way to get any service. We didn't require any, but men kept bobbing their heads in and out of the cabin as Cyril sat like a pasha greeting each one in turn until the boat became too rocky and he had to lie down.

In France, the first thing one notices is the tops of the willows which have been recently pollarded and resemble nutty crunch bar chocolate. On the train, we get into conversation with a bright scruffy Bostonian who attacks England, saying the English know nothing about food or painting. How about Turner, Constable, Hogarth and Gainsborough . . . ? He turned out to be a publisher, George Novack and, when asked by Cyril what he thought of English critics, could only think of V S Pritchett. It was exhilarating arriving in Paris, humid, brightly lit and a steady downfall of sleet. We bought snacks on the platform.

Am up early, dressed and just belting up my overcoat when we get to the Spanish frontier. We change trains at nine in the morning. Cyril immediately begins grumbling about the armed police and the inadequacy of the bookstall. 'A country of philistines,' he says. The Talgo a long windowed moving caterpillar. We sit in twos in a long line, metal trays are placed over our knees. We order *huevos* and gaze out at the Basque countryside. Granite mountains, scrubby evergreen ilexes, large open spaces with clusters of giant boulders looking as though they had been coughed up from the bowels of the earth. Then vast stretches of umbrella pines. Piles of swedes were stacked on all the platforms, and groups of desultory travellers loafed about, or put their faces close to the Talgo with inquisitive stares. We might have come from another planet.

We reach Madrid at 6.30 after passing the Escorial which stood out in all its grandeur gleaming in the sunlight. It was strange to come upon a large city, surrounded by a vast plain, in the centre of such wild country. Madrid very much alive. Fountains, crowded streets. Bill Davis met us on the platform, very dandified in a loose, knee-length, grey gabardine overcoat. He was much thinner, full of self-confidence and jauntily swinging a silver-topped cane, directed us to a large American roadster. The flat was spacious and white, full of evergreen plants and modern paintings. Annie (Cyril's American sister-in-law when he was married to Jeannie) had on an old gabardine skirt and blouse, with gold chain bracelet and necklace that she always wore, in case, she said, she should ever get stranded in a foreign country without her lord and master. We saw the children. Both a dead spit of Bill. The first meal, *langostina* with mayonnaise, steak cooked by Bill with mashed potatoes, spinach and fruit salad. The conversation Burgess and Maclean, and Bill saying all the time, 'And what do you think of so-and-so, Cyril?' Pop unpacks his suitcase and brings out a trousseau, a pair of orange silk pyjamas trimmed with black, hand-stitched with his initials. (Philip Mountbatten has a pair just like them, he tells me.) The next exhibit was a pair of scarlet leather slippers so stiff and ill-fitting that he can barely squeeze his pretty broad feet into them, let alone walk. Luckily, the floors are polished wood parquet, so that he is able to skate. I absolutely forbid him to wear the pyjamas while I am sharing the same room, as they make me dizzy. He says they will suit him better when he is sunburnt. He complains about his sinus, is tomato-red under the eyes (a further clash) and has scales flaking off his cheeks with patches of dandruff round the temple. The following morning he eats a two course breakfast and says he needs some sunshine.

Sunday, February 8
A very delicious day. (Probably the most enjoyable of the whole trip. Everything still new and interesting.) We rise late, then set off to lunch the other side of the Guadarramas. I borrow a very splendid pair of sunglasses that I intend to keep. A dream pair, just sitting on the bridge of the nose without producing lines under the eyes. A slight mist covers the ground, but it is warm and sunny, the mountains faintly obliterated by a haze. Halfway up the Guadarramas the road is blocked by heaped snow and we are unable to continue. We retreat and lunch at Miraflores; a summer resort. Impeccable meal, ordered cautiously. Bill unaccommodating with advice as though he did not want to be held responsible. Start with *hors d'oeuvres*, including some excellent tinned tunny fish, followed by a *tortilla* filled with diced potatoes, veal cutlets, salad soaked in water and vinegar (better than it sounds), Spanish lettuces being very good and crisp, and finally a speciality of the house, rice pudding with a lemon flavour. The Castille wine, Riscal, was drunk nonstop throughout the trip. We then motor to Annie's dreamhouse: a vast turreted circular castle, owned by the Marquis of Alcapulco, now inhabited by peasants, cows, sheep and goats, and the whole place smothered in animal pellets. It was in a very ruinous state, but Annie says she only intends to live in one of the ten wings, and would be content to do it up one room at a time. Cyril says that will take a lifetime, at the end of which one would have no money left and have to depend on charity.

Later a visit to the Prado. A conducted tour by Bill who walks ahead in dapper dress swinging a cane. I lingered at Goya's *Shooting of La Moncloa*. Cyril absorbed in the Bosch paintings.

Sunday, February 15   Malaga
In bed with 'flu. Have been stricken ever since leaving Madrid. As we leave the house, I complain of a sore throat and insist on stopping at a chemist. Everyone thinks I am making unnecessary fuss. Leaving Madrid, we motor across a dull plateau, a dun-coloured, endless vista of wild country fringed with foothills, very

aware of the ubiquitous sky fleeced with white clouds. When we crossed over the Andalusian border Pop gears us all for the observation game, tells us to cry out when we see some sign of a southern climate. The person who pipes up first is rewarded with ten pesetas, the unobservant ones paying the forfeit. The first sign being a palm followed by an aloe, Pop is the first to spot both and cries out, unable to stifle his pleasure at his own cleverness. I just concentrate on spotting a cactus, deciding that is the best tactic. Call out when I sight a prickly pear, but everyone looks so grumpy, I decide to drop out of the game. After leaving the plain, everything becomes green; eucalyptus of giant height with rustling silver branches fan the road. We pass through the Sierra Morena, driving through several Moorish towns of great beauty.

Stay the night at Ubeda in a converted palace with a patio. Pop and I on very bad terms, me irritable and ill. Spend a sleepless night – such dim lighting it is impossible to read. Annie says dim lighting is typical of Spain. Bill agrees and gurgles with pleasure, the idea of our discomfort being a huge joke. He drives in silence, occasionally emitting a grunt. Annie chatters nonstop. I periodically turn round to release a fresh barb at Cyril, or glare.

Next day passed through two ravishing towns, Baeza and Mancha Real, clusters of palms, clumps of aloes, prickly pears and regiments of olive trees. Dwarf blue and white irises border the road; there was an occasional carob and a sudden burst of bright yellow as we passed a climbing jasmine. We had a glimpse of the first orangery and a touch of spring, at last – almond trees in blossom, a wonderful sight, the pink flowers contrasting with the dark negroid barks. A very good lunch at Jaeh of *paella*, *merluza* (the inevitable hake) and *manchego* cheese. We end the meal with large glassfuls of orange juice. The people of Andalusia more sympathetic than in Castille and better-looking, maybe due to their having darker skins. Annie thoughtfully buys me a pair of white woolly gloves as I left the last pair behind in Ubeda. We visited the cathedral, a lot of elaborate wood carving, then push on south. The Sierra Nevada capped in snow. We stop the night in a fishing village and summer resort, Almuñecar. Cyril and I both with temperatures. Drink hot grogs and become muffled. We read that in England there is snow, an epidemic of 'flu and roads are cut off. Once more dim lighting in the hotel. We are the only guests, it being out of season. Pop now ill, flushed and bundled up in woollen clothes and overcoat with turned-up collar. Drink more hot grogs. Wake up to see the nets being hauled in, the bedroom looking right onto the sea. All the fishermen gather round with baskets, some leading donkeys onto the beach to cart away the fish. Pop shows us the custard apple trees at the back of the town. Many ravishingly pretty Renoir women with deep pools for eyes. Scores of beggars everywhere. After three days, when Cyril has retired to bed, Bill opens his mouth for the first time to elucidate on the things that give him pleasure: (a) farting loudly for people to hear and then turning round with a surprised leer; (b) peeing all over the lavatory seat to annoy women; (c) blowing his nose into his fingers and flinging the snot. As we left next morning, we saw two dogs copulating and Bill went on sniggering until several miles outside the town. On arrival at Torremolinos, Cyril immediately looks fluffed out and furious *à cause des anglais partout*.

We whizz through the main street deploring the newly-built villas, haunted by the possibility of running into David Tennant. Leave the bungalow world of Torremolinos and spend the night in a luxury hotel. A comfortable room at last looking onto the sea. Bright lighting and hot sea water bath. I retire to bed with Gerald Brenan's *South from Granada*.

In the evening, the Davises return from some trip to announce their car will have to be laid up, as it has a leak in the gearbox. They are fed up at the idea of being static. Cyril and I wink with pleasure, as we had been discussing earlier how we could get them to stay put for a few days. The plan is to return to Malaga, unfortunately one of the dullest towns in the south. There was nothing to see but a commonplace Gothic cathedral and a museum of nineteenth-century paintings, one Zurbaran, a few Riberas and a ravishing seventeenth-century Christ sculptured in wood.

My 'flu gets steadily worse. Spend three nights with dinner in bed, then we visit the Brenans for tea. It was a very cold day and we were all shivering; the garden was at its worst. It is the same shape as ours, but in place of a hawthorn hedge is surrounded by a wall. The only pleasing spectacle on such a windy day was the tall shiny ochre-coloured bamboo canes that swayed and creaked like a galleon in the wind. He had an avocado pear tree too, but the whole garden was dominated by an enormous deciduous tree with a greyish bark resembling a giant elm, that could be seen standing out against the skyline when approaching Churriana from Malaga. We all drank tea crouched round a circular table, enveloped in a blanket, under which was a large brazier full of smouldering charcoal.

Gerald Brenan did most of the talking, said we were the first guests they had had since arriving back five weeks before. He was terribly pleased to see people, just as Cyril is after being deprived of company for five days. I was at my most tactful and asked to borrow Mrs Brenan's book, promising to return it before we left Malaga. The visit was considered a success and Cyril and I found it refreshing to see intelligent people for a change.

The car was eventually ready and we pushed on to Gibraltar. I had a fresh outbreak of fever and sat in the front seat with a suffering face. Bill dropped us at the Rock Hotel for lunch and disappeared to deal in some currency transaction. Cyril was in high spirits; he and Annie had a bibulous many-course lunch while I looked on. It was rather a nice contrast to Spain, everything clean and well-run. Strange seeing the English PC uniforms at the frontier. They looked like men in a musical comedy.

From Gibraltar we drove along the coast high up above sea level. We passed through Tarifa under a Moorish arch, looked at the crenellated Moorish towers, were stopped by the Spanish police, then motored on to Cadiz through the flat, bull-breeding country. Cadiz was a lovely city with vistas of long narrow streets and everything dazzling white, with iron-grilled windows looking onto neat squares with palms and shrubs and wooden benches where women sat nursing babies. We stayed in a small well-run *parador* with comfortable rooms and soft hot water. I ate dinner in bed of *langostina*, followed by the most divine 'knuckly' baby lamb cooked in garlic and butter with artichoke centres and small round baked potatoes, followed by tangerines. Very soon after, I fell into a deep sleep from which I awoke feeling completely restored.

I had a hot bath, washed my pyjamas and, with renewed spirits, was conducted round the town by 'my old Pop and Barrel'. Bought a pair of perfectly hideous green- and red-striped sandals and visited the museum where we saw some Zurburan saints originally intended for the monastery at Jerez. We had lunch at a summer resort. Drank sherry and mineral water sitting in the sun facing the sea, watching the donkeys being driven down to the water and loaded up with sand. In the evening, we had drinks at the tiled café mentioned in William Sansom's book of short essays, *Pleasures*

Strange and Simple. I felt ready for a night out but there is never anywhere to go in these Spanish cities and the old folks are never in the mood for it.

Tony Bower was mentioned at lunch and a few cats were let out of the bag in the way of 'home truths'. It was a question of what Tony Bower had said to us about the Davises in England, followed by what Tony Bower had said about the Connollys to the Davises in Spain. Tony had stated that Bill led a secret life in Madrid and not only kept a mistress in the form of Sabena, the servant, without Annie knowing, but that, each time he disappeared out of the flat, he made a beeline for one of the brothels. That he was always drunk and beating people up. Annie was quite injured and indignant at the reference to Sabena, stressing that she had engaged her as a servant herself. They had been warned by Tony to put a time limit on our visit, as Cyril was inclined to be a squatter and would most certainly overstay his welcome. I was described as having two sole interests: (a) money, and (b) sex. And, of course, my dear, the marriage was going *terribly* badly.

Pop and I are beginning to feel Spain is a blighted country, wonderful for scenery and architecture, but full of gibbering monkeys. The pleasure one has from sightseeing is counteracted by irritation caused by the succession of beggars. Swarms of children follow us through the villages, each one anxious to act as a guide. We pick our way across cobbled streets, with unsmiling, cross faces, like Pied Pipers, while everyone ogles with curiosity.

The cathedral in Seville was rather disappointing. Even the Columbus tomb was installed in 1900, his body having been brought back from Cuba. There were some gilded Baroque gates of great beauty and some seventeenth-century Doric pillars in pinky-brown Alicante marble. We pressed on to the Alcazar, which had been terribly restored. But the gardens were very peaceful with fountains and orange trees and box hedging. Here we had a guide who was both bored and courteous, and very grateful when over-tipped. Bill told Cyril it shocked him to think of us seeing all the obvious things, that neither the cathedral nor Alcazar were worth visiting. The following day Bill himself conducted a tour in as bored and courteous a manner as the guide, showing us two palaces and a Roman house with perfectly preserved mosaics of fish.

155

We had two of the nastiest dinners there, in the main street near the hotel where we saw the bullfighter, Litri. He looked very young, barely twenty, shy with a rather big hawk nose, gawky and badly dressed. One day we lunched outside Seville at one of the roadhouses with a *corral*, where they keep the bulls during the season just before a fight. It was a very hot afternoon and we sat on the terrace overlooking the *corral*, where an old sow and mule lay stretched on a bed of moist dung. The mule, with a distended penis, kept wandering round the *corral* making a terrible noise.

We had another session of 'home truths'. The Berniers were brought up. It was a question of what Peggy Bernier's sister had revealed to Bill, what Cyril had said to the Berniers. There was a reference to Cyril doing an imitation of Bill and Annie when we were dining at the Berniers. It was all true, but we managed to convince them no malice had been intended. Later, Pop had to go back to the hotel to do his review and we went to see Italica, a Roman ruined city with some well-preserved mosaics, fifteen miles outside Seville. The guide said they were the best Roman mosaics in the world for they included fifteen different colours!

In Seville, we made enquiries about flamenco singers and were told of two possible places. The music hall and a brothel called La Terrasse. We went to the nightclub-cum-brothel but our escorts were bored so, after one bad brandy and several mediocre cabaret turns, we left. In it was one dreadful-looking man, resembling a travelling salesman whom I fancied. Before leaving the city, we saw an eighteenth-century bullring. The walls were sandy-ochre with white portals, curved dark red tiles and brick red sand. It must be lovely to watch a bullfight there on a hot day with hot sun and lots of blood about.

We arrived at Cordoba around six in the evening. We dined at a small restaurant called Gomex, which had huge stuffed bulls' heads attached to the walls. The one above where we sat was towering and black, and had lost its ear.

Towards the end of dinner, Cyril hears a guitarist playing in an adjoining room and goes in to investigate. The guitarist tells him there are two good flamenco singers in the town. The better singer is not to be found but, after a great deal of telephoning on the part of the waiters, we are informed that the second best is on his way. In a short while, a spry dwarf appears; he has carefully smarmed hair, sticking-out ears and is newly washed. He at once drew up a chair, we offered him a brandy and, beating time with his palms on the rim of his seat, he began to sing. Bill moved away from our table and slouched in a chair a few feet away, and was such a dampener that I asked him why he didn't go to bed. His face looked flushed and pained for a moment, but he eventually departed with good grace, handing over to Annie a wad of notes. While we had been dining, two businessmen wearing black Cordoba hats had remained standing at another table drinking sherry. One was very talkative and kept putting his face very close to the other, and we gathered they were discussing prices. They were completely absorbed in their conversation but, when the singing began, we suggested they join us. Both of them removed their hats before sitting down; one of them bowed and kissed Annie's hand and then mine. They were a great help with the 'oles' and Cyril was very happy conducting the concert. The singer kept his eyes tight shut as he sang but opened them wide on the last notes as they rose from his stomach in a great swell of feeling at the end of each song. There was a chef standing outside the kitchen. He had a plate and dishcloth in his hand and, whenever the warbling notes came out, he writhed about as though he were being tickled, clasping his hands across his stomach and shaking his head, as much as to say, 'I don't know how he does it.' Suddenly one of the businessmen brought out a jewel box and handed round a collection of precious stones. We all inspected them politely. Then the guitarist offered to take us to a nightclub. Annie was very drunk and seemed absolutely dead set on prolonging the evening. An argument arose between the three of us until Cyril adamantly stormed back to the hotel. Assuming him to be the moneybags, the two artists were rather perplexed, but the singer insisted on taking us to a square, called the Place of Sorrows, where a ten-foot Christ was being crucified in floodlighting. To our surprise, he flung himself to the ground and, kneeling at the foot of Christ, bowed his head and muttered a prayer, and rose with tears streaming down his face. The nightclub turned out to be a brothel full of black-haired women who made every effort to be friendly. Taking the guitarist onto the dance floor, Annie kept saying, 'Where's the flamenco. I wanna hear flamenco . . .' We could hear music coming from a private room, 'I wanna go in there,' Annie said, 'why can't we go in there? I wanna hear flamenco.' Finally, she pushed her way in where a blind man sat, a guitar on his knee, surrounded by whores. 'Play sommink,' screamed Annie. Everyone laughed as they realised she was drunk. 'It's five o'clock,' said one of the women. When we

157

walked out, the singer tugged me up some narrow steps, where we were faced by an angry woman in black who started waving her arms in the air and screaming, so we quickly descended and encountered Annie coming out of the nightclub who, seeing me, carried on screaming where the other woman had left off. 'So, you bin in a brothel,' she shrieked, as if she hadn't seen me for several hours. 'If that's the kind of person you are, I'm off.' She swept round a bend of the street and was out of sight.

April 9
We got back to England to hear that old Queen Mary had died and her favourite operetta, *Cavalcade*, was being played on the radio, but we turned it off when the *Titanic* began to sink.

Pop sounds amiable as he calls to me through the hole in the wall to ask how I slept. Mrs Lea is less frowning and mutters less since her Easter holiday. I enjoy my breakfast, fresh dairy butter, warm toast and tea piping hot. I finish off the remains of the Oxford marmalade. Pop says he doesn't enjoy his. The butter tastes of marrow, tea lukewarm, and toast dry and cold. That I have eaten all the marmalade, but the accusation is said without bitterness because he has awoken in a good humour.

The grey weather persists. From the window, stained, yellowy humps of grass made uneven by the worm casts. The leaf buds are constipatedly holding back. The nectarine against Kupy's hut has already broken out in peach curl. In a fury, Cyril sends Coombes a telegram. 'Nectarine blighted as usual. Please come as promised.'

Back in England for five weeks. We are all the time awaiting something; is it the sun that never appears? Cyril says it's the grave. He has a fan letter from a Dutchman complimenting him on his Coleridge review, in which he has described *The Ancient Mariner* as a barbarous jingle. Today, we finished off the Spanish ham that Bill gave us. It was minced, mixed with cream, egg yolks and mustard. The guinea chicks eat the last rinds. Have difficulty enticing Pop out of the bath. Mrs Lea bangs about in the kitchen, hopping from one foot to the other, holding a dishcloth, every two minutes saying, 'Is he out yet?' When I ask her if she would like to go to the Coronation, she says decisively not. How dangerous the stands look. And what a lot of money is being spent. She is sure the Queen does not want it, either. 'Science fiction! That's what it is,' says Pop, emerging from the bath carrying his book and dressing-gown, a ragged towel partially draped round his *brioche*, beads of water glistening on his fat back. 'It gets me, baby,' he says.

May 20

Waiting, waiting, waiting for the spring? The summer? Whatever it is, it does not arrive. We have been having a trying time owing to Cyril's book of *Horizon* comment. Yesterday, the first review. Philip Toynbee in *The Observer*, full of malice and unspecified criticism. All through the day, Pop's hurt feelings exposed in different shades of pink all over his face. He lies on his bed in his kennel, groaning. I talk about it all the time to make it easier and give him what consolation I can. Assure him the rest of the reviews will be good.

Weidenfeld gave a party. It was a combined party for Cyril's *Golden Horizon*. Was taken by Chuff who was wearing a new suit. Host offers a lukewarm Martini or sherry. Henry Yorke approaches. 'You two together again!' he beams. 'Any news of Poppet?' 'We don't correspond.' 'Why is that?' His face lights up, 'I suppose you tried to get off with Pol.' HE HE HE! I beam at Dig Yorke; we never have anything to say. No one else approaches except Cyril who grabs my arm and says, 'Keep away from that fellow,' indicating Chuff. 'Everyone is asking if we are separated.' We return to the crowd. I greet Kitty. Jack Lambert is friendly. The Davenports snooty. I mutter inanities. Baroness Budberg friendly. Tom Hopkinson friendly. His wife, ditto. Joan friendly for once. V S Pritchett friendly. Jocelyn Baines friendly, but on the defensive. June in powder-blue chiffon, very much the insipid English beauty. Chuff buffeting and blinking with bent head, a tired bull's stance. Ann Fleming and Peter Q converse on the stairs in a reclining pose, *à la debs'* dance, in a heart-to-heart. Father d'Arcy and Isaiah Berlin in the distance.

The end of May

Yesterday, the ash came into flower. Have been reading the final volume of Koestler's autobiography. A continuous repetition of the names of dead comrades and the circumstances in which he knew them. He hears his voice as a warning to the world.

Raindrops on the roseleaves like jewelled blobs. Cyril has gone to London to get some advance money from Weidenfeld. We are quite broke. The telephone cut off. Bills pouring in. We invite ourselves to the Campbells. Arrive at Ashford to find a Sunday train service and Charing Cross in the thick of the Coronation. A taxi pulls up.

'You're in luck,' shouts the driver. 'I'm the only taxi in London today.' The procession route is barricaded off like a sacred walled city, the surrounding streets deserted, a lot of stray colonial-looking men standing in doorways sipping coffee out of thermos flasks, the streets littered with empty cartons, silver paper and squashed stubs. We cross to the Paddington Station Hotel where the Coronation service is being transmitted on television. To my surprise, it is really impressive. The Queen glittering, stately, a cleric walking calmly on each side, trainbearers and a general impression of rigid limbs and stiff necks all bearing weights . . . After sipping some disgusting coffee in the hotel lounge, stocked with motoring magazines, we board another train. We are met by Mary's cowman. Two grey ducks quack at us, a litter of black 'dak' puppies like fat little puddings tumble out of the kitchen. I am shown the young bantams; how pretty they are. On entering the house, we are again struck by the filth. The stairs up to our rooms coated in dust. Dust seems to seep into one's clothes. When one gets out of the bath, one is appalled by the floating filth on the surface. A long passage has to be traversed before reaching the communal eating room and Cyril remarks on the reek of chicken-shit as we go into each meal. The evening of our arrival, we are told there would not be much of a meal, as we were being taken to a fireworks display. So, we just ate *oeufs Mornay*, me helping to peel the eggs. It was a five-mile drive. We reached a large Queen Anne house beside the river, coloured bulbs were strung along the water front, a gramophone was playing and the music transmitted through a pick-up. As soon as we arrived it started to rain. A group of people stood about the hall, Ralph and Frances Partridge among them. We were offered nothing.

Clusters of expectant faces wait about in the rain. Everyone making conversation. The fireworks went on for over an hour. One felt frozen. 'They're no good. They've become damp,' the hostess wailed. 'It's the noise that matters,' I said. 'They are wonderful,' said an old man from the village. She sighed with relief. 'Do you really think so!' It was all she wanted to hear. Nearing midnight, we were invited into the warm, brightly-lit, log-fired drawing room and offered beer and cake! Our hosts had both been in the Abbey and showed us their coronets. Then, Mary wanted to go on to a village dance with her cowman, but Robin made a fuss. We were all tired. The fireworks were certainly very fine; it was a pity it had rained. The following day, Robin showed me his roses. He takes great care of them, pinching off each greenfly in his fingers. It was an expensive visit as Cyril had taken a large parcel of champagne and claret. But the Campbells are cosy. The last evening, we motored thirty miles to dine with the Pritchetts. Mary had described Mrs VSP as being the best cook she knew. We had plovers' eggs, tinned turtle soup and the most delicious duck, with a rich walnut dressing. Robin never spoke. We all stood about a great deal reading *Vogue* and *Harper's* magazines. On the last evening at the Campbells, a rat scuttled across the kitchen. Mary said, 'Take no notice, it's one of our pets.' I backed 'Ambiguity', the winner of the Oaks, picking on the name, and it came in at eighteen to one.

On Friday, we were taken to Marlborough, where we caught a double-decker bus to Salisbury. At the station we ran into Eddie Sackville-West and all three of us squeezed into the restaurant car. We ate a thoroughly nasty meal. I covered everything with Heinz mayonnaise; Eddie was shocked, 'Do you really like it?' he asked. 'Not at home, but always on trains,' I told him. A taxi met us at the station in Cornwall. We had a ten-mile drive to Newton Ferrars. It was so cold that I sat, with ice-cold feet, huddled up in my sheepskin coat. Bertie Abdy came in from the garden when we arrived. We saw his beautifully-polished leather slippers carefully laid out in the hall. There were some good-hearted jokes about the size of his feet – they did seem rather long and pronglike. He was wearing a thick, stone-coloured, cowl-necked pullover, of the Simpson variety. We all sat round a well-stocked teatable. There was a delicious-looking honeycomb on the table and I expressed a wish to have some for my breakfast (but I never did). I did not like Diane Abdy's taste in interior decorating; it was a little Eric Woodish, only on a more luxuriant scale. Cyril was ticked off for carrying one of our suitcases up the stairs instead of leaving it to the butler. We dressed for dinner, the host wore a very becoming bottle-green dinner jacket with velvet facings. After dinner, we were shown the library which was full of precious *objets d'art*. Next morning, the midget hostess greeted me in trousers and was levered up on high green cork-wedge shoes. The food was disappointing, although in a typical English-good-cook way the puddings were excellent, particularly the *crème brûlée*. Sunday was spent motoring to the far end of the Cornish 'boot' and back in order to hear a musical festival which consisted of a young man seated at a piano, dreamily playing Arthur Bliss sonatas, surrounded by pots of pale hydrangeas. We stopped at St Michael's Mount on the way. How beautiful the smooth sands looked and the sea so calm and grey. We chugged across in a small motorboat as the tide was up and were greeted by a walrussy host with a rich fruity voice who, with much pride, showed everyone his mounting cliff garden; the mesembryanthemums were very knotted and tight, laid out like deep purple-and-pink prayer mats, firm juicy succulents protruding from out of the rocks. Once at the top we seemed to be at a great height. Horror! Inside the fortress it was a cross between Peniscola and the Escorial, only less impressive. The heavy oak furniture. The chunky stone walls. Seated at a long oak table refectory-fashion, we ate tea, surrounded by portrait-burdened walls, paintings done by Opie, with one portrait of the present Lady St Levan done by Moynihan. After tea, a tour; a chapel; a chart room; a map room; some eighteenth-century costumes of great beauty. Afterwards, Cyril said, 'One more room full of compasses, and I should have flagged.' With boredom gnawing at my vitals and the horror of having to cope with any more fresh faces that had to be 'looked into' and 'talked at', I decided to depart.

Monday was a day of tension. Cyril and I wrangling in whispers because of my going, every sound penetrating the walls. The cook and the butler rowing in the kitchen and the Abdys conversing in their quarters about the servant trouble. I caught a train to Truro and was met by Nancy.

My stay with Nancy, a cipherine friend from Cairo, was not altogether a success. I felt her uneasiness, as when she is nervous she develops an unconscious sniff, and then she kept repeating, as if to assure herself, 'Oh, it is nice to see you!' And I was glad to see her. Her mother was a tall, bony, purple-faced woman, continually wandering through whichever room we were talking in, carrying a large dog's bowl. 'Do you see how alike we are?' Nancy asked. 'People talk to Mummy for hours under the impression they are addressing me.' Nancy's Uncle Harry was there, grunting, with swollen pouches under his eyes. They all talked across me at dinner, in the typical English fashion; I suppose they are so used to meals alone together that one probably *is* invisible to them. I had a bad night, waking in the early hours to a stampede of rats. I sweated a lot and had a final impression of having been visited by a vampire after discovering two small red scratches on my thigh. We ate some home-grown strawberries. 'What are these?' I asked. 'Climax or Sovereign?' 'Oh, I don't know,' said Mrs T. 'Number

Threes,' said Harry. 'They come in numbers now.' Harry told us he'd tried to see the Coronation on a neighbour's television. 'It was hopeless,' he said, 'like rain falling.'

Go down to Hythe to see my mother. She tells me she has just missed winning the tote double. She irons my blouses. I watch horrified as she presses creases. She says she likes ironing and won't let me do it. She tells me how much she now likes living alone and how she wondered when Daddy died if she would ever be able to.

I meet Cyril later in the Sandgate bookshop. He is laden with calf-bound first editions bulging out of his pockets. 'You are being self-indulgent today,' I say. We go over to the hotel opposite and are joined by Edgell Rickwood[*] and his wife. 'Are they all unreadable firsts or readable seconds?' 'A bit of each,' Cyril says. He has some Lamb *Letters to Coleridge*. Coleridge is the new craze at the moment.

Mr Rickwood has sex appeal. He was wearing a flecky-brown pullover, the kind a schoolmaster might wear, horn-rimmed specs and his eyes were blurred like a dead fish's. He focuses on the ground, or so it seems, and talks in whispers, as though he has such a low opinion of himself that he doesn't want anyone to hear what he has to say. He does not think *The Ancient Mariner* such a bad poem. Taken as a whole, it has a hypnotic effect. Cyril picks out two bad lines and says, 'You can't call that good.' Mrs Rickwood dashes in, carefully made-up face and black hair screwed back with a large tortoiseshell comb which should have been supporting a mantilla. She is extraordinary and seems to want to swallow us all up; she says everything with great force and looks permanently belliger-ent. Her small black eyes bore into one and when she speaks she seems to chew the air. 'What has become of Honor Tracy?' she asks. Cyril says he didn't know her. 'I used to know Brian Howard very well . . . I adore Basle,' she says, 'though you have to know the right parts, the special parts. I know them all.' She snapped her jaw at us and glared like an animal at bay with nutty eyes hooded by a heavy brow. Suddenly, Cyril announced we were going to see a Joseph Cotten film in Hythe. We order a ham sandwich and rush out. 'Rickwood has sex appeal,' I say to Cyril. 'Not any more,' C says, 'he's been sucked dry by communism.'

---

[*]Editor of a literary monthly of the 1920s, *The Calendar of Modern Letters*.

May 28   Whitsun Weekend

Yesterday, we went to lunch at St Margaret's Bay. Lucien Freud was there, looking very clean and sunburnt. He has sly bluey-green cats' eyes. If he is not there, he is invariably talked about and although he ran everybody down (bar Sonia) he was at his most sweet-natured. Ann Fleming and James Pope-Hennessy sat at either end of the table. Lucien next to James and myself beside the hostess, thereby placing two women and two men cheek-to-cheek. It was a poor lunch, as usual, with under-ripe melon, dried-up lobster and milky mayonnaise, a mushy insipid onion and lettuce salad, cold meat and inferior red wine. Ann immediately began reeling off her luncheon parties of the previous week. Her great pride this time was one consisting of Joan Rayner, Peter Watson, Koestler, Tom Hopkinson and his wife. 'Why the Hopkinsons?' we asked. She was anxious to see what Mrs H was like. 'Oh, just idle curiosity,' said her sister, Laura Dudley,* who was sitting on Cyril's right. Apparently, Ann had not thought much of Mrs H. She liked Koestler. Laura Dudley said he became a fearful bore when drunk. He was not drinking, Ann said. LD said that you never notice he is drunk until he suddenly begins to lay down the law and hold the floor. Ann had wanted to take Lucien to the lunch but Ian, who had not attended, had objected. James Pope-H has bitten-down finger nails and a face the colour of mud. He described Weidenfeld as being oleaginous. They discussed Philip Toynbee's review of Cyril's *Golden Horizon* book. They thought Philip had behaved 'monstrously' and that he must be 'a nasty piece of work!' Sonia's disappearance was discussed. C said it indicated that at last she was happy. Lucien said he was pleased for her to have found someone, but with her disposition he didn't believe she had found much happiness. Then HAPPINESS was thrashed out. For how long was it possible to remain in a state of happiness? Ann thought it was not possible for longer than a fortnight. James P-H said he could be perfectly happy by himself and that places gave him as much pleasure as people, that he had recently spent a blissfully happy time alone in some watering place. They were all horrified. 'James is like a candle talking to a lot of moths,' said Cyril, and everyone laughed. 'I thrive on tension,' said Ann, 'but it's so exhausting. One needs a lot of vitality.' 'We all like tension,' said Cyril, 'and thrive on tugs-of-war so long as the rope is evenly balanced. When

---

*Then married to the Earl of Dudley.

the tension and vitality go, there is your happiness, as with Sonia.' They were all very exhilarated with the discussion and rose from the table flushed like radishes. Ann once stated that all she cared about was power and that she would like to be fabulously rich in order to wield as much power as possible. When she enters a roomful of people, she immediately has to squat in their midst on the floor, she likes to be the core. The other day, at Joan's party, when Ann went into ecstasies about a painter called Devas whose paintings she described as being 'so cosy', Robin Ironside sharply replied, 'I don't know that I agree that "cosy paintings" make for cosiness.'

◇◇◇ Chapter XVI ◇◇◇

Overnight in France

Diary

June 1, 1953
Early last week, Joan Rayner telephoned and asked if we were prepared to leave for France. It turned out to be a plan she and Cyril had hatched together, that we should accompany her across the Channel, have lunch at Montreuil and see her off on the 'rest of the summer' tour round Europe. Cyril's overdraft is so immense that he cannot cash any more cheques and no money is due before three weeks. But Joan has lent him twenty pounds, which will enable her to have company en route but does not help him to live within his means.

In preparation, we go to London. I have my legs shorn. Hair set and manicure. Very extravagant, I am sure, but perhaps I can be permitted these small indulgences to maintain a little confidence. London is empty, grey and tawdry with dirty flags and tattered streamers fluttering from the buildings. There are no taxis, the buses infrequent. The Ritz is full of people dressed up, waiting for transport. I am squeezed between two people on the bus, the man on my right presses into me, looking steadfastly out of the window at the park. I realise he is trying to get off with me; he is quite attractive, a road mender type. Laden with parcels (a new suit) I reach Charlotte Street later than instructed. Cyril glares, as he opens the door of Joan's flat. We harangue each other all the way up

the stairs. Joan glares, when I enter the sitting room. We finish a
bottle of warmish champagne. Everything is packed up. The flat
looks bleak, awaiting new tenants. We all pile into Joan's new
second-hand Bentley (original owner Philip Dunne). Me at the back
directing the way. Once out of the built-up areas we speed up. I feel
cold, but in spite of repeated entreaties for the window to be closed
there is always a fraction left open. Neuralgic pain starts in my
head. I undo parcel and wrap a small velvet jacket round my head.
We make for the Boughton pub. All pile out, Cyril having spent
most of the journey praising the good food there. After consulting
the menu, C tells Joan that we have only dined there once (implying
that if anything goes wrong he will not be held responsible). I have
to contradict him. (Don't see why he should get away with such a
blatant lie, being one of the first people to criticise others for similar
offence.) Joan looks at me very crossly. I am spoiling their fun. We
eat a meal just like any other there. Bad, but Cyril is pleased because
on his advice the owner has got in some good claret. It is 1934 and
expensive. I drink it with smoked trout, my first course being
marmite soup. A lot of port drunk afterwards. Cyril offers the
owner a glass of port and tells him what was wrong with the
dinner. The man betrays neither surprise or dismay; he says most
of his clients don't know what good food is, but that he is slowly
teaching them. Flushed and content, Cyril pays the bill. I sometimes wonder, is he such a gourmet, after all? We press on. Cyril
exaggeratedly well-mannered toward Joan in marked contrast to
his attitude toward me, which is worse than that of a man to his
dog. I am cross when we arrive at the cottage. While I go to put the
geese to bed, I purposefully let them stumble into the house in the
dark so that they both fall over a laundry basket barring the
passage. When I get back, Joan says she would like a glass of water
to take to bed, 'if it is not too much trouble' and might she have a hot
water bottle 'if it is not too much trouble'. A lot of mewing goes on
between them as to what book she shall read in bed. They run
through a hundred possibilities. I say sharply that the outhouse is
crammed with miscellaneous reading matter and she only has to
LOOK. She goes off without saying good night. Cyril and I wrangle
over the lamps. He insists on putting a smoking Aladdin in her hut.
I protest. There is a tug-of-war until I wrest it away. 'You bloody
bitch,' I am told.

The following morning I am up early, after a bad night. I feed the
animals. Tell Mrs Lea to make an extra breakfast. Still in my
dressing-gown typing when Joan enters the bathroom. I call out

that the water is not very hot and would she like a kettle? She replies, 'No.' I tell her I will fetch a clean towel. Confronted by me at the bathroom door, she frantically rubs her face. *'Ton amie. Eh! Elle a beaucoup de rides, n'est-ce pas!'* I say to Cyril, and he actually laughs. I am still typing when Joan appears fully dressed. She is in a *panique*, says we are already late. Cyril is still in bed. He calls out for her to go up to his room. A flap. I quickly dress, wearing the new grey suit with pleated skirt, white shoes, white sweater and, without washing, run to the car that Joan has successfully manoeuvred in the right direction.

We stop once for petrol. Joan buys several cans of oil, says it is much cheaper in England. We arrive in Folkestone Harbour to find the gates closed and a barrier across the road. Cyril rushes off to buy two tickets. Eric Wood, whom we have invited to join us, is already on the boat. An *AA* man appears; he tells us it is too late to take a car over, but that we can go as passengers. Cyril contemplates this, but Joan's face darkens. Up to then she had been quite light-hearted. We had even exchanged a few giggles. Now the wrinkles reappeared. While I sympathise with the distraught driver, Cyril rushes off to rescue Eric Wood. A consultation takes place beside the hampering vehicle. The *AA* man suggests two alternatives. Calais or Le Touquet. Joan discards Calais because of the cobblestones. I see that with a lot of persuasion she will agree to Lympne. By the time the two men have claimed back their tickets, the fatal decision has been made. We split up in two cars, Eric Wood wearing a dark suit with a pink rosebud in his buttonhole and a clerical coat. To my embarrassment, Cyril has pointed out I am wearing a new suit and tells them the cost. Obligatory compliments are paid. A lot of hanging about at Lympne and several brandies drunk. Go to the cloakroom and glimpse myself in a long mirror. Picture the tailor's wife in the new suit and decide it looks suburban. Back at the bar, I consult Eric Wood; he agrees. 'It's not YOU, my dear.'

At 1.30, we all settle into the plane, wedged together in a small lilac box. Joan grips the arms of the plush seat and tightly shuts her eyes as we take off. Cyril leans towards me and shouts, 'Nice AIR.' He has bad breath. I point a finger in my mouth and mimic him, saying, 'NICE AIR.' He realises what I am getting at and actually smiles. When we arrive, after showing our passports, we tumble into Joan's car and make straight for the Grenouillère restaurant. Joan thinks she remembers the way. She was there three weeks ago. Cyril thinks he knows the way from the map. Joan suddenly swerves off the main road and gets deep into the country.

Everything very luxuriant, more advanced than in Kent. Cyril tells her she has taken the wrong turning. 'Wasn't there an arrow?' she asks. No one remembers seeing an arrow. She is ordered to turn back. We drive along for several miles. Joan: 'This is wrong.' We stop and ask a *boulangerie* the way. He has not heard of the Grenouillère. We drive on. 'Can't you remember the way from before?' Cyril says irritably. We ask some road menders. They point down the road Joan originally took. We then see a large arrow pointing to the right. The Grenouillère is empty, but there are dying embers of a fire, a nice bar, lots of mixed bottles behind it, a fat chef, wearing a chef's cap and a pleasant Madame serving drinks. We order Cinzanos. The menu is brought. On the wall, a newspaper cutting of Farouk with Madame Kahil seated on his right. It was taken the year I joined them in La Baule. Cyril orders the wine. Joan advises me to have the *truite meunière,* which is their speciality. I have the trout, with roast lamb to follow, spinach and delicious new potatoes. The trout is a dream cooked in wine, cream, butter and fennel with a strong flavour of tarragon vinegar. The meal almost ruined by an acid champagne *nature,* chosen by the master, that we drink with gross helpings of brawn and *pâté maison,* chosen by Joan. The meal did not exactly go off with a swing. Eric was laborious and somehow created a false impression. The meat was juicy, slightly pink and full of taste and the Burgundy with it was excellent. It was not a stimulating lunch. I think there was some love lacking. I complain about the acid champagne. Joan glares. Cyril agrees and apologises. We have Calvados to finish.

On the way to Montreuil, Cyril suggests staying the night. Horror! I am against it. Joan is pleased. Eric is thinking of his cat. We both vote against it. Cyril is furious. A row starts. I am attacked and accused of having no taste and no intelligence, but am simply a slave to an indomitable will. 'Have you no spirit of adventure?' I am asked. 'What is there adventurous in a continuous round of multi-course meals, with dyspepsia to follow?' I buy some espadrilles which turn out later to be too small. Eric and Cyril go off to a bank to change some money. With me still protesting we drive to the aerodrome. Approaching the runway I say, weakly, 'Well, do whatever you want.' So we stay. Having decided to return the grey suit, I get out of the car as we reach Le Touquet and slip off the skirt, borrowing, at the same time, Eric's clerical coat and folding the suit neatly on my lap remain semi-dressed for the remainder of the jaunt. It was a watery day. Montreuil was provincial and grey with a pretty main square and a statue of Haig in the centre. We wandered round in the rain. Cyril then suggested that we spend the night on the outskirts of Normandy at a place called Mesnil-Var, as he had never been there and the *Michelin* recommended a Hostellerie de la Vieille Ferme. Determined not to suffer any more discomfort than I could help, I now placed myself in the front seat of the car. We embark on a long drive. Eric says that now that we have given in to the 'mad Irish boy's' whim he had a small request – to stop at a perfectly simple roadside café and have a drink. I am all for this. The other two scowl. I am always frustrated in this request because of Cyril's snobbery leading him to the most expensive restaurant. I stress that I must halt and buy a toothbrush. The two 'food snobs' not in favour of either stop.

After a fuss, Eric and I get our way. Me running half-naked across a main street with clerical coat flying, having borrowed some francs from the driver and Eric being allowed three minutes in a waterside café for a *fine à l'eau*, drunk in haste and despair. We press on into the night, Joan bent double over the steering wheel, squinting before her like a 'mad learner'. 'Tell me if anything comes towards us,' she says to me, 'sometimes I don't see things.' Darkness descends. Cyril directs the way from the back. We get lost. I have to get out and peer at signposts which have Mesnil-Val pointing in several directions at once. We arrive at a place called Criel four times, each time halting in the main part of the town to ask the way. We back. We turn. We stop on a deserted heath. We call at a house. We turn, Cyril all the time confidently directing; 'bear left here, turn right.' Joan groans and sighs. Eric laughs hysterically. 'Mad Irish boy!' Cyril haughty and cross and righteous. Me silent. 'You must laugh at your husband sometimes,' Eric says to me. 'She is always too furious to laugh,' Cyril says bitterly. At ten o'clock we arrive. La Ferme is empty, but it is sympathetic in a checkcloth way. Madame helpful and anxious to serve. Joan grumpy as hell. A great parking fuss ensues. I decide to cut myself off from everyone as much as I can. Cyril asks if we can have four rooms for the night. Eric (thinking of the extra expense) questions this. Cyril explains it away by saying that I object to his snores. Since I have not been consulted, I protest and say he prefers to sleep on his own anyway, and why must I take the blame? A large menu placed before us. The men decide to eat a five-course set meal. Joan and I not hungry. I sigh. Cyril turns on me and says something unpleasant. 'I don't see why I should eat five-courses just to please you,' I say. We all order *moules marinière*. The small *moules* and the best. Eric objects. He likes the giant Dutch type. Cyril says we must have some white wine for the fish and red for the meat. Eric scorns this by saying that it is only the English who live up to being such wine snobs and that you don't find the French fussing about the wine all the time. Cyril glares as only a wine snob can glare at someone he considers a complete philistine. The meat is high. There is an argument on the subject of homosexuals. Joan gets whiney. Eric calls them 'fairies' – after all he is one himself. Fairies have spoilt things for themselves by becoming so blatant and that there was a time when they were included in the most select gatherings by the best hostesses and no one was any the wiser, that they constituted a magic circle, but now they were asked because it was known that they were fairies and people thought them interesting. In time, he said, he thought society would turn on them. A homosexual is just the same as anyone else was Joan's contention, neither more interesting, nor less, and she could not see what all the fuss was about.

A lot of Calvados drunk. Madame falls asleep by the fire, nursing her cat. Cyril says we ought to go to bed. We all drift up to an annex and spread out into our cubbyholes. We gather together in Joan's, which is the largest. Eric wants to talk about 'LOVE'. He tells us once again that he is impotent. 'Did it happen suddenly?' I ask. 'Or was it gradual?' Joan looks cross, as much as to say, 'She is now on her favourite topic.' Eric tells me it set in at forty. Cyril accuses me of being provocative, walking about in Eric's clerical coat, thereby stressing my nakedness underneath. Who could I be wishing to provoke? After all, by taking off the suit (which I intend to take back), I am saving Cyril having to pay for it. I ask Joan if I might borrow her cold cream. She produces a pot of Pond's. Eric pretends to be shocked. 'You don't use Pond's! How squalid. You should always use Arden's.'

We scattered and everyone went to bed. I slept exactly one hour throughout the night. The next day it rained. Had the grey suit wrapped into brown paper and then explored the village. It was *triste*. I wandered to the sea. It was rippleless and grey. There was a long stretch of sand and high cliffs, and some men installing sewage pipes. I bought some espadrilles and a bar of Toblerone. Returned to La Ferme to hear Joan and Cyril with a map discussing plans for the day. I asked irritably if we couldn't leave soon.

Later, running into Cyril in the village, he said Joan's comment had been, 'If she had been as anxious to leave early yesterday, it would have been more to the point.' Boiling with fury, I stormed back to the annex and, bursting into her room, said, 'If you think I was responsible for missing the boat, I would just like to tell you I

171

was up two hours before you.' Meeting Cyril in the passage, I said for Joan to hear, 'I suppose we won't start for ages. She will be spending at least an hour doing her face.' Eric, unaware of what was going on, turned up soon after fully dressed. Feeling he was responsible for the dismal dinner of the night before, Cyril made a point of being particularly amiable to everyone. In this mood we set off for Abbeville, which had a façade for a cathedral and all the sadness of a many-times bombed town. In a steady drizzle, we all got out of the car to inspect the ruin, each one shivering with cold, before collapsing into a café to drink Cognac and some muddy coffee. Here we parted from Joan and from then on I enjoyed the trip. We took a bus to Montreuil. With Cyril laying on the charm, we walked in the rain to another meal at the Grenouillère. It was even better than the day before. We visited Sterne's Inn and admired the Ravilious-like butcher shops with their blue tiles, striped awnings and painted shutters. We walked. We joked. It rained. It didn't matter. We took the plane. We talked. Eric went home to his cat and we were all sad to part.

September 13
A quick one-page journal as the bath is running and Joan, if you please, is arriving any minute from Lympne. September 10 (three days ago) Pop's fiftieth birthday and seemed to call for a celebration; he had planned to give a big party for forty or so of his would-be friends at the Ritz. Luckily, this venture never materialised and the party was whittled down to six. Peter Watson was the first on the list but failed to turn up, excusing himself by ringing up the Etoile at the last moment to say he was ill, so we were left with Sonia and Janetta (on whom one had taken pity after Derek's desertion), Robin Ironside (as being a bright spark though non-present giver) and when Peter failed to turn up, thereby casting a blight on the evening, Graham, Joan's brother, was contacted, but he also was unable to come.

It started off a *triste* little party, a special meal having been ordered by the host the day before. Bayonne ham with Charentais (English hothouse) melon, followed by a kind of *bouillabaisse* done with mullet (which turned out to be simply delicious) with a main course of partridge with, if you please, *salade Niçoise*. The birds were good; no one ate their salad. The two girls (now inseparable) arrived rather tipsy and giggly, and on their best behaviour. Janetta had brought Cyril a smart suitcase (which Cyril had asked for) as a present and there were some jokes about that. 'A suitcase that Jo

172

Cotten would be proud of,' Cyril demanded, 'or that buggers would envy.'

After dinner we adjourn to Sonia's, her flat having been improved with the addition of Cyril's patterned Axminster carpet from Sussex Place; the marks of the kitchen stove are pointed out, it having left black weals across the middle, and everyone was amused.

Kenneth Tynan's visit to Oak Coffin. He arrives Friday night on the 7.15 having eaten on the train. We seemed to have been awaiting his arrival for hours. Cyril puts some champagne in the porch to get cold. I pine to drink it having stayed in bed all day without eating. At last, the sound of the taxi stopping in front of the gate. Cyril: 'This is my discovery of the perfect drink. A very light, agreeable and unacid wine.' (Taittinger *blanc de blanc* '47.) Tynan, sounding shy: 'How long have you had this cottage?' An explanation follows. It is not his, but 'my wife, Barbara, bought it before the war.' Tynan says little after that, mainly in the affirmative. Tynan: 'Is there anything that contains all the facts about you?' Cyril: '*Enemies of Promise. Who's Who.* Who else have you done besides Graham Greene?' (Write-up for *Harper's*.) Tynan: 'I've done about a dozen of them.' Then, he talks about a book he's doing on bullfighting, comparing it to other forms of art. Cyril: 'You know Spanish?' 'Only bullfight Spanish.' They discuss Virginia Woolf's *Diaries*. Cyril: 'It was quite reasonable of her to have been against critics.' He says she had described him as the 'Cocktail Critic'. C compliments Tynan on his skit of the radio critics. Says how much he enjoyed it. Goes on to tell Tynan how annoyed he is when *The Unquiet Grave* is referred to as the 'Perfect Bedside Book'. Talks of Eton. Says that anyone he got on badly with there he would get on badly with now. Cyril: 'Have dramatic critics got worse since Max Beerbohm, do you think? Plays have got worse, haven't they?' Tynan: 'No, but more numerous, I should say.' Cyril talks of the complacent drama critics like Ivor Brown. Does an imitation of Pryce-Jones. '"I thought it MADLY agreeable. I couldn't have enjoyed myself more." Have you noticed how all the drama critics have adenoidal voices and how when they discuss homosexuality they always refer to it as "sexual abnormality"?' He tells Tynan about his new anthology of short stories. Goes through the list. Forgets the name of one of the authors. I feel his embarrassment. Afterwards, he told me he was afraid he was going to forget the names of all of them. Tynan: 'How about including *Rasselas*?' Cyril: 'Perfect but dead.' Talks about his *Coup de Vieux*. Tynan: 'What charge are you answering?' Cyril: 'Coming man who hasn't come.'

October 5

I wake up early. Lie in bed. Feel guilty brooding on clothes. Wonder if I am very greedy, as six months ago I had one new suit made. I have just got a new dress from Mattli and I am now visualising a further suit for next spring. But this is after three years of no clothes and poverty. I tell Cyril it is compensation for being in this country and that since I don't spend money on anything else it is reasonable (never buy cigarettes and don't drink). He has just had a new brown gabardine suit made and spent an enormous amount for his red leather skating slippers, crimson pyjamas and shirts (with initials – not to mention the sums he spends in *antiquaries*). I go down to the kitchen before Mrs Lea arrives and make two breakfasts on separate trays, carefully finishing off the buttered toast under the grill at the end. Take Cyril's tray into his room putting on ugly face, pretending to be Mrs Lea, grumpily laying it down on the bed and, after flinging the curtains back, stump out of the room muttering. Cyril laughs. 'How would you like to celebrate our marriage anniversary?' he calls, when I go up again with my own tray. 'Good heavens!' I exclaim, 'what can be the matter with you?' 'Well, you seem to be sweet and in a good humour. If you're going to be nice to me I'd like us to celebrate our anniversary. When is it, by the way?' 'I think it's the tenth,' I say. Later the post comes and there is a present of an eighteenth-century bowl from Lady Elizabeth Glenconner (Worcester, I think). He is pleased to have a present. I admire it and one minute later start grumbling at the mess he has made undoing the package.

I have to tell Mrs Lea to please clean the base of the lavatory which is thick with dust. 'What do you mean?' she hisses, 'I clean it every day.' 'How is it so black then?' I ask her. Muttering, she goes in there with a pail of water. One hour later I see Cyril studying a cookery book. 'I wish you could make *crème brûlée*,' he says to me. 'Well, read it out and tell me how.' 'I've told you several times but you're too lazy to try anything new.' 'It's not a question of laziness. I'm just sick of cooking. Besides, I have lost interest now you do the housekeeping. If you want me to care about cooking again you should be clever and give me a housekeeping allowance.' 'I used to give you money (two pounds at a time) but you hoarded it in your bag.' 'And then gave it back to you when you asked for it. The trouble is, you're too mean.' He jumps from his chair and rushes across the room. 'You call me mean, when all my money goes on buying you clothes?' and he picked up two books, *Gale Warning*, by Dornford Yates, and a science fiction novel, *The Weapon Shops of Isher*, hurled them across the room and ran upstairs muttering, 'bloody bitch, nagging shrew', and from then on silence. I consulted my diary, and found that today is our marriage anniversary and *that* I fear is how it is going to be celebrated.

Yesterday, daylight saving came to an end and we went back to normal winter time. I put on my woollen underpants. The geese, the fowl and the guinea chicks are getting mad with excitement over some mouldy apples. We went to London on October 1 and stayed at the Ritz as Ann Fleming was giving a dinner for Cyril's fiftieth birthday. The guests Peter Quennell, Elizabeth Glenconner, the Campbells, Joan Rayner, Maurice Bowra and, as I fell out at the last moment with gastric flu, the Foreign Secretary's wife, Clarissa Eden. The after-dinner guests were Alan Pryce-Jones, who took Cyril a book on old-fashioned gardens, Cecil Beaton, who gave him some vintage brandy, Lucien Freud, Caroline Blackwood and Francis Bacon, who each took him a pot of caviar, Stephen Spender and Elizabeth Cavendish, Ali Forbes, Freddie Ayer, Sonia and her lover who, apparently, was given the English freeze-up. Ann Fleming: 'Who is that pink-faced man over there? I tried for five minutes to talk to him, my dear, and then just GAVE UP.' Cyril tiptoed in very late clutching his goodies (another magnum of brandy given by Evelyn Waugh who did not actually turn up) like a typical tipsy husband after a night out.

October 14
Have been in bed ill for three days. Doctor Balfour summoned. A lady doctor of the Stephen Potter kind. My heart sank when I heard her arrive. The noisy, effusive, jocular hoots of assurance as she backed the car into the hedge. Clump! up the stairs. Cyril had scrabbled into my room in advance. I saw him looking down the stairs as though at some fabulous monster – and there she was, a large bulky woman on crutches, hopping on one leg. I felt as though I ought to get out of bed and help her in. 'May I sit on the bed?' as she collapsed down puffing. 'We have brought you lots of efficacious things here,' delving into a sham hide bag. 'Some little footballs.' She was very proud of that analogy because she repeated 'little footballs' several times. She grasped my wet wrist to feel the pulse and thrust a thermometer into my mouth as she proceeded to

175

ask a stream of questions. She then shook the thermometer hard and exclaimed in triumph 'Excellent! Excellent! No temperature. What a good thing!' It would have been the one thing that would have cheered me up! When I told Cyril that I had no faith in her, he said, 'You don't have to, it's modern medicine we have faith in now.' He stood over me while I took some stomach powder. 'What a terrible place to be ill in,' I kept muttering. 'It's a terrible place to be in without being ill,' he returned. Throughout the day, he made a sudden halt before my bed and presenting an angry stomach said, 'What am I going to eat today? . . .' 'Would you be very kind and make me a hot-water bottle? . . .' He disappeared into the kitchen. Then there was a long silence and I wondered what he was up to. 'How do you cook liver?' he called. 'Do onions take the same time to cook? . . .' 'Do you think you could please bring me a bottle? . . .' Half an hour later: 'My liver is wonderful,' he shouted up. There was a pause. 'Like some? . . .' 'Would you be an angel and make me a few Epsom Salts? . . .' In desperation, I dragged myself out of bed and crept down the stairs. I met Cyril coming out; he half backed in again when he saw me and looked as though he would have liked to prevent my advance. An empty fruit tin was perched so that a thin trickle of juice had gone over the edge; an empty bottle of claret lay on its side; small blobs of flaky cream cheese dropped all over the floor; a large hunk of goose shit brought in on a shoe; a plate with the remains of some fat; squeezed-out halves of oranges piled all over the sink; grease spots all over the cooker and breadcrumbs strewn round like confetti. 'You've managed to turn the place into an Irish hovel,' I hissed to a receding back. 'You're a filthy one with your filthy tongue,' I heard from two doors away. He then telephoned a number of people using my illness as an excuse to put them off. Having done that, he rang Joan and made a lunch date for the same day. 'You seem to have taken a turn for the better,' he told me to appease his conscience. 'I will bring some Muscat grapes from London.' 'Quand même, would you mind bringing me up a bottle? . . .' 'What is there for me to eat this evening?' The way he fled along the path to catch the taxi!

Mr Coombes came with his bill, pretended to do a bit of gardening but was mostly hanging round the back door. There was a whispered conference between him and Mrs Lea when the taxi went. ''E really 'as gone,' she croaked, ''opped it.' Then she too scurried away as though she had wild devils after her.

The only person who has saved me from complete boredom is Thurber. Before that I was reading *The Captive Mind* by Milosz. I think this book is responsible for my 'flu. I became muffled in a black blanket. The future was black. And of course the past was too black to contemplate. I only have to see the book lying on the bed now still open at where I left off with its spine split in two facing up to feel black despair.

It is Saturday. I am almost completely recovered. Got fully dressed yesterday and spent a lovely afternoon in the garden killing worms. This morning I was up early and striding across the grass to let the fowl and her flock out. I then stood at the kitchen window watching them gobbling up the worms. What strange pleasures there are in life!

December 1953
We spend Christmas Eve at the Grand Hotel in two little centrally-heated single rooms, with wash basins, like luxury maids' rooms, a bathroom along the passage. I make a fuss about getting out of trousers, saying I have nothing suitable to wear. Eventually compromise and change into the old black and white pleated check. It was lucky I did. Everyone had changed into low-cut wear with many furry tippets. Cyril donned his dinner jacket, but came downstairs very late, after a long soak in the bath. Both of us ill-humoured after drinking some *blanc de blanc* in our room. Throughout the meal neither of us spoke and we even managed to sit back to back. Very quick service; extra staff employed for the occasion. Woken in the morning by a Church Army band outside the window playing 'Onward Christian Soldiers'. A walk on the leas. Arrive at the Flemings in good time for lunch. A large gathering of three generations. Ann Fleming's father and step-mother. Ann's daughter, Fionn. And, in Ann's words, 'I can't imagine a Christmas without Peter.' Mr Quennell in person and a rather nice blokey friend of Ian's – best, best friend apparently. Since doing the *Atticus* column, Ian seems to have become a very dried-up and red-veined plain family man. Has lost any semblance of glamour or good looks, a bottlenecked figure with a large bum. Very bad manners – by that I mean a heap of something is plonked on one's plate so that it trickles over the side. Atmosphere hearty. We are offered a Bloody Mary. Cyril holds forth on our previous evening, making it sound funny, but not coming out of it in such a good light as he thinks . . . 'And then I said to her, "I suppose you'd like to take a look at the ballroom," and a look was all she took . . .' We had been told about their wonderful new pair of cooks. A rancid stuffing with the

turkey, bottled chipolatas and another brown sauce with bits of turkey liver floating in it. The Christmas pudding was good, but the brandy butter was made with sham cream. Then, after tea, present giving. *The Awkward Age* from Peter, a Henry James he gave me ten years ago, although I didn't tell him so. From Ian some sexy black pants with black lace and a hideous beige galoshes bag. A pair of nylon stockings from Ann. And then, because Cyril had previously said to Ann 'I wonder how Peter will find a solution between meanness and avoiding to appear so,' he gave me an extra present of some bath essence. We gave Ian a bottle of Taittinger *blanc de blanc* which he had mentioned in his book, without ever having drunk any. Ann was given an eighteenth-century Wedgwood pâté dish which I would have liked to keep.

We left at six and broke down on the hill – out of petrol. We both got out of the car and walked off in separate directions, me taking a short cut so that I reached the garage first. I cried all the way driving to Eric Wood. Felt everything was miserable. Eric had arranged all his Christmas cards round the fake pillars in his sitting room and when I asked him how many he had sent he said about a hundred. A bowl of white Christmas roses were set in a Dresden dish. I am glad we didn't stay long enough to see them droop. The same man from last Christmas was there, a *louche*, sadistic-looking, elderly queer with a loose jutting mouth, speaking little and seemingly bored. The dinner was a definite improvement on the Flemings. To start, something *en gêlée*, followed by an underdone joint of beef, braised celery and broad beans in a white sauce; a delicious mousse to follow. I had left off my woollen underwear and was christening my new red, striped, velvet trousers, so felt cold in the unheated dining room. Eric Wood read aloud Oscar Wilde's *Selfish Giant* and we did our best to condemn it as whimsical.

Next day Cyril spent pacing the grounds, as the new proud owner, and came back with plans for pulling down every surrounding house in the neighbourhood and making an annex for guests, a summer house on the hill and a guests' garage on the opposite side of the road. Eric just acquiesced and went on mixing drinks. I enjoyed the latter part of the morning. 'Have a little drinky?' Eric said, and gave me a strong Martini while I watched him prepare the lunch, and we talked and I unwound some wool for knitting a scarf. I got a little drunk and felt benevolent, with the hope that perhaps life had something good still to offer.

After lunch, we went off to look at a house for sale near Dover. A converted oast being sold for £3,200. Cyril had already promised me that he would make up the extra £700 if I should sell the cottage for £2,500. I told him not to expect much for £3,200 but he was determined the house should be a 'dream'. It was bang on the road opposite a bleak field of barley. It had a good nuttery of hazels and we saw grey squirrels swinging from the top branches of some poplars. They looked so pretty leaping from one branch to another. We went back to have supper with Eric Wood and were shown the phoney Greek pillars again that look so out of place. After supper Cyril wandered round the garden and came back to tell us he had heard some strange snortings in the long grass beyond the Greek temple, so we both went back to investigate and a huge hedgehog shuffled onto the path. Cyril, in the attitude of someone pouncing on a large ferocious animal, tiptoed forward and flung a sack over it and gingerly swept up the beast. 'Wasn't I brave?' he said to me. Eric would not let us take it into the house as he said it was a flea and lice carrier, so we tucked it into the back of the car. When we got home, Cyril unrolled the sack and tilted it onto the grass and the hedgehog, to my intense surprise, scuttled away in the direction of the holly trees and has never been seen since. It was almost as sad as the tame sparrow being swallowed up by Kupy.

The geese were killed on Saturday. Cyril had strongly objected to their being killed at all, but I promised him he wouldn't hear, as Mrs Lea had informed me they would not screech while it was going on. 'It's too difficult for me to do,' she said, 'you have to lay a stick across their necks and step on it.' Around ten o'clock we heard a car draw up. 'Who is that?' Cyril demanded. 'I hope it's not the man for the geese.' We heard voices in the kitchen and then silence. I went down to investigate. 'Is that your nephew come to kill the geese? If so tell him to take them away with him.' 'I'm afraid he's gone, Madame.' 'And the geese?' 'They're dead.' 'Take them away.' I wailed, covering my eyes to blot out the sight of the poor geese. So, she hid them in the outhouse. I then had to break the news gently to Cyril. 'As long as I don't have to see them again,' he said. Later we were having a combined bath and he said, 'You won't tease me, will you? But I think I'd like to eat one of those geese, after all, and,' he added, 'I would like it to be the largest.' But, in the end, Cyril expressed a preference for the smallest. He was most adamant about it; he would eat that one or nothing. When I asked him why,

179

he said the little one was obviously the most female and there might be something erotic about it. But, the other was simply 'a big obstreperous rival male'. I have ordered the butcher to send the other one to Marjorie and John Davenport.

◇◇◇ Chapter XVII ◇◇◇

I Tatti

Everything to Lose: Diaries 1945–1960, Frances Partridge

January 1954

We went over to Stokke one evening, where the Connollys, Freddie and Joan Rayner were staying. A return visit by the Campbells and Freddie next day, full of complaints of the Connollys. They had insisted on bringing their coati but it was not allowed to sleep in the nice hutch lined with straw prepared for it and had to share their bedroom, where of course it shat on the coverlet. Barbara sulked in her room and refused to come down to meals. She had asked to be taken to the early train on Monday, which meant getting up at seven.

When Monday came and we drove Janetta to the station, we found the whole Stokke party pacing up and down the platform, their faces lavender with cold. Robin told me in tones of stifled horror that they had got up at seven and called Barbara, only to be told by Cyril that she was sleepy and had decided to take the NEXT train. So here they were, but Barbara refused to get into it, saying she had left some kind of basket behind at Stokke. 'She's going on the one-seventeen though,' Robin said between clenched teeth.

Diary

January 6, 1954
Icy cold. Mrs Lea stamping about the house muttering. We have just spent a horrible four days at the Campbells. I never wanted to

go, but was tricked into it. The other guests, Freddie Ayer and Joan Rayner. Vast unheated house like a boys' preparatory school, a twin-bedded room with a two-barred fire giving out no heat. No privacy and Robin bursting in at all hours without knocking, bringing someone with him to inspect his dead father's suits, a chest of silver and a cupboard full of shoes. A succession of meaty-coursed meals into which we all troop like penancing monks. Whimsical talk between Joan and Freddie, the latter very talkative and flamboyantly egomaniacal; says he is pleased with himself because he has been doing some satisfactory work lately. Robin, who doesn't like me, is all the time on the nag. To make conversation, knowing Joan to be interested in cooking, I say, 'Do you ever use any cooking GADGETS?' She gives me a cold stare and drawls, 'Only a FORK.' In order to rouse them, I suggest that the inherited silver tea caddy (left by Robin's father) would be pretty gilded; Joan does not approve of metals being made to seem what they're not. I think to myself that she should be made to take a course of cleaning silver solidly for a year and then give us her views. Robin says he would like to see my powder box 'since it's been gilded'. I say, 'But you've seen it already.' 'Not since it's been put to some good use,' he says. Heavy irony. He knows I don't use powder. Joan and I never discard our coats. Nothing is drunk at the fatal hour and all good feeling for the coming year seems lacking. Cyril embraces Joan and glares at me. The Partridges arrive with Janetta who looks thin and peaky. Something unpleasant about Mr P. What is it? Conceit? Complacency? Just don't feel I've got anything to say to anybody. Robin's puritanism a drag. Seems to disapprove of all his friends' wives; in fact, he is uncharitable about most women. Joan, though, is sacred (well-bred, intelligent, has a private income, is a generous provider of food and drink. Has the right friends . . . Maurice Bowra . . . Cyril . . . is also considered to be a beauty! And is too bluestocking to take an interest in CLOTHES).

Since having my hair cut, Cyril now looks pointedly at other women and leaning back fixes their pelts with an admiring stare. I agree I look hideous and get sulkier as the weekend drags on. After three sleepless nights, because of snores and hens, I make a fuss and stress I have to sleep alone. The house party considers this request unforgivable. Am henceforth in total disgrace. Cyril gets taken his breakfast. Not me. I am accused of being lazy for not talking to people. When we are in the kitchen alone, Robin says, 'You ought to live abroad, you know.' 'How can I when Cyril is tied to England?' 'Why don't you run away with some Egyptian?' I react by jokingly saying, 'We don't meet Egyptians at Elmstead.' 'Oh, well,' says Robin, 'you could probably find one at the Ritz.' I retire to my room to read, with frequent interruptions as members of the house enter unannounced. Robin says peevishly, 'What have you been doing to the curtain?' It had fallen off a hook. Seeing a gap in the window, he snaps, 'Shut it up, for goodness' sake.' 'That's a man's job,' I reply, meaning for someone taller. 'There is no such thing as a man or a woman, only PEOPLE,' he says sharply.

Sunday, I invent a dentist's appointment and say I have to leave. Cyril makes a fuss so I stay on. But I ask to be called at seven to catch an early train. Unfortunately, that night I take two strong sleeping pills, so that when called am unable to get up. At eleven am awoken by Cyril who drags me out of a happy state of oblivion saying, 'Mary is FURIOUS.' She had taken the trouble to wake up early and worse still I had left the fire on all night. My defence: I was convinced that Mary rose every morning at seven, as she had to feed the animals, I told her later I always rose at that hour and apologised, but Mary remains snappy. Then Cyril and I had a row over strapping up Kupy, so I left it to him and, in the fury of departure, my basket got left behind. Cyril drew my attention to its absence, as he climbed out of the taxi, which made me suspect he knew all the time, as this enabled him to depart alone with Joan. The Partridges and the Campbells then retreated to the pub. More in disgrace than ever, I returned to the house and there was the basket sitting outside the Kupy hutch!

As they see me off, Mary says, 'Come again when you're not so cross.'

Spend the rest of the day crying from one train to another. Get out at Newbury in mistake for Reading, miss the connection, take a bus, arrive in London at five o'clock. Clean up at the Ritz. No sign of any Egyptians with whom to elope and, not wishing to embark immediately on another train to Ashford, I walk to the Carlton Cinema and see *Julius Caesar* with Gielgud as Cassius and Brando as Mark Antony.

January 14
Have made a plan for the next 20,000 words of my book. I wonder if I shall manage it all right. The first twenty read quite well but seem too slight. I find it funny. But I don't expect anything will come of it.

Yesterday, as I was typing, Mrs Lea passed through the sitting room carrying a dustpan and brush. 'I'm not disturbing you, am I?' 'No,' I replied, without looking up. 'You'll make a lot of money,' she said, and laughed. 'Maybe,' I said. 'Well, you may,' she repeated. And we both laughed.

Last night I said to Cyril that it was having to give up sex that made me so ill-humoured. 'Well,' he said, he had had to give up society and entertaining. 'But, I thought you considered too much of your life had been taken up with time wasting.' We talked about death. Cyril says there were two courses to take; one, preparing yourself for death all your life, digging your grave, so to speak; and the other was to accept it as being an endless sleep.

Three people who can make Pop cry in the following order: Mozart, Watteau and Horace. I ask why. 'Because of their perfectionism,' he says.

January 21
Very depressed. Heard yesterday of Angelica's suicide. Can think of nothing else. It has a morbid fascination for me. Want to talk about it and visualise it happening. Angelica wandering about her basement flat in a grubby blue dressing-gown, slightly bent forward with the stooping walk she had. Probably drunk, preparing the death chamber. Sealing the windows and the door, and then turning on the unlit cooker, opening the oven, with a drawn taut expression on her face and then climbing into the bed she had made up in the kitchenette after drugging herself with sleeping pills. It seems quite incomprehensible after lunching with her and Johnny last Thursday. She appeared so unmorbid and gay, but on the defensive, seeking cause for offence whenever by chance I mentioned anything that might be considered criticism. On finding a tape measure about the flat, for something better to do, I began taking our waist and hip measurements. 'How strange,' I said, 'you are broader at the top than me and yet you haven't so much bosom,' and she replied rather sharply, 'I do very well with what I've got.' And then Johnny asked me whether it wouldn't be natural for me to love someone like Angelica with her beautiful legs. I paused, at a loss, seeing the statement was intended to be taken seriously. I saw her face cloud into a frown as though I were deliberately preparing

184

an insult when, in desperation, I said, 'I find it difficult enough to love a man, let alone a woman,' which somehow saved the situation because she burst out laughing, as if I had said something *bien drôle*. They half-heartedly tried to entice me into the bed and I left them both lying naked between the bedclothes like a scene in a play, two very white bodies, their dead-white arms entwined above the sheet, with two pallid faces and Angelica's dead-black hair topping it all, like a black cap. I made as dignified an exit as I could and, sidling round the door as I went, thanked them for a very nice lunch and said I hoped to see them again soon. Then Johnny, two-facedly, said, 'Give my love to Cyril.' I telephoned Poppet this morning for further details. She sounded distant and none too pleased to hear from me, but none too upset either. Poppet said Angelica was worried about money and was £200 overdrawn. Also she had an obsession about cancer. She told me about the preparations and said a note had been left for Madeleine saying, 'Don't call the police, call Mr Maclaren.' Cyril said it was like someone preparing themselves for a journey, a journey without luggage, with the note left behind.

April 26
Ice-cold wind penetrating all the cracks like dagger thrusts. Swaying bare branches of the beech tree and a vista of bare twigs topped by a murky grey sky. Kupy has turned self-destructive and chases round in circles, biting her tail till she draws blood, eating it like asparagus, as C describes it; have tried putting flowers of sulphur on her tail, but to no avail. It drips blood and is eaten down to the tendon. Tried to cover it over with a French letter, but no good. We have made Eric Wood an offer of £5,000 for his house, but he refused, admitting he anticipated getting £6,000. But when we lunched there Saturday he said not a soul had been to look at it. 'You'll get it yet,' I comforted C. My new toy – a Roleiflex camera – affording infinite pleasure. Took my mother and the twins to tea at Fullers. Very dull little girls. My mother her usual maddening self. 'Where is Cyril this afternoon?' 'He's gone to see some friends at St Margaret's Bay.' 'Oh yes, the Fletchers,' she says, in a knowall way. Asked me what my book was in the back of the car. '*The Iliad*,' I said. 'Fancy reading that old-fashioned book!' Who had we been to lunch with? 'A painter called Eric Wood.' 'But he lives right here in Saltwood, quite near to me.' She looked towards me in a fury as though she'd caught me out in a lie. 'Not this one,' I said. 'Of course he does,' said my mother, 'an elderly man with a beard.' 'Not the

Eric Wood we lunched with.' 'Then it must be his brother,' she insisted.

May 20
On May 15 the beech tree and weeping lime came into flower, and we bought a baby badger from Spong Farm. We paid two pounds and the Bryce son was unable to conceal a cunning smile as he took the money. The badger died last night, four days later. It cried so at night, not when it was dying, but before. We did not coddle it nearly enough. Cyril having made me as funky as himself by expatiating at length on how its teeth interlocked when it bit you. Poor little baby badger, its teeth were hardly formed and we only dared to peer at it through the chink of Kupy's cold hut. I did not realise it was not eating enough. It would lick the honey from the spoon and tried to tug at a finger of my glove which was a substitute for a nipple. What cowards! What shame! Kupy had just given us each a nasty nip, which had upset one's nerve.

We have had a few hot days. But now it has clouded over and there is an east wind. We had Mary McCarthy and Bowden Broadwater to lunch last Sunday. She is very alive, and he is restful and fastidious, combs his hair forward with a funny flattened look to cover the baldness on the top of his head. They loved England but then she has been made a great fuss of, and, when I complained that one could not find anything in the shops except in toned-down colours for the English, Broadwater said he was leaving with five new suits. They very generously brought us two delicious bottles of old whisky, Bourbon and Scotch, and insisted on doing all the washing-up after the lunch.

BIG NEWS. KUPY GONE TO A ZOO IN ILFRACOMBE.

August 19
Had an appalling night. C installed himself in my bed. He was only allowed in after I had scrubbed the soles of his feet. He now never wears shoes about the house and picks up all manner of filth; it was so engrained that I had to flake off the black clots with a brush. And what a fuss! Dragging his foot away every second and howling with pain. Then he woke me in the early morning by putting his Chinese coolie legs across my thighs.

◇◇◇

We catch the 9.25 train in good time, leaving the car on the return side of the platform and buy the newspapers. I order eggs and bacon in the restaurant car, as C has ordered some, and I know I will be tempted when I see his. He goes off with the usual review copies to sell at the booksellers. Collects me at the hairdresser's. I am told I was looking far better before I went. Shows me the photographs he has collected and suggest we go to the Ritz to have a shufty. Pleased with them on the whole. The portraits of people are definitely the best. We leave the Ritz at one and disappear into the rain. Immediately start grumbling, say I usually like walking, but have not the proper shoes. C says okay and calls a taxi. Think I look tired and plain, wearing the fawn suit (that I hate since Bill said it was inferior gabardine). What a bore it is, I grumble, my being included in the luncheon at the Ivy (as I am no longer hungry). Complain I am half dead and won't have anything to say. Aldous Huxley was there waiting in a crowded foyer. I go upstairs to try and improve my face, notice I am stared at (because of the bright canary jacket worn over the suit), run my hands through my hair, decide I look simply dreadful and there is absolutely nothing to be done, eyelashes sticking together and hair too curly and neat. AH takes us to a far corner table (a fearful draught from the window) and to my horror see it is laid for *five*. Before I have time to recover Mary Hutchinson walks in, very dolled up, but quite pleasantly, in gunmetal grey and a small fitting hat, the kind of hat all dowdy Englishwomen wear that I tried very hard to criticise but failed utterly. She has simply taken trouble. She hardly greets me, which always makes me discomfited, but, determined to make an effort, I smile, to show I am not going to give in to my aversion, which I am sure she knows I feel and probably reciprocates. We are placed opposite each other, AH on my left. Menus are handed round, one each. AH says he thinks it is a day for soups, but what will we have to drink? Should we order before Raymond arrives? C says definitely yes. AH and I agree on dry sherry. MH nothing and C in an exacting way says he wants some kind of cocktail; the expression on the face of the waiter as well as the host indicate they think he is going to be difficult, but it all ends with a quick decision for a Martini. Then I order a melon to start, followed by plain grilled sole, while the others pick out avocado pear, prawn cocktail and minestrone respectively, and all three agree on roast lamb, their voices united in pleasure so that I am made to think I've ordered unwisely.

Raymond Mortimer arrives in a tweedy suit, greets everyone very warmly, including Mary Hutchinson, laughs in a deep, warm way and seems pleased to be there. Orders melon (am kept company, thank God). Cyril says, 'Do you think that is a wise choice?' Raymond says he doesn't want to be wise. Has a kidney dish to follow. Everything mellow, middle-aged and well-mannered. The conversation mainly lofty gossip. When asked by Cyril if he found any place in North Africa worthy of permanent habitation Raymond, who was there early in the spring, replies 'definitely not'. Agadir a horrid place but remarkable climate, Mogador ravishing town but flat, treeless. I don't think anyway he shares C's craving for expatriation. 'What do you think of the Channel Isles?' C asks. Everyone: 'Horrid.' Raymond: 'Nothing but hothouses and tomatoes.' C: 'But a warm climate.' Aldous (referring to bananas grown in Cornwall): 'Plants are fearful liars. Because tropical things can be grown there it doesn't mean the climate is warm but that there is no frost.' 'That's it,' says C, 'they blanket the leaves for protection.' C says if he could really choose he would live in California. Mary Hutch raises her gingery eyebrows in exaggerated surprise and, looking at me, asks, 'Would you like to live in America?'

Raymond says that the *Sunday Times* has come to the conclusion that both of them were quite irreplaceable and their one dread was that they would be killed together in a taxi. C tells Raymond that when Trevor-Roper, who was about to write an article on ethics or morals, and was cited as a co-respondent, the *Sunday Times* did not consider he was suitable any longer and decided in view of Raymond's irreproachable reputation as a discreet homosexual he was the one best qualified. R was amused. Huxley talked about his grandparents, of how his grandfather was out strolling with a friend and the friend's hat blew off landing in a lake; whereupon there was a discussion as to whether to retrieve the hat and wear it wet, or go home without. The latter was decided upon. The next time they met, the friend said to Huxley's *grand père*, 'Do you know after I last saw you and the loss of my hat, I developed a cold in the head?' Whereupon Huxley's grandfather replied, 'If you had chosen to wear your hat home, you would now have pneumonia.' The point being, how strange the Victorians were to think that if you went out without a hat you would inevitably catch cold. Aldous said he recalled his grandmother saying that she wished birth control had been current in her younger days. But he criticised her for having always refused to meet George Eliot. Raymond said that most of her life Eliot could only receive in her own house and only toward the end was she accepted everywhere. Huxley had been disappointed in Europe, particularly in Italy, where it was so noisy. He had liked the Lebanon very much. When Cyril asked him his plans, he said lecturing and finishing his essay on mescalin. Everyone agreed that Norman Douglas was a horrid man. Huxley: 'When I last saw him in Italy he absolutely refused to be interested in anything but drink and sex.' Raymond said he hadn't liked Nancy Cunard's book[*] on him, but all the other reviewers had boosted it. Isherwood's last book had made him squirm. The trouble now is that no one writes at all well. Cyril disagreed that Bertrand Russell wrote well, but Huxley said it was rare for a philosopher to write at all. Nobody liked D H Lawrence. Aldous told the story of Lawrence visiting Aldington when he was living with two women in Provence. Lawrence was shocked and complained that the atmosphere had been so *louche* that even the donkeys had permanent erections. No one had a good word to say for Maugham. Cyril said, 'The trouble with writers who reach old age is that they spend their time running down their dead contemporaries.' He then added, 'Longevity is the revenge of talent on genius.' Raymond: 'Who said that?' C: 'I say it now.' Aldous: 'Then I think we all ought to applaud.'

Only this morning, C had complained that now I had taken up photography, only his ugliness would be perpetuated and not his epigrams. C asked Aldous about his eyes, were they any better? Much better, he said, but that when he went blind in one eye for six months, it had been a most painful experience. He had seen Arthur Waley. Raymond: 'What an odd fish.' C: 'Did he talk at all?' Aldous: 'A lot.' C: 'What about?' Aldous: 'Oh, his work, I think.' 'What is he doing now? . . .' 'Still translating. They now translate into modern Japanese Waley's English version of ancient Japanese.' Everyone thought it odd to be an expert on a country one had never visited. No one thought much of Malraux. Talk the hind leg off a donkey. 'You can't live through art alone,' Aldous said, and that most of the text of Malraux's books was clichés and double-Dutch. He and Raymond had both enjoyed the Edward VII room at the British Museum. 'Cults of ugliness such as Picasso's have run through the ages.' And he remarked on how extraordinary it was that similar things had been produced simultaneously all over the world, when there could not have been any link. Huxley said what a disappointing city Athens was; it had no antiquity apart from the Acropolis. Raymond liked it, though, and mentioned the small Turkish

---

[*]*Grand Man: Memories of Norman Douglas.*

189

quarter at the foot of the Acropolis. We were almost the last in the restaurant. Raymond said to Mary Hutch, 'You must come and see me in Islington.' Mary H said to us, 'You must both visit me in my new home, where I shall have a proper kitchen.' I said we would be delighted.

This morning I received a letter from Eric Oliver with a wobbly arrow pierced with a heart. He has given me two Staffordshire figures, one called Flora and a Charles II gold coin which I was going to give him back, but Cyril says I should give it to Farouk when we get to Rome as, having been deprived of his collection of coins, which are up for sale in Egypt, all a collector wants to do is to start collecting again. For in two days we are off to Italy. Cyril has been commissioned by the *Sunday Times* to do an article on the recent excavations at Herculaneum.

The first pleasure was waking up in the sleeper to see an exotic landscape of palms, cypresses, umbrella pines, calm sea and sunshine, with the occasional belltower or bombed building and pink stucco houses with green shuttered windows flitting by like candy.

At the Hotel Eliseo, Cyril lies prostrate on his bed fully dressed with firm shut eyes, what I call his 'dying duck' expression, occasionally emitting a loud groan to imply he is in a state of depression. After the first day's bill, which is enormous, we move to the Inghilterra, where Cyril once more stretches out on the single bed, closes his eyes and proceeds to groan. Irritated by this, I go out to a bank on the Piazza di Spagna and buy a Lake Como shawl, for we have arrived in Rome in the middle of January: icy cold wind, frozen, more so than when we were in Merry England.

C refuses to give me any money, but luckily before leaving I pawned the ugly Chuff watch for £25, £7 of which I gave the pawnbroker to get Cyril's mother's watch out of pawn. The big check shawl is soft and bulky. I am dressed like an Arab in a Tangiers gale, so that people stare. C rings no one and complains that his money is running out. He is supposed to be on his way to Herculaneum to investigate the up-to-date diggings. I begin to think I would be happier in Rome alone but, feeling persecuted, fail to ring Farouk. Nonstop blame-shifting goes on – how it is my fault that so much money has been spent, as owing to my not paying for my own meals on the train he had to change an unnecessary cheque. Arriving at a bank, after visiting the Sistine Chapel (a disappointment to both of us), C yells, 'If it wasn't for you looking at those tombs [the Egyptian sculpture in the Vatican] we would have reached the bank in time.' I go alone in the rain to the Piazza del Popolo to see the Santa Maria del Popolo church and then fail to find the Sansovino tomb that is mentioned by Wölfflin, even after asking one of the priests attached to the church.

We eventually get to Naples where it is milder, gayer, less cosmopolitan and constricted. Neopolitans stare and stare as though we were walking about nude. A balmy southern atmosphere, too; there is nothing southern about Rome in the winter. The rain had washed Naples clean and it did not have the dirt and dustiness of the summer. Cyril said he liked it as well. The *louche* bars, sailors, seafood, guitar players in restaurants and sentimental singers. The Hotel Metropole was warm (it was recommended by the Inghilterra), modern, with flowered wallpaper on a powdery blue ground; everything modern in the bathroom, comfortable with boiling water and the most instant service; the furniture was gimcrack, though, and things kept falling to pieces; handles came off drawers, a leg propping the bed up broke (without any provocation), and a glass pane that slid into the slots of the shelves slipped out and smashed (for which we had to pay). I walked about the first day drugged (after sleeping tablet) but without an overcoat and how the men stare! Am struck by the amount of noise everywhere; it is the same in Capri in the summer, too. It is mainly those horrid little Italian Vespa bikes, the backfiring of traffic, the dogs that bark and the voices that shout, and then always in the distance a pick being plied (nonstop building everywhere). At the Hotel Inghilterra it was a torture all night, the revving of cars, when the people disgorged late from the cinemas; the rain pattering on the rooftops, 'like people trying to burn steel hoops on a bonfire', Cyril said. His only flash of humour on the trip, up to now.

After taxiing round to the Metropole and dumping the luggage, we go out again to one of the bathing-beach restaurants, indoors behind wide glass windows, speckled with lights, the sea lapping the sides of the concrete waterway. Music throughout the meal and, as almost everywhere in Italy, a tenor sang sentimental Neopolitan songs, but C got cross and left his jumble of *moules*, mullet, octopus and squares of fried toast floating about in green herbed fish soup on the plate. The wine was brought in small quarter-pint bottles intended for ginger beer. We had not been in the hotel long before the hall porter told us that one of the guests had just been robbed; the handle of his car ripped off and all the petrol coupons taken. I make Cyril take an inventory to see if his watch had been pinched, or his Boucheron cufflinks out of pawn. I get an idea for a short story – about a man who thinks he is being robbed by the Neapolitans, when really it is his wife who picks his pockets. Went to a hairdresser. They tried to sell me things all the time. 'You liker de tonic for de grease?' 'No, thank you.' 'You liker de shampoo for de grease?' 'No, thank you.' 'You liker de shampoo for de dry?' 'I would like an ordinary shampoo, thank you.' 'You liker de tonic for de face?' 'No, thank you.' Then another tormentor approaches. 'You taker de massage for de face?' And when I say, 'No', 'You taker de manicure for de sure.'

Went to the museum. Ravishing things to see. Roman wall paintings impressionist and Guardi-ish. Steep mounting alleys that rise in steps as far as the eye can see, with clean washing strung across, barrows rooted to the corners laden with oranges, tangerines, bananas and lemons hanging in festoons shaped like Chinese lanterns. The *épiceries* crammed with fresh cheeses – Bel Paese, Provolone and mozzarella; truncheons of garlic sausage decorating the portals, barrel organ drawn by sturdy grey donkeys, the neon-lit cafeterias where they squeeze one fresh juices and music plays from a radio box.

We visit Paestum. Board a breakfast train in brilliant sunshine, wear my thick white hand-knit pullover and lean towards the window to get the heat from the sun; *pain grillé*, a miniature pot of ersatz-tasting plum jam and coffee *molto caldo*, special care being taken to heat the cup and saucer as well. Pass orange groves, artichoke fields and rows of cauliflowers (the small kind, broccoli); strings of *pomodori* attached to the outside walls of the houses hanging like glazed udders; wander round Salerno. Well-cared for, sunny with a long promenade, men lounging about on wooden seats and sea-washed sands the colour of slate; bathed there once during the war and the water was full of medusa. Catch another train after being pestered by rows of midget men to take a horsedrawn cab. The cathedral was closed for repairs; it looked as though they might be turning it into another Vézelay, where the restored capitals now look as though sculpted by Epstein. We seem to be the only travellers on the train ever to pay for a ticket and the other occupants of the carriage hold up vouchers, some passing themselves off as officials. Cyril says, 'A sign of decadence. A country run by bureaucracy.' On the way back a perfectly fit man posing as a beggar entered each carriage in turn demanding alms. Most people paid. 'Is there anything wrong?' I ask. 'No,' they say. A man holds forth in Italian: 'In Boston, which is one of the richest cities of the world, there is a street devoted entirely to beggars who lie out on the pavement all night.' Cyril corroborates this fact, letting the carriage know that he too has been there. Paestum was very disappointing to both of us, but the museum was exciting with some quite recent archaic metopes of dancing maidens playing flutes. There was some desultory digging going on and one of the men held up a coin he had just found in the soil. We had a horrible lunch, the worst so far in Italy. Tasteless veal in a sickly Marsala gravy, spaghetti too hard and tinned tomato sauce, with some wet puff-ball cheese. As we were leaving Cyril shouted over his shoulder at the waiter, 'caro e malo' (dear and bad) so that he came running after us to claim the matches he had given me to light my cigarette.

For the second night running we went to bed early and had a meal brought up on a tray; scrambled eggs and tea. I bought some yoghurt (have a passion for it here) and Farouk telephoned, having received the letter I had written in Rome. He said he was in the far north at a skiing resort, was friendly and gay and we arranged to meet in Rome. A *libeccio* wind blew all through the night.

Rain! Rain! Rain! On the quay were men supporting trayloads of coral and cameo brooches. 'You like a good contraband watch, mister, fifteen dollars to you, mister.' 'I have one already.' 'Like to see the spring, mister?' Bringing out his grandmother's Victorian watch, Cyril says, 'I have a good contraband watch already, thank you.'

Pick-up men pester one all the time; there are those who draw silently up to the kerb in tiny Fiat cars like black silver fish and musty men slip out, peer into a shop window, gaze over their shoulders at you without speaking and then climb back in, drive a few paces and repeat the theme. There are the ones on foot, who stop, pause, turn, halt: 'Where you go, Miss? I show you sommink?'

Go to Capri to meet the pastry cook. A terrible journey. Rough sea. The boat dipped and rose. I was sick. A handsome fatherly sailor in high Wellington boots held my head. Standing on the

Marina Grande in readiness for my arrival was a funny little chap in a black overcoat, carrying a gamp, who with small mincing purposeful steps led me away. Is this the little bourgeois fellow I have come to see? Where is the slouching fat pastry cook of the summer season?! Having contemplated remaining the night on the island I am resolved to get away on the last boat. 'I thought you would come back,' Cyril said, 'as this hotel has base-appeal.'

The next day was spent at Pompeii, the peak of our visit. A car is hired; alas, it is Sunday, and shoals of sailors are being led through the turnstile and counted like sheep. 'You like to stop five minutes at the cameo factory?' our driver asks. 'Decidedly no.' We glare out of our respective windows at the many fields of broccoli. On arriving at Pompeii, Cyril tries to find his way about by studying his guide. I hear someone explain, 'This is where the judges sat.' 'Why couldn't you tell me that?' I say crossly to C, who is still studying his guide map. Then, we make for the House of Vettii, where women are forbidden to enter. While I am inspecting the erotic murals with the aid of a torch, a large troupe of businessmen are shepherded in and I am caught. There is a fearful to-do, much to my bewilderment, as they struck me as being quite unaphrodisiac. So, we had to go before a head man like naughty children but, when Cyril brandished the slip of paper given to him by the curator of the Museo Nazionale in Naples, we were allotted our own guide. I adored the brightly coloured murals of the fourth style Pompeiian art; the garden wall paintings of birds, mimosa, cherry, pomegranate, fig and lemon trees, red arbutus berries with birds perched on the branches and a serpent shown circling a tree after a bird's nest. When all the other sightseers had gone off to lunch, we wandered about the deserted streets. Noting the phallic symbols at the corners of the streets and the tubular shaped urns into which the Pompeiian men urinated, the guide related that the urine was afterwards used for washing clothes. A priapus symbol was nearly always put at the entrance to a rich man's house, to ward off ill luck. When I asked Cyril if Botticelli could have been influenced by Pompeiian art, he said he could not have seen any. We visited the House of Mysteries and then took a bus on to Sorrento, then rushed back to the opera at San Carlo. A man sharing our box asked how it is we speak such good English. 'But we are English.' To which he giggled as at an obscene joke and said, 'I thought you were Germans. I often mistake the two.' The following day we take the train to Florence, to stay with Bernard Berenson at I Tatti.

'It's strange to be the sole survivor of an epoch,' said Berenson, after dinner the first night. 'I have begun to take myself seriously, which I never did before.' We had been invited by telegram to stay for two nights. They talked about mutual friends. When, reprovingly, C mentioned someone who had been made very unhappy by his wife's infidelity during the war, Berenson thought it quite justified. He said to me, 'Could you be faithful to someone who talked like a Bishop? Can anyone be faithful to anyone, anyway? Fidelity belongs to an era of slavery.'

It is snowing today; through the grey sleet we can see the mountains covered with snow and the cypresses; in the wind they sound like the rustling of the sea. Berenson, at ninety, is wonderful looking. Tiny and very spruce, he moves in a kind of upright sprint in the manner of someone who is accustomed to being the centre of attention; is very clothes-conscious; wears narrow, black suede shoes. I noticed him looking at my old leather walking shoes with displeasure. He appears almost hairless, except for a white beard and for someone with such a slight figure has a very thick neck. He used his sensitive hands to stroke his face in mock anguish when subjects like psychoanalysis cropped up; when talking to a woman he likes to hold her hand or stroke her hair. He told us that his visual sense was such that, in his youth after his first visit to the Prado, he could remember in detail every picture he had seen. Talking of Ezra Pound a guest maintained that he had been mad from the age of ten. 'It has always been the excuse made for him by his friends,' said C. But the lady went on, 'You can see it in his handwriting.' 'I see vulgarity,' piped BB, 'a great deal of ignorance and some appallingly bad grammer, but no madness.'

At dinner, we had fresh peas from the garden. Italy, Berenson said, was a very productive country with practically all the natural resources that she needed; like the beggar who, when he dies, turns out to be a millionaire. We talked about the Roman paintings. Everyone admired the Villa Livia fresco now in the Terme Museum, Rome. Like a vision in a dream, someone said. 'Some of them are like old Chinese wallpapers,' C said. Berenson agreed but, laughing, stated they were not quite as good as that. He insisted that the Romans were completely uncreative, that all the painting had been done by Greeks, that some of them were copies from Greece executed by Greeks, as Pompeii was originally a Greek city and anyway the Romans considered painting to be an unworthy occupation. The Villa of the Mysteries was a copy; the execution was inferior to the conception, copies of about the time of Augustus. C was surprised. 'Always remember,' Berenson stressed, 'when the execution is inferior to the conception you may be sure a copy has been made.' He then stated that it was only at the beginning of the nineteenth-century that painting became a respected profession. C disagreed, referring to the great painters of the Renaissance. Berenson said that they were esteemed as geniuses all right, but artisans all the same. You would find that Michelangelo, for example, would never have been seated at the Pope's table. Many of the great painters would never have come face to face with their noble patrons. C countered with Velasquez. 'What a snob he was!' said Berenson. He thought Anatole France was a very great writer and that he would have a revival. But he did not think much of any of the present French writers, except Montherlant. Gide had capitalised himself fully during his lifetime, there was nothing more to be squeezed out of him. Valéry, of course, everyone praised – a man indifferent to success or notoriety. He was very against Virginia Woolf's *Diaries* and did not think any writer should be so obsessed about their work; he criticised her for harping on her sales all the time. He thought it was wrong to have published them leaving out so many personal passages. 'She ought to have remained a critic,' he concluded, 'she was very good at that.' Maugham was dismissed as not worth a serious discussion, never having written a memorable phrase. His essay on Zurbaran was utterly trite.

The first night they kept trying to make C open a full bottle of whisky that had been put beside him. When he declined, Nicky Marieno said, 'But we had been told you had become a very heavy drinker and so we arranged to have something strong in the house specially.' She had also heard that he had become exceedingly fat but admitted, 'You don't seem so fat to me.' 'It's just the jowl,' said Berenson. 'If you were a few inches taller no one would think of you as being fat at all. It's your head which looks out of proportion.'

The Routine of the day is that we all foregather for lunch at one o'clock, having been left to our own devices till then. But it is not easy to remain in bed as the servants disturb us, bringing clothes that have been pressed, preparing baths, stoking the fire. C gets up early and goes to work in the library. After lunch we retire; congregate for tea or, as C puts it, 'go on parade again' at a quarter to six; disappear again at seven; dinner is at a quarter to nine; we are summoned to it by a gong.

Robert de Montesquiou was mentioned. 'What a dear fellow,' mused Berenson. 'Such a brilliant talker, but a failure as a writer. A true aristocrat, confident of the superior quality of his mind and the distinction of his appearance. What a stimulating companion he has been! But garrulous and exhibitionist in a social gathering, demanding all the attention. What a wonderful profile he had! . . .' It was through Montesquiou that he had met Proust. 'What has been your impression of your morning?' Berenson addressed me, as I sat next to him at lunch. 'Too many books in the library.' Everyone looked across in dismay. 'So many one wants to read and so little time,' I explained. 'I really have achieved something with the library. I shall be leaving something behind that is really worthwhile.' Then he laughed. 'It provides anyone with standard intelligence with what an American would call, "a good liberal education".' C talked about Petronius and got so excited that he did not eat his food in time and the fruit had to be passed round while he was a course behind. When he had finished an Italian guest exclaimed, 'Very interesting!' 'Aren't you proud,' said Berenson, 'of having a husband who is as well-informed as he is frivolous?'

Again I was admonished for reading art books. 'I have never read a thing about painting all my life,' said Berenson. But he recommended Burckhardt. 'You'll be learning Chinese soon,' he suddenly said to me with disgust. 'Do you like to be a doormat to your husband?' Anticipating my answer, he concluded, 'Then you don't love him.'

On our last evening C told Berenson he should write his memoirs, reminiscences of personalities, as he possessed such a gift for bringing people to life. 'I have very little concentration left,' he replied, 'and the little that I have is going into compiling a catalogue of Italian painting.' He paused. 'I have so little time left and it is to be in four volumes. So I must think of nothing but that. And it exhausts me so to write.' When it was suggested that he dictate, he said, 'I can't understand how anyone can work through dictation, it is a most uninspiring medium. I need someone to draw out the memories. It is as though they were at the bottom of a well and needed extracting.' That he could not do himself. Someone asked whose works would be read in a hundred years. Portions of Proust would survive, but there was a great deal of him that needed weeding out. What he has to say about the time factor was quite unique, said C. Berenson said that he had met Proust in Paris with

Montesquiou, whose voice Proust even imitated. 'A peacock's screech,' he said. 'Shrill and high-pitched.' C said that many of those who had met Proust had not taken to him very much. Was there something repellent about his appearance? 'He was very dirty,' Berenson agreed. 'Wore no tie; and dirty open-necked soft collars; and *dans le monde* sat in a corner not speaking but watching everybody, and then later he took up with such boring women! What Proust had done could have been a great deal better.

'The tragedy of the present was that the world was run by journalists who, being culturally ignorant about the past, failed to comprehend what was happening in the present. Even politics were governed by journalists; diplomats did not count any more. Just journalists and revolutionaries . . . Too many people wrote; and they wrote solely for the present; no one gave a thought for the future . . .' If he had unlimited money he would leave a trust for writers *not* to write. He had no use for Eliot now. 'A terrible humbug.' Auden was no good either. 'Is Sanskrit such a wonderful language as it is reputed to be?' Cyril asked. 'Some maintained it was more expressive and melodious than Greek.' 'Horrible language,' said BB, 'mathematical and spoken like a chant.'

How he hated metaphysics! 'Meterfussers,' he called the metaphysicians. He thought the Flaubert cult a great exaggeration, that reading him was 'like swimming in turtle soup'. He had read the *Education Sentimentale* many times and still had the impression it could have been reduced to a long short story, *Il tire par les cheveux*. But he liked *Bouvard et Pécuchet* most. We asked him if he liked Verrocchio's *David* as much as we did. But he did not share our enthusiasm and described it as being 'equivocal'. Cellini's *Cosimo* was very much praised. Michelangelo's *David* was a 'hobbledehoy'. There had been more balderdash talked about painting in the last fifty years than ever before; if a hundred years elapsed without another word being said on the subject, it would be no loss to the world. How overpraised the late Renaissance had been! The absurd reverence for Raphael, Leonardo and Michelangelo – out of all proportion. The Douanier Rousseau was a complete fraud. But Van Gogh was a great painter.

C went into his room to say goodbye for the last time and told him that when he had stayed at I Tatti in the 'twenties he had been anti-culture. He had felt that I Tatti was the dead hand of the past on creative young people. He was more influenced by Huxley, Lawrence and Joyce than by Pearsall Smith and Berenson. But now he had come round to see that 'I Tatti was infinitely more precious than anything *avant garde* which had such a short life'. BB said, 'Culture is like a match burning in infinite darkness.' C: 'Why do people always want to blow it out?' 'They don't want to, they just have to blow.' C asked, 'What are your plans?' 'Trying to finish my catalogue of Italian paintings, though each night I go to bed wondering if I will be here the next day . . .'

'The snow has melted. Look, BB. And the birds are singing. It's spring today.' Berenson: 'This bed is where I do my singing. Peep peep.'

⋄⋄⋄ Index ⋄⋄⋄